STUDIES IN HENRY JAMES

R.P. BLACKMUR

STUDIES IN HENRY JAMES

Edited with an introduction by Veronica A. Makowsky

A NEW DIRECTIONS BOOK

Manufactured in the United States of America
First published clothbound and as New Directions Paperbook 552 in 1983
Published simultaneously in Canada by George J. McLeod, Ltd., Toronto

Grateful acknowledgment is given to the publishers of books where the
essays reprinted here first appeared. For a list of these acknowledgments,
please see page 250.

Library of Congress Cataloging in Publication Data
Blackmur, R. P. (Richard P.), 1904–1965.
    Studies in Henry James.
    (A New Directions Book)
    1. James, Henry, 1843–1916—Criticism and inter-
pretation—Addresses, essays, lectures.   I. Title.
PS2124.B54 1983   813'.4   82–18911
ISBN 0–8112–0863–X
ISBN 0–8112–0864–8 (pbk.)

New Directions Books are published for James Laughlin
by New Directions Publishing Corporation
80 Eighth Avenue, New York 10011

TABLE OF CONTENTS

Editor's Introduction 1

The Critical Prefaces of Henry James (1934) 15

The Sacred Fount (1942) 45

In the Country of the Blue (1943) 69

Henry James (1948) 91

The Loose and Baggy Monsters of Henry James (1951) 125

The Golden Bowl (Grove Press) (1952) 147

Introductions to the Laurel Henry James Series (1958–1964)

The Wings of the Dove 161

The American 176

Washington Square and *The Europeans* 185

The Portrait of a Lady 193

The Tragic Muse 202

The Ambassadors 213

The Golden Bowl 221

Appendix 231

Bibliography 243

Acknowledgments 250

EDITOR'S INTRODUCTION

Without a college education, or even a high school diploma, Richard Palmer Blackmur (1904–1965) became one of the most influential critics of his age and a Professor of English at Princeton University. Obviously he managed to educate himself quite well without benefit of schoolmasters or institutions, but he was not entirely without preceptors. Instead of formal instruction, Blackmur chose education by emulation. His teachers were two of the magisterial figures of American literature, Henry Adams and Henry James. In their lives and works he hoped to discover the key to the relationship between life and art. Whether he called the opposing forces art and life, the imagination and reality, or the artist and society, the quest for their most fruitful relationship was the principal theme of Blackmur's criticism, particularly his works on James and Adams. As his failure to complete a book on either Adams or James indicates, the interaction between art and life escaped his fixed formulation, but the attempt evoked some of his most brilliant and characteristic criticism.

While still a teenager in Cambridge, Massachusetts, Blackmur discovered Adams and James and began to use them as divergent approaches to the same end, the union of reality and the imagination. For Blackmur, Adams exemplified reality pursued so obsessively that the pursuit was transmuted into art. Almost despite himself, the historian who had sought a completely scientific and rational explanation for human history had created two great works of the imagination, *The Education of Henry Adams* and *Mont-Saint-Michel and Chartres*. Blackmur tried to emulate Adams's art of reasoned cultural criticism in his *Henry Adams* and some late essays such as "The Swan in Zurich."

Blackmur regarded James as Adams's antithesis, the supreme artist whose passionate cultivation of the imagination could transform reality. As his introduction to *The Wings of the Dove* indicates, Blackmur felt that his sense of reality had been permanently changed by his reading of James.

> When I was first told, in 1921, to read something of Henry James—just as when I had been told to read something of Thomas Hardy and something of Joseph Conrad—I went to the Cambridge Public Library looking, I think, for *The Portrait of a Lady*. It was out. The day was hot and muggy, so that from the card catalogue I selected as the most cooling title *The Wings of the Dove*, and on the following morning, even hotter and muggier, I began, and by the stifling midnight had finished my first elated reading of the novel. Long before the end I knew a master had laid hands on me. The beauty of the book bore me up; I was both cool and waking; excited and effortless; nothing was any longer worthwhile and everything had become necessary. A little later, there came outside the patter and the cooling of a shower of rain and I was able to go to sleep, both confident and desperate in the force of art.

So began at age seventeen R. P. Blackmur's lifelong reading of Henry James, a reading which never lost its passion and intensity as it matured in appreciation and judgment.

Blackmur was fortunate enough to begin his study of the Master at a crucial juncture in James criticism. In the decade after the novelist's death in 1916, interest in his works had revived with the publication of four posthumous volumes. In 1917 two unfinished novels, *The Sense of the Past* and *The Ivory Tower*, appeared, supplemented by James's notes for their completion, as well as the third volume of James's autobiography, *The Middle Years*. With Percy Lubbock's edition of *The Letters of Henry James* in 1920, the canon was established and critics began their retrospective rearrangements of James's career. Although critical movements do not pass with the precision of a changing of the guard, some trends can be discerned between James's death in 1916 and Blackmur's first published essay on James in 1931.

In 1918 the Henry James Number of *The Little Review* proclaimed and reinforced James's emerging status as a major author. Two generations of critics meet in this issue, but their views of James are remarkably similar. They establish James's importance by firmly relegating him to the past as a representative of an elegant, leisured age which had been brutally extinguished by the advent of modern times, dramatically precipitated by the First World War.

The Henry James Number begins with a voice from the past, that of Ethel Coburn Mayne, one of James's fellow contributors to *The Yellow Book*, the quarterly of Aubrey Beardsley and other decadents. Mayne holds that James did his best work in the 1890s, which she nostalgically regards as a golden age when art was gloriously ascendant over life. The onslaught of modern times ruined Henry James by causing him to develop his hesitant, evasive, late manner as an inadequate defense. "The bull in the china shop has smashed up the Aeolian harp. . . ." As this metaphor suggests, Mayne's criticism is impressionistic, not analytical.

Like Mayne, two younger contributors to the James Number, Ezra Pound and T. S. Eliot, view James as a representative figure and devote little attention to his fiction. Pound's quintessential James is the author of *The American Scene* (1907), which, he writes, "more than any other [volume] gives us our peculiar heritage." In *The American Scene*, James recounts his feelings of horror and extreme vulnerability upon returning to the mechanized America of skyscrapers and elevators after an absence of

twenty years. For Pound, James represents the battle of the individual against a culture which increasingly enforces homo-
geneity. The struggle is doomed, Pound believes, because "artists
are the antennae of the race, but the bullet-headed many will
never learn to trust their great artists."

Although Pound does provide an annotated list of James's
work, in this essay he is more interested in content than technique,
as his summary of *The Ambassadors* indicates: ". . . rather clearer
than the other work. Étude of Paris versus Woolett. Exhortation to
the idle well-to-do, to leave home." In another piece in the Henry
James Number, "The Notes to *The Ivory Tower*," Pound does
consider James's method. He organizes James's notes for his
unfinished book into an outline for the construction of a novel,
complete with topics and subtopics, a format Blackmur would
refine in his essay on James's critical prefaces.

Eliot also uses James to attack modern life, but his target is
more specific, the peculiar faults of America, "a large flat country
which no one wants to visit." In this essay, he is less interested in
James's fiction than in James's expatriation as a precedent and
justification for his own decision to live in England. Eliot's
description of James's attitude toward Hawthorne could as easily
characterize Eliot's feelings about James. "The first conspicuous
quality in it is tenderness, the tenderness of a man who escaped
too early from an environment to be warped or thwarted by it,
who had escaped so effectually that he could afford the gift of
affection." Eliot, however, does devote some attention to the
qualities of James's thought. His famous dictum that James "had
a mind so fine that no idea could violate it" became the touchstone for Blackmur's assertion that in art's precarious balance of
reason and imagination, James emphasized human emotions and
values, rather than the doctrinaire abstractions characteristic of
Henry Adams.

In the decade after *The Little Review*'s Henry James Number,
much James criticism continued to rehearse the tired arguments
over James's "Americanness" and his relevance to twentieth-
century life. Van Wyck Brooks gives the question a Freudian twist
in *The Pilgrimage of Henry James* (1925). According to Brooks,

James's expatriation and difficult style were the consequences of his inability to confront his childhood fear of America, which Brooks equates with reality. In *Portrait of the Artist as American* (1930), Matthew Josephson provides a more sympathetic version of this argument. Although he finds James's decision to emigrate regrettable, he believes the America of the "Gilded Age" was inhospitable to James's genius.

Two critics, however, suggested approaches to James which the New Critics, including Blackmur, would later develop. As early as 1918, in *The Method of Henry James*, Joseph Warren Beach attempted to lay bare James's technique and development with chapters entitled "Point of View," "Dialogue," and "Eliminations." Although Beach's argument is teleological and stresses structure at the expense of what John Crowe Ransom would later call "texture," the book does emphasize the fiction as an artistic achievement instead of the man as a cautionary or exemplary figure. In his introduction to *The Letters of Henry James* (1920), Percy Lubbock begins the reverent portrayal of James as the high priest of the religion of art, with sacerdotal terms such as "shrine," "mystery," "fervent faith," and "vocation." According to Lubbock, James "did not scruple to claim that except through art there is no life that can be known or appraised." Lubbock introduces the view of a text as a higher reality which is independent of its audience or creator, a separation the New Critics would later enforce.

In these years of increasing interest in James's fiction, R. P. Blackmur was continuing his self-education and establishing himself as a critic. He clerked at various Cambridge bookstores until 1927, when he became an editor of the distinguished little magazine *Hound & Horn*. With the publication of his essays on modern poetry, later collected in *The Double Agent* (1935), Blackmur's reputation as a critic was secured. These essays also helped establish an innovative critical method which became known as the New Criticism. In its heyday in the 1940s and '50s, the New Criticism dominated the quarterlies and the campuses and numbered such distinguished critics as Allen Tate, Robert Penn Warren, and Cleanth Brooks among its adherents.

In his pioneering essays of the early 1930s, Blackmur was primarily responding to the difficulty and obscurity of modern poetry which seemed to require a different type of criticism, an inspired exegesis which would illuminate meaning and elucidate technique. The poem was primary; the critic's knowledge of the poet's life and beliefs was important only if it helped explicate the poem. In "A Critic's Job of Work" (1935), Blackmur explains and defends his method, which he calls the "technical approach," as he lists its advantages.

> It readily admits other approaches and is anxious to be complemented by them. Furthermore, in a sense, it is able to incorporate the technical aspect, which always exists, with what is secured by other approaches—as I have argued elsewhere that so unpromising a matter as T. S. Eliot's religious convictions may be profitably considered as a dominant element in his technique of revealing the actual. The second advantage of the technical approach is a consequence of the first; it treats of nothing in literature except in its capacity of reduction to literary fact, which is where it resembles scholarship, only passing beyond it in that its facts are usually further into the heart of the literature than the facts of most scholarship.

Blackmur also applied his technical approach to some works which were often considered as complex and difficult as modern poetry, the fiction and criticism of Henry James.

Blackmur's first published essay on James was "The Critical Prefaces of Henry James" (1934). To Blackmur, these prefaces to James's collected works (the New York Edition, 1907–1909) comprised "the most eloquent and original piece of literary criticism in existence." His criteria for this appraisal amount to a précis of the values and methods of the New Criticism: "The things most difficult to master will be the best." He praised James for close attention to the texture of his fiction: "not the furthest eloquence nor the most detached precept, but flows from the specific observation and the particular method." In his discussion of the "germination" of *The Ambassadors*, Blackmur suggests that through such concentration upon individual passages, the critic can enter the work as fully as its creator did. "If we can expose the substance of these two discussions we shall have been in the process as intimate as it is possible to be with the operation of an artist's mind. In imitating his thought, step by step and image by image, we shall in the end be able to appropriate in a single act of the imagination all he has to say." Although this is a heady claim for the powers of criticism, Blackmur's reverence for literature prevents him from raising the critic to the stature of the artist; for Blackmur, the critic's powers, no matter how extraordinary, exist to facilitate appreciation of the text.

Blackmur performs this critic's job of work with thoroughness and distinction in "The Critical Prefaces of Henry James." In the first section he explains "what kind of a thing a James Preface is, and what kind of exercise the reader may expect a sample to go through." The second section remains unsurpassed as a useful guide to James's artistic credo. In a refinement of Pound's method for arranging the notes for *The Ivory Tower*, Blackmur organizes the prefaces by topics such as "The International Theme" and "The Plea for a Fine Central Intelligence." The analytical divisions of the second section enrich the third, in which Blackmur reintegrates his categories through an explication of James's preface to *The Ambassadors*.

Although published eight years later, "*The Sacred Fount*" (1942) is a companion piece to "The Critical Prefaces" in method and theme. Reading the novel as a fable or fictive version of James's artistic beliefs, he found that "only in the critical Prefaces is the tone of assurance at all comparable." The organization of the argument is again tripartite. Blackmur first lays the groundwork with a summary of current critical opinions of the novel, generally considered James's most puzzling and obscure. He then proceeds to order and analyze James's ghost stories as manifestations of the dark netherside of the artist's own personality. Finally, he returns to *The Sacred Fount* and elucidates it within the context of the occult tales. Although critics remain in radical disagreement about interpretation of the novel, Blackmur's essay is still the best introduction to this difficult work because of his ability to relate it both to James's theory of art and his practice in other fiction.

"In the Country of the Blue" (1943) marks the beginning of Blackmur's growing ambivalence toward James. Superficially, the essay reflects Lubbock's portrait of James as the votary who sacrifices all for the religion of art. Blackmur, however, suggests that such an extremity of faith paradoxically acts against its ostensible object, the work of art, by attenuating its link with reality.

> His very faith in his powers kept him from using them to their utmost and caused him to emphasize only his chosen, his convicted view. That is why he is not one of the very greatest writers, though he is one of the indubitably great artists. . . . That is why, too, as his faith increased he came less and less to make *fictions* of people and more and more to make *fables*, to draw parables, for the ulterior purposes of his faith.

Blackmur's priestly diction conveys none of Lubbock's inspired enthusiasm; instead it reflects Blackmur's increasing conviction that since James emphasized imagination at the expense of reality, his works could not represent the equilibrium between the two forces which was Blackmur's ideal.

Blackmur's doubts about James are also reflected in his curiously ambivalent title and its amplification. "If [the artist] sees, his vision disappears in his work, which is the country of the blue. That is why the only possible portrait to paint of the artist will be a portrait of him as failure. Otherwise there will only be the portrait of the man." Although the country of the blue might initially seem a kind of heaven, the artist's reward for his labors and sacrifices, it is really a frigid circle of hell which Blackmur reserves for what James called "that queer monster the artist." The artist is monstrous because his special gifts do not enrich his humanity, but are devoured by his insatiable art. According to Blackmur, this capacity for self-surrender, amounting to self-annihilation, "is what brought James himself, for the moment of expression, into the blue," a prospect at once awe inspiring and strangely chilling.

"In the Country of the Blue" also reflects a change in Blackmur's methods. Ironically, as the "close reading" of the New Critics became literary orthodoxy, Blackmur became more interested in broad theoretical and cultural questions. He may have felt, after years of hand-to-mouth freelancing, that his acceptance by the Princeton faculty in 1940 gave him a secure basis for *ex cathedra* pronouncements. Whatever the reason, he begins to address the social concerns of Henry Adams in the late manner of Henry James. "In the Country of the Blue" begins with a wide-ranging discussion of the artist's role in American and European civilization and does not reach its ostensible subject, James's tales about artists, until its second half.

"The Loose and Baggy Monsters of Henry James" (1951) follows a similar pattern. Blackmur introduces a more elaborate version of his old interest in the interaction between art and life when he discusses the novels' technical or executive form, "the underlying classic form in which things are held together in a living way with the sense of life going on." He indicates his belief that the critical pendulum has swung too far in one direction when he refers to "a period like our own when works tend to be composed and are largely read as if the only conscious labor were the labor of technical form: the labor of the game of the mind, the play of its conventions and the play of its words." Blackmur suggests that when James excoriated Thackeray, Dumas, and Tolstoy for writing "such large loose baggy monsters," he helped initiate an over-reliance upon form at the expense of life which caused the artistic failure of some of his own novels, such as *The Tragic Muse*. When he deplores James's emphasis upon form and his influence upon critical trends of the 1940s and '50s, Blackmur is anticipating today's critical reversal in favor of looser, more rhetorical fiction which has returned the Victorian novelists to literary esteem. In the second half of the essay, however, Blackmur demonstrates that James's highly wrought forms do succeed when infused with intense feelings, as in the late masterpieces, *The Ambassadors*, *The Wings of the Dove*, and *The Golden Bowl*.

Although he reacted against a myopic concern with form and was increasingly preoccupied with larger cultural issues, Blackmur never lost his ability to seize the detail which illuminates the whole. His various introductions to James are as valuable to the James devotee as they are to the novice. The first introduction was the masterly survey of James's life and fiction which Blackmur wrote for the *Literary History of the United States* (1948). He begins "Henry James" by stating the shared quest of author, critic, and reader: "The story of that struggle to realize life as emotion and to create it as art is the abiding story of Henry James, as near as we can come to the Figure in his Carpet." He traces James's variations upon this dominant motif through what he identifies as James's three principal themes: "the international theme, the theme of the artist in conflict with society, and the theme of the pilgrim in search of society."

Blackmur's diminishing enthusiasm for James is clearly demonstrated in his introductions to various editions of James's novels, particularly in his two introductions to *The Golden Bowl*. In the first, written for the Grove Press edition of 1952, Blackmur praises the rarefied atmosphere of the novel, calling it "a poetic drama of the soul's action." He regards Maggie Verver as an admirable, if tragic, figure: "The supremacy of her effort is the measure of her failure with the possible as it is proof of her success with the impossible." He considers the suffering that Maggie causes her most intimate friends and relations a necessary part of the glorious tragedy of her awakening consciousness. When forced into the realm of action, consciousness becomes conscience, as in the last scene of the novel in which Maggie buries her head on her husband's breast: "Surely this mode of love grew out of moral beauty and high conscience, but as Maggie applied it, it required sacrifice of life itself till nothing but the created shade was left. . . . It was a shade embracing a shade, but in the shades of poetry."

The "shades of poetry" no longer seemed sufficient compensation or explanation for the pain Maggie perpetuates when Blackmur wrote an introduction to the Laurel edition of *The Golden Bowl* (1963). Highly wrought art is no longer a higher reality, but a perversion of humanity: *"The Golden Bowl* is a novel of the daily world James partly knew and partly created; and if it goes beyond the human it does not go to God, but to the inhuman." Blackmur's reading of the novel's final scene is also radically different:

> There is no beauty in [Maggie's] daily life; so, like Iago, she removes it from possibility—so far as they believe her—from the lives of her father, from Charlotte, and from her husband. She exhibits as if it were riches the poor bare forked spirit of unaccommodated man. Looking into Maggie's eyes one does not see oneself staring back; one sees (in James's own phrase) the Medusa face of life: the face that crumples us into zombies. No wonder Maggie buried her eyes in her husband's breast; at the last moment James reports of her, she could not bear her own triumph over what she held dear.

In little over a decade, Maggie has been transformed in Blackmur's mind from secular saint to green-eyed monster.

An explanation for this remarkable reversal of interpretation can be discovered when the Laurel introductions are considered as a coherent series. By the late 1950s, Blackmur had come to believe that James's novels were not liberating dramas of awakening consciousness, but claustrophobic morality plays of imperious conscience. This thesis is best expressed in his discussion of the role of the governess in Miles's death at the conclusion of *The Turn of the Screw*: "The abyss over which he fell at the moment of death is that of the intolerable consciousness which may often be brought best to us by human cruelty become conscience and motive in a personality driven, possessive, possessed." In the Laurel introductions, Blackmur explores the various permutations of consciousness in Christopher Newman, Isabel Archer, Merton Densher, Lambert Strether, and others. Finally, in the introduction to *The Ambassadors* (1964), he concludes that James's view of human nature is restricted and restricting: "Whoever wins in this novel—in this mode of human relations—wins within a loss. One monster is replaced by another monster, more private, within the bosom; and it is the human loss in getting from one to the other which James's novel measures."

Blackmur's decreasing admiration for James certainly provides one explanation for his inability to fulfill the contract with New Directions for a book-length study of James which he had signed in 1940. An equally compelling reason, I believe, lies in the intense personal identification with James which Blackmur manifests in his essay for the *Literary History of the United States*. Many of his comments about James could as easily apply to himself. Like James, Blackmur had a "reputation for finickiness, difficulty beyond the necessities, unreality, and remoteness," which meant he could never "escape violently opposed opinions as to the character of what he wrote." He believed James's fussiness arose from the minimal formal education which caused him to make his mind his "primary and trustworthy sense." Blackmur, who was also self-educated, continues, "This is the hallmark of the homemade mind, and it serves very well for home affairs, but in the affairs of the wide world it drives its victims partly to makeshift and partly to reliance upon naked humanity."

To Blackmur, James represented the aspects of himself which kept him a perpetual outsider, the astute observer and critic of society who could never be a full participant. His affinity with his fellow stranger in the "wide world" caused Blackmur to describe the last years of James's life in a way which presages his own solitary death in Princeton: "At his life's end he had a number of friends but none close, many acquaintances but none important to him, and considerable influence on the younger writers of his time. . . . But essentially he died, as he had lived, lonely both in art and in life, a very special case indeed." By the 1950s, Blackmur no longer needed James as a mentor and feared his example as a man.

Blackmur's long-rumored book on Henry James was really little more than a rumor. Unlike his *Henry Adams*, which was two-thirds complete at his death, Blackmur's *Henry James* does not exist as any coherent portion or portions of a lengthy, integrated work. In the 1930s and 1940s he did plan a full-length study of James, but over the years the plan became reduced to a collection of essays entitled *Studies in Henry James*. According to a list in Blackmur's papers at Princeton, the collection was to include chapters called "Ambassadors, Sacred Fount, Country of the Blue, The Spoils of Poynton, Wings of the Dove, The Golden Bowl, the Turn of the Screw, Portrait of a Lady, The Tragic Muse, The Bostonians, The early novels, [and] Maisie and the Awkward Age." Some of these chapters exist as Blackmur's published essays, but some were simply never written.

Among Blackmur's papers at Princeton, I also found a handwritten essay dating from the early 1940s, which seems to be a draft of the introduction to his proposed book. I have included "The Spoils of Henry James: A Special Case of the Normal" as an appendix. In this introduction, Blackmur rejects the emphasis on James's personal idiosyncracies so common in earlier criticism. Instead he suggests that James's life and works reacted upon each other to form "a special case of the normal." By "the normal," Blackmur means modern man's plight as an "unaided intelligence" in a world characterized by an "absence of the supernatural order." As an artist, James was a "special case" who met the challenge of the new chaos with a "permanent development, a new dimension, of sensibility." By concluding the essay with the last line of Yeats's "Three Movements," Blackmur indicates that this new development was not entirely salutary.

> Shakespearean fish swam the sea, far away from land;
> Romantic fish swam in nets coming to the hand;
> What are all those fish that lie gasping on the strand?

An excessive reliance on form and convention made James, as the precursor of the modern artist, a fish out of water.

Although Blackmur did not write a full-length study of James, his published essays are a treasury of a lifetime's insights. Unfortunately, for many years they remained buried treasure since they were largely inaccessible to the general reader in defunct

---

journals and out-of-print books. Collected here in a single volume, these essays are once again available to students of James's fiction and Blackmur's criticism.

The copy text for each essay is the last published version where more than one version exists, although the differences are not significant. I have not altered the published essays except to make spelling consistent, to correct obvious typographical errors, and to make one addition. I have inserted three paragraphs about *The Aspern Papers* into the introduction to *The Wings of the Dove*. These paragraphs, indicated by brackets, are taken from Blackmur's introduction to the Laurel edition of *The Aspern Papers* and *The Spoils of Poynton* (1958), which is otherwise a slightly reduced version of the introduction to *The Wings of the Dove*. For the reader's convenience, I have added paragraph divisions and regularized punctuation in the manuscript fragment, "The Spoils of Henry James."

Although I have chosen to arrange the essays in chronological order to highlight Blackmur's critical development, I have attempted to make the book equally useful to students of James by providing an index which directs the reader to all of Blackmur's comments on a single novel or story. The reader who wishes to find all of Blackmur's criticism of *The Ambassadors*, for example, should consult the entries in the index under that title. All significant discussions of any work are indicated by the page numbers in boldface.

I would like to thank A. Walton Litz and Peter Putnam, without whose assistance this collection would not have been possible. For presenting me with some of the Laurel Henry James and encouraging me to collect them all, I am grateful to Samuel Hynes. I would also like to express my appreciation for the aid I received from the staffs at the Departments of Rare Books and Interlibrary Loan at Princeton's Firestone Library and the Interlibrary Loan Department of Middlebury's Starr Library.

Veronica A. Makowsky
Middlebury, Vermont
July 1982

THE CRITICAL PREFACES OF HENRY JAMES

The Prefaces of Henry James were composed at the height of his age as a kind of epitaph or series of inscriptions for the major monument of his life, the sumptuous, plum-colored, expensive New York Edition of his works. The labor was a torment, a care, and a delight, as his letters and the Prefaces themselves amply show. The thinking and the writing were hard and full and critical to the point of exasperation; the purpose was high, the reference wide, and the terms of discourse had to be conceived and defined as successive need for them arose. He had to elucidate and to appropriate for the critical intellect the substance and principle of his career as an artist, and he had to do this—such was the idiosyncrasy of his mind—specifically, example following lucid example, and with a consistency of part with part that amounted almost to the consistency of a mathematical equation, so that, as in the *Poetics*, if his premises were accepted his conclusions must be taken as inevitable.

Criticism has never been more ambitious, nor more useful. There has never been a body of work so eminently suited to criticism as the fiction of Henry James, and there has certainly never been an author who saw the need and had the ability to criticize specifically and at length his own work. He was avid of his opportunity and both proud and modest as to what he did with it. "These notes," he wrote in the preface to *Roderick Hudson*, "represent, over a considerable course, the continuity of an artist's endeavour, the growth of his whole operative consciousness and, best of all, perhaps, their own tendency to multiply, with the implication, thereby, of a memory much enriched." Thus his strict modesty; he wrote to Grace Norton (5 March 1907) in a higher tone. "The prefaces, as I say, are difficult to do—but I have found them of a jolly interest; and though I am not going to let you read one of the fictions themselves over I shall expect you to read all the said Introductions." To W. D. Howells he wrote (17 August 1908) with very near his full pride. "They are, in general, a sort of plea for Criticism, for Discrimination, for Appreciation on other than infantile lines—as against the so almost universal Anglo-Saxon absence of these things; which tends so, in our general trade, it seems to me, to break the heart. . . . They ought, collected together, none the less, to form a sort of comprehensive manual or *vademecum* for aspirants in our arduous profession. Still, it will be long before I shall want to collect them together for that purpose and furnish *them* with a final Preface."

In short, James felt that his Prefaces represented or demonstrated an artist's consciousness and the character of his work in some detail, made an essay in general criticism which had an interest and a being aside from any connection with his own work, and that finally, they added up to a fairly exhaustive reference book on the technical aspects of the art of fiction. His judgment was correct and all a commentator can do is to indicate by example and a little analysis, by a kind of provisional reasoned index, how the contents of his essay may be made more available. We have, that is, to perform an act of criticism in the sense that James himself understood it. "To criticise," he wrote in the Preface to *What Maisie Knew*, "is to appreciate, to appropriate, to take intellectual possession, to establish in fine a relation with the criticised thing and make it one's own."

What we have here to appropriate is the most sustained and I think the most eloquent and original piece of literary criticism in existence. (The only comparable pieces, not in merit of course but in kind, are by the same author, "The Art of Fiction," written as a young man and printed in *Partial Portraits*, and "The Novel in 'The Ring and the Book,'" written in 1912 and published in *Notes on Novelists*; the first of which the reader should consult as an example of general criticism with a prevailing ironic tone, and the second as an example of what the same critical attitude as that responsible for the Prefaces could do on work not James's own.) Naturally, then, our own act of appropriation will have its difficulties, and we shall probably find as James found again and again, that the things most difficult to master will be the best. At the least we shall require the maximum of strained attention, and the faculty of retaining detail will be pushed to its limit. And these conditions will not apply from the difficulty of what James has to say—which is indeed lucid—but because of the convoluted compression of his style and because of the positive unfamiliarity of his terms as he uses them. No one else has written specifically on his subject.

Before proceeding to exhibition and analysis, however, it may be useful to point out what kind of thing, as a type by itself, a James Preface is, and what kind of exercise the reader may expect a sample to go through. The key fact is simple. A Preface is the story of a story, or in those volumes which collect a group of shorter tales, the story of a group of stories cognate in theme or treatment. The Prefaces collocate, juxtapose, and separate the different kinds of stories. They also, by cross reference and development from one Preface to another, inform the whole series with a unity of being. By "the story of a story" James meant a narrative of the accessory facts and considerations which went with its writing; the how, the why, the what, when, and where which brought it to birth and which are not evident in the story itself, but which have a fascination and a meaning in themselves to enhance the reader's knowledge. "The private history of any sincere work," he felt, "looms large with its own completeness."

But the "story of a story" is not simple in the telling; it has many aspects that must be examined in turn, many developments that must be pursued, before its center in life is revealed as captured. "The art of representation bristles with questions the very terms of which are difficult to apply and appreciate." Only the main features can be named simply. There is the feature of autobiography, as a rule held to a minimum: an account of the Paris hotel, the Venetian palace, the English cottage, in which the tale in question was written. Aside from that, there is often a statement of the anecdote and the circumstances in which it was told, from which James drew the germ of his story. There is the feature of the germ in incubation, and the story of how it took root and grew, invariably developing into something quite different from its immediate promise. Then there is an account—frequently the most interesting feature—of how the author built up his theme as a consistent piece of dramatization. Usually there are two aspects to this feature, differently discussed in different Prefaces—the aspect of the theme in relation to itself as a balanced and consistent whole, the flesh upon the articulated plot; and the aspect of the theme in relation to society, which is the moral and evaluating aspect. Varying from Preface to Preface as the need commands, there is the further feature of technical exposition, in terms of which everything else is for the moment subsumed. That is, the things which a literary artist does in order to make of his material an organic whole—the devices he consciously uses to achieve a rounded form—are rendered available for discussion, and for understanding, by definition and exemplification.

These are the principal separate features which compose the face of a Preface. There are also certain emphases brought to bear throughout the Prefaces, which give them above all the savor of definite character. Again and again, for example, a novel or story will raise the problem of securing a compositional center, a presiding intelligence, or of applying the method of indirect approach. Again and again James emphasizes the necessity of being amusing, dramatic, interesting. And besides these, almost any notation, technical, thematic, or moral, brings James eloquently back to the expressive relation between art and life, raises him to an intense personal plea for the difficulty and delight of maintaining that relation, or wrings from him a declaration of the supreme labor of intelligence that art lays upon the artist. For

James it is the pride of achievement, for the reader who absorbs that pride it is the enthusiasm of understanding and the proud possibility of emulation.

None of this, not the furthest eloquence nor the most detached precept, but flows from the specific observation and the particular example. When he speaks of abjuring the "platitude of statement," he is not making a phrase but summarizing, for the particular occasion, the argument which runs throughout the Prefaces, that in art what is merely stated is not presented, what is not presented is not vivid, what is not vivid is not represented, and what is not represented is not art. Or when, referring to the method by which a subject most completely expresses itself, he writes the following sentence, James is not indulging in self-flattery. "The careful ascertainment of how it shall do so, and the art of guiding it with consequent authority—since this sense of 'authority' is for the master builder the treasure of treasures, or at least the joy of joys— renews in the modern alchemist something like the old dream of the secret of life." It is not indulgence of any description; it is the recognition in moral language of the artist's privileged experience in the use of his tools—in this instance his use of them in solving the technical problems of *The Spoils of Poynton*. James un- failingly, unflaggingly reveals for his most general precept its specific living source. He knew that only by constantly retaining the specific in the field of discussion could he ever establish or maintain the principles by which he wrote. That is his unique virtue as a critic, that the specific object is always in hand; as it was analogously his genius as a novelist that what he wrote about was always present in somebody's specific knowledge of it. In neither capacity did he ever succumb to the "platitude of state- ment."

It is this factor of material felt and rendered specifically that differentiates James from such writers as Joyce and Proust. All three have exerted great technical influence on succeeding writers, as masters ought. The difference is that writers who follow Joyce or Proust tend to absorb their subjects, their social attitudes, and their personal styles and accomplish competent derivative work in so doing, while the followers of James absorb something of a technical mastery good for any subject, any attitude, any style. It is the difference between absorbing the object of a sensibility and acquiring something comparable to the sensibility itself. The point may perhaps be enforced paradoxically: the mere imitators of the subject matter of Proust are readable as documents, but the mere imitators of James are not readable at all. It is not that James is more or less great than his compeers—the question is not before us—but that he consciously and articulately exhibited a greater technical mastery of the tools of his trade. It is a matter of sacrifice. Proust made no sacrifice but wrote always as loosely as possible and triumphed in spite of himself. Joyce made only such sacrifices as suited his private need—as readers of these Prefaces will amply observe—and triumphed by a series of extraordinary *tours de force.* James made consistently every sacrifice for intelligibility and form; and, when the fashions of interest have made their full period, it will be seen I think that his triumph is none the less for that.

There remains—once more before proceeding with the actual content of the Prefaces—a single observation that must be made, and it flows from the remarks above about the character of James's influence. James had in his style and perhaps in the life which it reflected an idiosyncrasy so powerful, so overweening, that to many it seemed a stultifying vice, or at least an inexcusable heresy. He is difficult to read in his later works—among which the Prefaces are included—and his subjects, or rather the way in which he develops them, are occasionally difficult to coordinate with the reader's own experience. He enjoyed an excess of intelligence and he suffered, both in life and art, from an excessive effort to communicate it, to represent it in all its fullness. His style grew elaborate in the degree that he rendered shades and refinements of meaning and feeling not usually rendered at all. Likewise the characters which he created to dramatize his feelings have sometimes a quality of intelligence which enables them to experience matters which are unknown and seem almost perverse to the average reader. James recognized his difficulty, at least as to his characters. He defended his "super-subtle fry" in one way or another a dozen times, on the ground that if they did not exist they ought to, because they represented, if only by an imaginative irony, what life was capable of at its finest. His intention and all his labor was to represent dramatically intelligence at its most difficult, its most lucid, its most beautiful point. This is the sum of his idiosyncrasy; and the reader had better make sure he knows what it is before he rejects it. The act of rejection will deprive him of all knowledge of it. And this precept applies even more firmly to the criticisms he made of his work—to the effort he made to reappropriate it intellectually—than to the direct apprehension of the work itself.

2

Now to resume the theme of this essay, to "remount," as James says of himself many times, "the stream of composition." What is that but to make an *ex post facto* dissection, not that we may embalm the itemized mortal remains, but that we may intellectually understand the movement of parts and the relation between them in the living body we appreciate. Such dissection is imaginative, an act of the eye and mind alone, and but articulates our knowledge without once scratching the flesh of its object. Only if the life itself was a mockery, a masquerade of pasted surfaces, will we come away with our knowledge dying; if the life was honest and our attention great enough, even if we do not find the heart itself at least we shall be deeply exhilarated, having heard its slightly irregular beat.

Let us first exhibit the principal objects which an imaginative examination is able to separate, attaching to each a summary of context and definition. Thus we shall have equipped ourselves with a kind of eclectic index or provisional glossary, and so be better able to find our way about, and be better prepared to seize for closer examination a selection of those parts of some single Preface which reveal themselves as deeply animating. And none of this effort will have any object except to make the substance of all eighteen Prefaces more easily available.

There is a natural division between major subjects which are discussed at length either in individual essays or from volume to volume, and minor notes which sometimes appear once and are done, and are sometimes recurrent, turning up again and again in slightly different form as the specific matter in hand requires. But it is not always easy to see under which heading an entry belongs. In the following scheme the disposition is approximate and occasionally dual, and in any case an immediate subject of the reader's revision.

To begin with, let us list those major themes which have no definite locus but inhabit all the Prefaces more or less without favor. This is the shortest and for the most part the most general of the divisions, and therefore the least easily susceptible of definition in summary form.

The Relation of Art and the Artist. The Relation of Art and Life. Art, Life, and the Ideal. Art and Morals. Art as Salvation for its Characters. These five connected subjects, one or more of them, are constantly arrived at, either parenthetically or as the definite terminus of the most diverse discussions. The sequence in which I have put them ought to indicate something of the attitude James brings to bear on them. Art was serious, he believed, and required of the artist every ounce of his care. The subject of art was life, or more particularly someone's apprehension of the experience of it, and in striving truly to represent it art removed the waste and muddlement and bewilderment in which it is lived and gave it a lucid, intelligible form. By insisting on intelligence and lucidity something like an ideal vision was secured; not an ideal in the air but an ideal in the informed imagination, an ideal, in fact, actually of life, limited only by the depth of the artist's sensibility of it. Thus art was the viable representation of moral value; in the degree that the report was intelligent and intense the morals were sound. This attitude naturally led him on either of two courses in his choice of central characters. He chose either someone with a spark of intelligence in him to make him worth saving from the damnation and waste of a disorderly life, or he chose to tell the story of some specially eminent person in whom the saving grace of full intelligence is assumed and exhibited. It is with the misfortunes and triumphs of such persons, in terms of the different kinds of experience of which he was master, that James's fiction almost exclusively deals.

It is this fact of an anterior interest that largely determines what he has to say about *The Finding of Subjects* and *The Growth of Subjects*. Subjects never came ready-made or complete, but always from hints, notes, the merest suggestion. Often a single fact reported at the dinner table was enough for James to seize on and plant in the warm bed of his imagination. If his interlocutor, knowing him to be a novelist, insisted on continuing, James closed his ears. He never wanted all the facts, which might stupefy him, but only enough to go on with, hardly enough to seem a fact at all. If out of politeness he had to listen, he paid no recording attention; what he then heard was only "clumsy Life at her stupid work" of waste and muddlement. Taking his single precious germ he meditated upon it, let it develop, scrutinized and encouraged, compressed and pared the developments until he had found the method by which he could dramatize it, give it a central intelligence whose fortune would be his theme, and shape it in a novel or a story as a consistent and self-sufficient organism. James either gives or regrets that he cannot give both the original *donnée* and an account of how it grew to be a dramatic subject for almost every item in the New York Edition.

Art and Difficulty. Of a course, a man with such a view of his art and choosing so great a personal responsibility for his theme would push his rendering to the most difficult terms possible. So alone would he be able to represent the maximum value of his theme. Being a craftsman and delighting in his craft, he knew also both the sheer moral delight of solving a technical difficulty or securing a complicated effect, and the simple, amply attested fact that the difficulties of submitting one's material to a rigidly conceived form were often the only method of representing the material in the strength of its own light. The experience of these difficulties being constantly present to James as he went about his work, he constantly points specific instances for the readers of his Prefaces.

Looseness. Looseness of any description, whether of conception or of execution, he hated contemptuously. In both respects he found English fiction "a paradise of loose ends," but more especially in the respect of execution. His own themes, being complex in reference and development, could only reach the lucidity of the apprehensible, the intelligibility of the represented state, if they were closed in a tight form. Any looseness or laziness would defeat his purpose and let half his intention escape. A selection of the kinds of looseness against which he complains will be given among the minor notes.

The Plea for Attention and Appreciation. The one faculty James felt that the artist may require of his audience is that of close attention or deliberate appreciation; for it is by this faculty alone that the audience participates in the work of art. As he missed the signs of it so he bewailed the loss; upon its continuous exertion depended the very existence of what he wrote. One burden of the Prefaces was to prove how much the reader would see if only he paid attention and how much he missed by following the usual stupid routine of skipping and halting and letting slide. Without attention, without intense appreciation an art of the intelligent life was impossible and without intelligence, for James, art was nothing.

The Necessity for Amusement. James was willing to do his part to arouse attention, and he labored a good deal to find out exactly what that part was. One aspect of it was to be as amusing as possible, and this he insisted on at every opportunity. To be amusing, to be interesting; without that nothing of his subject could possibly transpire in the reader's mind. In some of his books half the use of certain characters was to amuse the reader. Henrietta Stackpole, for example, in *The Portrait of a Lady*, serves mainly to capture the reader's attention by amusing him as a "character." Thus what might otherwise have been an example of wasteful overtreatment actually serves the prime purpose of carrying the reader along, distracting and freshening him from time to time.

The Indirect Approach and *The Dramatic Scene.* These devices James used throughout his work as those most calculated to command, direct, and limit or frame the reader's attention; and they are employed in various combinations or admixtures the nature of which almost every Preface comments on. These devices are not, as their name might suggest, opposed; nor could their use in equal parts cancel each other. They are, in the novel, two ends of one stick, and no one can say where either end begins. The characterizing aspect of the Indirect Approach is this: the existence of a definite created sensibility interposed between the reader and the felt experience which is the subject of the fiction. James never put his reader in direct contact with his subjects; he believed it was impossible to do so, because his subject really was not what happened but what someone felt about what happened, and this could be directly known only through an intermediate intelligence. The Dramatic Scene was the principal device James used to objectify the Indirect Approach and give it self-limiting form. Depending on the degree of limitation necessary to make the material objective and visible all round, his use of the Scene resembled that in the stage-play. The complexities of possible choice are endless and some of them are handled below.

The Plea for a Fine Central Intelligence. But the novel was not a play however dramatic it might be, and among the distinctions between the two forms was the possibility, which belonged to the novel alone, of setting up a fine central intelligence in terms of which everything in it might be unified and upon which everything might be made to depend. No other art could do this; no other art could dramatize the individual at his finest; and James worked this possibility for all it was worth. It was the very substance upon which the directed attention, the cultivated appreciation, might be concentrated. And this central intelligence served a dual purpose, with many modifications and exchanges among the branches. It made a compositional center for art such as life never saw. If it could be created at all, then it presided over everything else, and would compel the story to be nothing but the story of what that intelligence felt about what happened. This compositional strength, in its turn, only increased the value and meaning of the intelligence *as* intelligence, and vice versa. The plea for the use of such an intelligence both as an end and as a means is constant throughout the Prefaces—as the proudest end and as the most difficult means. Some of the specific problems which its use poses are discussed in the Prefaces to the novels where they apply. Here it is enough to repeat once more—and not for the last time—that the fine intelligence, either as agent or as the object of action or as both, is at the heart of James's work.

So much for the major themes which pervade and condition and unite the whole context of the Prefaces. It is the intention of this essay now to list some of the more important subjects discussed in their own right, indicating where they may be found and briefly what turn the discussions take. The Roman numerals immediately following the heading refer to the volume numbers in the New York Edition.* The occasional small Roman numerals refer to pages within a preface.

The International Theme (XII, XIV, XVIII). The discussion of the International Theme in these three volumes has its greatest value in strict reference to James's own work; it was one of the three themes peculiarly his. It deals, however, with such specific questions as the opposition of manners as a motive in drama, the necessity of opposing positive elements of character, and the use of naive or innocent characters as the subjects of drama; these are of perennial interest. There is also a discussion under this head of the difference between major and minor themes. In X (p. xix), speaking of "A London Life," there is a discussion of the use of this theme for secondary rather than primary purposes.

The Literary Life as a Theme (XV) and *The Artist as a Theme* (VII). The long sections of these two Prefaces dealing with these themes form a single essay. XV offers the artist enamored of perfection, his relation to his art, to his audience, and himself. VII presents the artist in relation to society and to himself. In both sections the possibilities and the actualities are worked out

*For possible convenience in reference I append the numbers and titles of those volumes which contain Prefaces. I *Roderick Hudson*; II *The American*; III *The Portrait of a Lady*; V *The Princess Casamassima*; VII *The Tragic Muse*; IX *The Awkward Age*; X *The Spoils of Poynton*; XI *What Maisie Knew*; XII *The Aspern Papers*; XIII *The Reverberator*; XIV *Lady Barbarina*; XV *The Lesson of the Master*; XVI *The Author of Beltraffio*; XVII *The Altar of the Dead*; XVIII *Daisy Miller*; XIX *The Wings of the Dove*; XXI *The Ambassadors*; XXIII *The Golden Bowl*.

with specific reference to the characters in the novels and the tales. The discussion is of practical importance to any writer. Of particular interest is the demonstration in VII that the successful artist as such cannot be a hero in fiction, because he is immersed in his work, while the amateur or the failure remains a person and may have a heroic downfall. The thematic discussion in XVI properly belongs under this head, especially pp. vii–ix.

The Use of the Eminent or Great (VII, XII, XV, XVI) and *The Use of Historical Characters* (XII, XV). The separation of these two subjects is artificial, as for James they were two aspects of one problem. Being concerned with the tragedies of the high intelligence and the drama of the socially and intellectually great (much as the old tragedies dealt death to kings and heroes) he argues for using the *type* of the historical and contemporary great and against using the actual historical or contemporary figure. The *type* of the great gives the artist freedom; the *actual* examples condition him without advantage. If he used in one story or another Shelley, Coleridge, Browning, and (I think) Oscar Wilde, he took them only as types and so far transformed them that they appear as pure fictions. The real argument is this: the novelist is concerned with types and only with the eminent case among the types, and the great man is in a way only the most eminent case of the average type, and is certainly the type that the novelist can do most with. To the charge that his "great" people were such as could never exist, James responded that the world would be better if they did. In short, the novelist's most lucid representation may be only his most ironic gesture.

The Dead as a Theme (XVII). Five pages (v–ix) of this Preface present "the permanent appeal to the free intelligence of some image of the lost dead" and describe how this appeal may be worked out in fiction. "The sense of the state of the dead," James felt, "is but part of the sense of the state of living."

On Wonder, Ghosts, and the Supernatural (XII, XVII) and *How to Produce Evil* (XII). These again make two aspects of one theme and the rules for securing one pretty much resemble those for securing the other. They are shown best "by showing almost exclusively the way they are felt, by recognising as their main interest some impression strongly made by them and intensely received." That was why Psychical Research Society ghosts were unreal; there was no one to apprehend them. The objectively rendered prodigy always ran thin. Thickness is in the human consciousness that records and amplifies. And there is also always necessary, for the reader to feel the ghost, the history of somebody's *normal* relation to it. Thus James felt that the climax of Poe's *Pym* was a failure because there the horrific was without connections. In both Prefaces the ghost story is put as the modern equivalent of the fairy story; and the one must be as economical of its means as the other. The problem of rendering evil in "The Turn of the Screw" (XII) was slightly different; it had to be represented, like the ghosts who performed it, in the consciousness of it by normal persons, but it could not be described. The particular act when rendered always fell short of being evil, so that the problem seemed rather to make the character *capable* of anything. "Only make the reader's general vision of evil intense enough, I said to myself—and that is already a charming job— and his own experience, his own sympathy (with the children) and horror (of their false friends) will supply him quite sufficiently with all the particulars. Make him *think* the evil, make him think it for himself, and you are released from weak specifications" (XII, xxi).

On the Use of Wonder to Animate a Theme (XI). This is the faculty of wonder on a normal plane and corresponds to freshness, intelligent innocence, and curiosity in the face of life; a faculty which when represented in a character almost of itself alone makes that character live. It is a faculty upon which every novelist depends, both in his books to make them vivid, and in his readers where it is the faculty that drives them to read. It is to be distinguished from the wonder discussed in the paragraph next above.

Romanticism and Reality (II). Seven pages in this Preface (xiv–xx) attempt to answer the question: Why is one picture of life called romantic and another real? After setting aside several answers as false or misleading, James gives his own. "The only *general* attribute of projected romance that I can see, the only one that fits all its cases, is the fact of the kind of experience with which it deals—experience liberated, so to speak; experience disengaged, disembodied, disencumbered, exempt from the conditions that we usually know to attach to it, and if we wish so to put the matter, drag upon it, and operating in a medium which relieves it, in a particular interest, of the inconvenience of a *related*, a measurable state, a state subject to all our vulgar communities." Then James applies his answer to his own novel (*The American*). "The experience here represented is the disconnected and uncontrolled experience—uncontrolled by our general sense of 'the way things happen'—which romance alone more or less successfully palms off on us." Since the reader knows "the way things happen," he must be tactfully drugged for the duration of the novel; and that is part of the art of fiction.

The Time Question (I, xii–xvi). Although the efforts dependent on the superior effect of an adequate lapse of time were consciously important to James, the lapse of time itself was only once discussed by him in the Prefaces, and there to explain or criticize the failure to secure it. Roderick Hudson, he said, falls to pieces too quickly. Even though he is special and eminent, still he must not live, change and disintegrate too rapidly; he loses verisimilitude by so doing. His great capacity for ruin is projected on too small a field. He should have had more adventures and digested more experience before we can properly believe that he has reached his end. But James was able to put the whole matter succinctly. "To give all the sense without all the substance or all the surface, and so to summarise or foreshorten, so to make values both rich and sharp, that the mere procession of items and profiles is not only, for the occasion, superseded, but is, for essential quality, amost 'compromised'—such a case of delicacy proposes itself at every turn to the painter of life who wishes both to treat his chosen subject and to confine his necessary picture." Composition and arrangement must give the *effect* of the lapse of time. For this purpose elimination was hardly a good enough device. The construction of a dramatic center, as a rule in someone's consciousness, was much better, for the reason that this device, being acted upon in time, gave in parallel the positive effect of action, and thus of lapsing time.

Geographical Representation (I, ix–xi). These three pages deal with the question: to what extent should a named place be rendered on its own account? In *Roderick Hudson* James named Northampton, Mass. This, he said, he ought not to have done, since all he required was a humane community which was yet incapable of providing for "art." For this purpose a mere indication would have been sufficient. His general answer to the question was that a place should be named if the novelist wanted to make it an effective part of the story, as Balzac did in his studies of the ville de province.

The Commanding Center as a Principle of Composition (I, II, VII, X, XI, XIX, XXI, XXIII). This is allied with the discussion of the use of a Central Intelligence above and with the three notes immediately below. It is a major consideration in each of the Prefaces numbered and is to be met with *passim* elsewhere. The whole question is bound up with James's exceeding conviction that the art of fiction is an organic form, and that it can neither be looked at all round nor will it be able to move on its own account unless it has a solidly posed center. Commanding centers are of various descriptions. In I it is in Rowland Mallet's consciousness of Roderick. In II it is in the image of Newman. In VII it is in the combination of relations between three characters. In X it is in a houseful of beautiful furniture. In XI it is the "ironic" center of a child's consciousness against or illuminated by which the situations gather meaning. In XIX it is in the title (*The Wings of the Dove*), that is, in the influence of Milly Theale, who is seen by various people from the outside. In XXI it is wholly in Strether's consciousness. In XXIII it is, so to speak, half in the Prince, half in the Princess, and half in the motion with which the act is performed.

The Proportion of Intelligence and Bewilderment (V). Upon the correct proportion depends the verisimilitude of a given character. Omniscience would be incredible; the novelist must not make his "characters too interpretative of the muddle of fate, or in other words too divinely, too priggishly clever." Without bewilderment, as without intelligence, there would be no story to tell. "Experience, as I see it, is our apprehension and our measure of what happens to us as social creatures—any intelligent report of which has to be based on that apprehension." Bewilderment is the subject and someone's intelligent feeling of it the story. The right mixture will depend on the *quality* of the bewilderment, whether it is the vague or the critical. The vague fool is necessary, but the *leading* interest is always in the intensifying, critical consciousness.

The Necessity of Fools (V, X, XI), and *The Use of Muddlement* (XI, XIX). These subjects are evidently related to that of Intelligence and Bewilderment. In themselves nothing, fools are the very agents of action. They represent the stupid force of life and are the cause of trouble to the intelligent consciousness. The general truth for the spectator of life was this: (X, xv)—"The fixed constituents of almost any reproducible action are the fools who minister, at a particular crisis, to the intensity of the free spirit engaged with them." Muddlement is the condition of life which fools promote. "The effort really to see and really to represent is no idle business in face of the *constant* force that makes for muddlement. The great thing is indeed that the muddled state too is one of the very sharpest of the realities, that it also has colour and form and character, has often in fact a broad and rich comicality, many of the signs and values of the appreciable" (XI, xiii).

Intelligence as a Receptive Lucidity (XI, XXI). The first of this pair of Prefaces almost wholly and the second largely deals with the methods of conditioning a sensibility so as to make a subject. In XI James shows how the sensibility of a child, intelligent as it may be, can influence and shape and make lucid people and situations outside as well as within its understanding. She, Maisie, is the presiding receptive intelligence, the sole sensibility, in the book, and is furthermore the sole agent, by her mere existence, determining and changing the moral worth of the other characters. In XXI Strether is outlined as the example of the adult sensibility fulfilling similar functions, with the additional grace of greatly extended understanding.

The Dramatic Scene (III, VII, IX, XI, XIX, XXI, and *passim*).
We have already spoken under the same heading of James's
general theory of the dramatic scene. It is too much of the whole
substance of the technical discussion in many of the Prefaces to
make more than a mere outline of its terms here possible. In III,
xxii and XIX, xxiii, there is developed the figure of windows
opening on a scene. The eye is the artist, the scene the subject, and
the window the limiting form. From each selected window the
scene is differently observed. In VII is discussed the theory of
alternating scenes in terms of a center (p. xv). In IX which is the
most purely scenic of all the books, the use of the alternating
scene is developed still further. At the end of XI there is a bitter
postscript declaring the scenic character of the form. In XXI there
is intermittent discussion of how to use the single consciousness
to promote scenes, and a comparison with the general scenic
method in XIX. It is principally to IX that the reader must resort
for a sustained specific discussion of the Scene in fiction and its
relation to the Scene in drama, and to XIX, of which pp. xii–xxiii
deal with the scenic structure of that book, where the distinction
is made between Scenes and Pictures and it is shown how one
partakes of the other, and where it is insisted on that the maximum
value is obtained when both weights are felt. Subordinate to this
there is, in the same reference, a description of the various re-
flectors (characters) used to illuminate the subject in terms of the
scene.

On Revision (I, XXIII). The Notes on Revision in these
Prefaces are mainly of interest with reference to what James
actually did in revising his earlier works. He revised, as a rule,
only in the sense that he re-envisaged the substance more ac-
curately and more representatively. Revision was responsible re-
seeing.

On Illustrations in Fiction (XXIII). This is perhaps the most
amusing note in all the Prefaces, and it is impossible to make out
whether James did or did not like the frontispieces with which his
collected volumes were adorned. He was insistent that no illustration to a book of his should have any direct bearing upon it. The

danger was real. "Anything that relieves responsible prose of the duty of being, while placed before us, good enough, interesting enough, and, if the question be of picture, pictorial enough, above all *in itself*, does it the worst services, and may well inspire in the lover of literature certain lively questions as to the future of that institution."

The Nouvelle as a Form (XV, XVI, XVIII). The nouvelle— the long-short story or the short novel—was perhaps James's favorite form, and the form least likely of appreciation in the Anglo-Saxon reading world, to which it seemed neither one thing nor the other. To James it was a small reflector capable of illuminating or mirroring a great deal of material. To the artist who practiced in it the difficulties of its economy were a constant seduction and an exalted delight.

On Rendering Material by its Appearances Alone (V). James had the problem of rendering a character whose whole life centered in the London underworld of socialism, anarchism, and conspiracy, matters of which he personally knew nothing. But, he decided, his wanted effect and value were "precisely those of our not knowing, of society's not knowing, but only guessing and suspecting and trying to ignore, what 'goes on' irreconcilably, subversively, beneath the vast smug surface." Hints and notes and observed appearances were always enough. The real wisdom was this:—that "if you haven't, for fiction, the root of the matter in you, haven't the sense of life and the penetrating imagination, you are a fool in the very presence of the revealed and the assured; but that if you *are* so armed you are not really helpless, not without your resource, even before mysteries abysmal."

And that is a good tone upon which to close our rehearsal of the major subjects James examines in his Prefaces. Other readers and other critics (the two need not be quite the same) might well have found other matters for emphasis; and so too they may reprehend the selection of Minor Notes which follow.

On Development and Continuity (I). Developments are the condition of interest, since the subject is always the related state of figures and things. Hence developments are ridden by the principle of continuity. Actually, relations never end, but the artist must make them appear to do so. Felicity of form and composition depend on knowing to what point a development is *indispensable*.

On Antithesis of Characters (I). The illustration is the antithesis of Mary and Christina in this book. James observes that antitheses rarely come off and that it may pass for a triumph, if taking them together, one of them is strong (p. xix).

On the Emergence of Characters (X, xiii). James's view may be summarized in quotation. "A character is interesting as it comes out, and by the process and duration of that emergence; just as a procession is effective by the way it unrolls, turning to a mere mob if it all passes at once."

On Misplaced Middles (VII, XIX). Misplaced Middles are the result of excessive foresight. As the art of the drama is of preparations, that of the novel is only less so. The first half of a fiction is the stage or theater of the second half, so that too much may be expended on the first. Then the problem is consummately to mask the fault and "confer on the false quantity the brave appearance of the true." James indicates how the middles of VII and XIX were misplaced, and although he believed the fault great, thought that he had in both cases passed it off by craft and dissimulation.

On Improvisation (XII, xvi). Nothing was so easy as improvisation, and it usually ran away with the story, e.g., in the *Arabian Nights*. "The thing was to aim at absolute singleness, clearness and roundness, and yet to depend on an imagination working freely, working (call it) with extravagance; by which law it wouldn't be thinkable except as free and wouldn't be amusing except as controlled."

The Anecdote (XIII, vi). "The anecdote consists, ever, of something that has oddly happened to some one, and the first of its duties is to point directly to the person whom it so distinguishes."

The Anecdote and the Development (XV, ix, XVI, v). In the first of these references James observes that whereas the anecdote may come from any source, specifically complicated states must come from the author's own mind. In the second he says that "The

Middle Years" is an example of imposed form (he had an order for a short story) and the struggle was to keep compression rich and accretions compressed; to keep the form that of the concise anecdote, whereas the subject would seem one comparatively demanding developments. James solved the problem by working from the outward edge in rather than from the center outward; and this was law for the small form. At the end of this Preface, there is a phrase about chemical reductions and compressions making the short story resemble a sonnet.

On Operative Irony (XV, ix). James defended his "supersubtle fry" on the ground that they were ironic, and he found the strength of applied irony "in the sincerities, the lucidities, the utilities that stand behind it." If these characters and these stories were not a campaign for something better than the world offered then they were worthless. "But this is exactly what we mean by operative irony. It implies and projects the possible other case, the case rich and edifying where the actuality is pretentious and vain."

On Foreshortening (VII, XV, XVII, XVIII). This is really a major subject, but the discussions James made of it were never extensive, seldom over two lines at a time. I append samples. In VII, xii, he speaks of foreshortening not by adding or omitting items but by figuring synthetically, by exquisite chemical adjustments. In XVII, xxv, the nouvelle *Julia Bride* is considered as a foreshortened novel to the extreme. In XVIII, xv, after defining once again the art of representation and insisting on the excision of the irrelevant, James names Foreshortening as a deep principle and an invaluable device. It conduced, he said, "to the only compactness that has a charm, to the only spareness that has a force, to the only simplicity that has a grace—those, in each order, that produce the *rich* effect."

On Narrative in the First Person (XXI, xvii–xix). James bore a little heavily against this most familiar of all narrative methods. Whether his general charge will hold is perhaps irrelevant; it holds perfectly with reference to the kinds of fiction he himself wrote, and the injury to unity and composition which he specifies may well be observed in Proust's long novel where every dodge is

unavailingly resorted to in the attempt to get round the freedom
of the method. The double privilege (in the first person), said
James, of being at once subject and object sweeps away difficulties
at the expense of discrimination. It prevents the possibility of a
center and prevents real directness of contact. Its best effect, perhaps, is that which in another connection James called the mere
"platitude of statement."

On Ficelles (XXI, xx). Taking the French theatrical term,
James so labeled those characters who belong less to the subject
than to the treatment of it. The invention and disposition of
ficelles is one of the difficulties swept away by the first-person
narrative.

On Characters as Disponibles (III, vii–viii). Here again James
adapted a French word, taking it this time from Turgenev. Disponibles are the active or passive persons who solicit the author's
imagination, appearing as subject to the chances and complications of existence and requiring of the author that he find for
them their right relations and build their right fate.

The rule of space forbids extending even so scant a selection
from so rich a possible index. But let me add a round dozen with
page references alone. On Dialogue (IX, xiii); Against Dialect
(XVIII, xvi); On Authority (XVIII, xviii); On Confusion of Forms
(IX, xvii); On Overtreatment (III, xxi; IX, xxii); On Writing of
the Essence and of the Form (III, xvii); On Making Compromises
Conformities (XIX, xii); On the Coercive Charm of Form (IX,
xvii); On Major Themes in Modern Drama (IX, xviii); On Sickness
as a Theme (XIX, vi); On Reviving Characters (V, xviii); On
Fiction Read Aloud (XXIII, xxiv); and so on.

The reader may possibly have observed that we have nowhere
illustrated the relation which James again and again made eloquently plain between the value or morality of his art and the
form in which it appears. It is not easy to select from a multiplicity
of choice, and it is impossible, when the matter emerges in a style
already so compact, to condense. I should like to quote four
sentences from the middle and end of a paragraph in the Preface
to The Portrait of a Lady (III, x–xi).

There is, I think, no more nutritive or suggestive truth in this connexion than that of the perfect dependence of the "moral" sense of a work of art on the amount of felt life concerned in producing it. The question comes back thus, obviously, to the kind and degree of the artist's prime sensibility, which is the soil out of which his subject springs. The quality and capacity of that soil, its capacity to "grow" with due freshness and straightness any vision of life, represents, strongly or weakly, the projected morality. . . . Here we get exactly the high price of the novel as a literary form—its power not only, while preserving that form with closeness, to range through all the differences of the individual relation to its general subject-matter, all the varieties of outlook on life, of disposition to reflect and project, created by conditions that are never the same from man to man (or, as far as that goes, from woman to woman), but positively to appear more true to its character in proportion as it strains, or tends to burst, with a latent extravagance, its mould.

These sentences represent, I think, the genius and intention of James the novelist, and ought to explain the serious and critical devotion with which he made of his Prefaces a *vademecum* —both for himself as the solace of achievement, and for others as a guide and exemplification. We have, by what is really no more than an arbitrary exertion of interest, exhibited a rough scheme of the principal contents; there remain the Prefaces themselves.

3

Although the Prefaces to *The Wings of the Dove* or *The Awkward Age* are more explicitly technical in reference, although that to *What Maisie Knew* more firmly develops the intricacies of a theme, and although that to *The Tragic Muse* is perhaps in every respect the most useful of all the Prefaces, I think it may be better to fasten our single attention on the Preface to *The Ambassadors*.

This was the book of which James wrote most endearingly. It had in his opinion the finest and most intelligent of all his themes, and he thought it the most perfectly rendered of his books. Furthermore in its success it constituted a work thoroughly characteristic of its author and of no one else. There is a contagion and a beautiful desolation before a great triumph of the human mind—before any approach to perfection—which we had best face for what there is in them.

This preface divides itself about equally between the outline of the story as a story, how it grew in James's mind from the seed of a dropped word (pp. v–xiv), and a discussion of the form in which the book was executed with specific examination of the method of presentation through the single consciousness of its hero Lambert Strether (pp. xv–xxiii). If we can expose the substance of these two discussions we shall have been in the process as intimate as it is possible to be with the operation of an artist's mind. In imitating his thought, step by step and image by image, we shall in the end be able to appropriate in a single act of imagination all he has to say.

The situation involved in *The Ambassadors*, James tells us, "is gathered up betimes, that is in the second chapter of Book Fifth. . . . planted or 'sunk,' stiffly or saliently, in the centre of the current." Never had he written a story where the seed had grown into so large a plant and yet remained as an independent particle, that is in a single quotable passage. Its intention had been firm throughout.

This independent seed is found in Strether's outburst in Gloriani's Paris garden to little Bilham. "The idea of the tale resides indeed in the very fact that an hour of such unprecedented ease should have been felt by him *as* a crisis." Strether feels that he has missed his life, that he made in his youth a grave mistake about the possibilities of life, and he exhorts Bilham not to repeat his mistake. "Live all you can. Live, live!" And he has the terrible question within him: "*Would* there yet perhaps be time for reparation?" At any rate he sees what he had missed and knows the injury done his character. The story is the demonstration of that vision as it came about, of the vision in process.

The original germ had been the repetition by a friend of words addressed him by a man of distinction similar in burden to those addressed by Strether to little Bilham. This struck James as a theme of great possibilities. Although any theme or subject is absolute once the novelist has accepted it, there are degrees of merit among which he may first choose. "Even among the supremely good—since with such alone is it one's theory of one's honour to be concerned—there is an ideal *beauty* of goodness the invoked action of which is to raise the artistic faith to a maximum. Then, truly, one's theme may be said to shine."

And the theme of *The Ambassadors* shone so for James that it resembled "a monotony of fine weather," in this respect differing much from *The Wings of the Dove*, which gave him continual trouble. "I rejoiced," James said, "in the promise of a hero so mature, who would give me thereby the more to bite into—since it's only into thickened motive and accumulated character, I think, that the painter of life bites more than a little." By maturity James meant character and imagination. But imagination must not be the *predominant* quality in him; for the theme in hand, the *comparatively* imaginative man would do. The predominant imagination could wait for another book, until James should be willing to pay for the privilege of presenting it. (See also on this point the discussion of Intelligence and Bewilderment above.)

There was no question, nevertheless, that *The Ambassadors* had a major theme. There was the "supplement of situation logically involved" in Strether's delivering himself to Bilham. And James proceeds to describe the novelist's thrill in finding the situation involved by a conceived character. Once the situations are rightly found the story "assumes the authenticity of concrete existence"; the labor is to find them.

"Art deals with what we see, it must first contribute full-handed that ingredient; it plucks its material, otherwise expressed, in the garden of life—which material elsewhere grown is stale and uneatable." The subject once found, complete with its situations, must then be submitted to a process. There is the subject, which is the story of one's hero, and there is the story of the story itself which is the story of the process of telling.

Still dealing with the story of his hero, James describes how he accounted for Strether, how he found what led up to his outburst in the garden. Where has he come from and why? What is he doing in Paris? To answer these questions was to possess Strether. But the answers must follow the principle of probability. Obviously, by his outburst, he was a man in a false position. What false position? The most probable would be the right one. Granting that he was American, he would probably come from New England. If that were the case, James immediately knew a great deal about him, and had to sift and sort. He would, presumably, have come to Paris with a definite view of life which Paris at once assaulted; and the situation would arise in the interplay or conflict resulting. . . . There was also the energy of the story itself, which once under way, was irresistible, to help its author along. In the end the story seems to know of itself what it's about; and its impudence is always there—"there, so to speak, for grace, and effect, and *allure*."

These steps taken in finding his story gave it a functional assurance. "*The* false position, for our belated man of the world —belated because he had endeavoured so long to escape being one, and now at last had really to face his doom—the false position for him, I say, was obviously to have presented himself at the gate of that boundless menagerie primed with a moral scheme which was yet framed to break down on any approach to vivid facts; that is to any at all liberal appreciation of them." His note was to be of discrimination and his drama was to "become, under stress, the drama of discrimination."

There follows the question, apparently the only one that troubled James in the whole composition of this book, of whether he should have used Paris as the scene of Strether's outburst and subsequent conversion. Paris had a trivial and vulgar association as the obvious place to be tempted in. The revolution performed by Strether was to have nothing to do with that *bêtise*. He was to be thrown forward rather "upon his lifelong trick of intense reflexion," with Paris a minor matter symbolizing the world other than the town of Woollett, Mass., from which he came. Paris was merely the *likely* place for such a drama, and thus saved James much labor of preparation.

Now turning from the story of his hero to the story of his story, James begins by referring to the fact that it appeared in twelve installments in *The North American Review*, and describes the pleasure he took in making the recurrent breaks and resumptions of serial publication a small compositional law in itself. The book as we have it is in twelve parts. He passes immediately to the considerations which led him to employ only one center and to keep it entirely in Strether's consciousness. It was Strether's adventure and the only way to make it rigorously his was to have it seen only through his eyes. There were other characters with situations of their own and bearing on Strether. "But Strether's sense of these things, and Strether's only, should avail me for showing them; I should know them only through his more or less groping knowledge of them, since his very gropings would figure among his most interesting motions." This rigor of representation would give him both unity and intensity. The difficulties, too, which the rigor imposed, made the best, because the hardest, determinants of effects. Once he adopted his method he had to be consistent; hence arose his difficulties. For example, there was the problem of making Mrs. Newsome (whose son Strether had come to Paris to save), actually in Woollett, Mass., "no less intensely than circuitously present"; that is, to make her influence press on Strether whenever there was need for it. The advantage of presenting her through Strether was that only Strether's feeling of her counted for the story. Any other method would not only have failed but would have led to positive irrelevance. Hence, "One's work should have composition, because composition alone is positive beauty."

Next James considers what would have happened to his story had he endowed Strether with the privilege of the first person. "Variety, and many other queer matters as well, might have been smuggled in by the back door." But these could not have been intensely represented as Strether's experience, but would have been his only on his own say-so. "Strether, on the other hand,

encaged and provided for as *The Ambassadors* encages and provides, has to keep in view proprieties much stiffer and more
salutary than our straight and credulous gape are likely to bring
home to him, has exhibitional conditions to meet, in a word, that
forbid the terrible *fluidity* of self-revelation."

Nevertheless, in order to represent Strether, James had to
resort to confidants for him, namely Maria Gostrey and Waymarsh, *ficelles* to aid the treatment. It is thanks to the use of these
ficelles that James was able to construct the book in a series of
alternating scenes and thus give it an objective air. Indispensable
facts, both of the present and of the past, are presented dramatically—so the reader can *see* them—only through their use.
But it is necessary, for the *ficelles* to succeed in their function, that
their character should be artfully dissimulated. For example,
Maria Gostrey's connection with the subject is made to carry itself
as a real one.

Analogous to the use of *ficelles*, James refers to the final
scene in the book as an "artful expedient for mere consistency of
form." It gives or adds nothing on its own account but only
expresses "as vividly as possible certain things quite other than
itself and that are of the already fixed and appointed measure."

Although the general structure of the book is scenic and the
specific center is in Strether's consciousness of the scenes, James
was delighted to note that he had dissimulated throughout the
book many exquisite treacheries to those principles. He gives as
examples Strether's first encounter with Chad Newsome, and
Mamie Pocock's hour of suspense in the hotel salon. These are
insisted on as instances of the representational which, "for the
charm of opposition and renewal," are other than scenic. In
short, James mixed his effects without injuring the consistency of
his form. "From the equal play of such oppositions the book
gathers an intensity that fairly adds to the dramatic." James was
willing to argue that this was so "for the sake of the moral
involved; which is not that the particular production before us
exhausts the interesting questions that it raises, but that the Novel
remains still, under the right persuasion, the most independent,
most elastic, most prodigious of literary forms."

It is this last sentiment that our analysis of this Preface is meant to exemplify; and it is—such is the sustained ability of James's mind to rehearse the specific in the light of the general—an exemplification which might be repeated in terms of almost any one of these Prefaces.

4

There is, in any day of agonized doubt and exaggerated certainty as to the relation of the artist to society, an unusual attractive force in the image of a man whose doubts are conscientious and whose certainties are all serene. Henry James scrupled relentlessly as to the minor aspects of his art but of its major purpose and essential character his knowledge was calm, full, and ordered. One answer to almost every relevant question will be found, given always in specific terms and flowing from illustrative example, somewhere among his Prefaces; and if the answer he gives is not the only one, nor to some minds necessarily the right one, it has yet the paramount merit that it results from a thoroughly consistent, informed mind operating at its greatest stretch. Since what he gives is always specifically rendered he will even help you disagree with him by clarifying the subject of argument.

He wanted the truth about the important aspects of life as it was experienced, and he wanted to represent that truth with the greatest possible lucidity, beauty, and fineness, not abstractly or in mere statement, but vividly, imposing on it the form of the imagination, the acutest relevant sensibility, which felt it. Life itself—the subject of art—was formless and likely to be a waste, with its situations leading to endless bewilderment; while art, the imaginative representation of life, selected, formed, made lucid and intelligent, gave value and meaning to, the contrasts and oppositions and processions of the society that confronted the artist. The emphases were on intelligence—James was avowedly the novelist of the free spirit, the liberated intelligence—on feeling, and on form.

The subject might be what it would and the feeling of it what it could. When it was once found and known, it should be worked for all it was worth. If it was felt intensely and intelligently enough it would reach, almost of itself, toward adequate form, a prescribed shape and size and density. Then everything must be sacrificed to the exigence of that form; it must never be loose or overflowing but always tight and contained. There was the "coercive charm" of Form, so conceived, which would achieve, dramatize or enact, the moral intent of the theme by making it finely intelligible, better than anything else.

So it is that thinking of the difficulty of representing Isabel Archer in *The Portrait of a Lady* as a "mere young thing" who was yet increasingly intelligent, James was able to write these sentences. "Now to see deep difficulty braved is at any time, for the really addicted artist, to feel almost even as a pang, the beautiful incentive, and to feel it verily in such sort as to wish the danger intensified. The difficulty most worth tackling can only be for him, in these conditions, the greatest the case permits of." It is because such sentiments rose out of him like prayers that for James art was enough.

THE SACRED FOUNT

Henry James had from the middle of his writing life to its end an increasing reputation for being difficult beyond reason: obscure in style, tenuous in theme, and subtle to the point of exasperation in both detail and general point of view. Somerset Maugham, who was entertained by him in Cambridge in 1910, gives the effect of judging his works when he describes James as escorting him up Irving Street and putting him on the Cambridge street trolley with the frightened and humanly inadequate bewilderment of an hysterical mother sending a small boy on a desperate journey. Maugham would have you feel that James's novels are like a vast ado about simple breathing. Henry Adams's wife, some thirty years earlier, was kinder in that she was more amusing when she remarked that it was not that Henry James bit off more than he could chaw but that he chawed more than he bit off. Ford Madox Ford, who professed to adore James as a master in the French sense, would speak of the time when his prose got gamey: quite as if his mastery had hung too long to be enjoyed by any but a depraved taste, and hung in an ivory tower at that. I do not think any one who has read James, however devotedly, has escaped a similar annoyed doldrums about his worth.

But I do not think, either, that there is anyone who has re-read James in even his most difficult works who has not found his doldrums redeemed, or buoyed up, by a sense of deep motion underneath. It is at such moments that all that had been exasperating in James's difficulty becomes rewarding. The reward is access of being.

It is one thing to state such an experience and another to represent it in more or less objective critical language. Criticism is the rashest of acts. Let us rashly fasten at once upon what would seem to have been the work in which James most nearly earned his reputation for difficulty in order to see, not how little, but how much we can work out of it; in order to see, that is, how much the difficulty is due not to the conception and execution of the artist, but to the reader's powers of attention. I mean the book called *The Sacred Fount*, which of all James's serious and accomplished books has been perhaps the least read, and, when read, the most misunderstood. Henry Adams, to whom James sent a copy as of regular habit, thought he understood it, but his one existing reference to it hardly suggests that he knew what it was that he understood. "Harry James has upset me," he wrote Mrs. Cameron, 6 May 1901. "John Hay has been greatly troubled by Harry's last volume, *The Sacred Fount*. He cannot resist the suspicion that it is very close on extravagance. His alarm made me read it, and I recognized at once that Harry and I had the same disease, the obsession of the *idée fixe*. Harry illustrates it by the trivial figure of an English country-house party, which could only drive one mad by boring into it, but if he had chosen another back-ground, his treatment of it would have been wonderfully keen. All the same it is insanity, and I think Harry must soon take a vacation, with most of the rest of us, in a cheery asylum." Rebecca West was less upset than infuriated by a story in which, as she describes it, "a week-end visitor spends more intellectual force than Kant can have used on The Critique of Pure Reason in an unsuccessful attempt to discover whether there exists between certain of his fellow-guests a relationship not more interesting among these vacuous people than it is among sparrows." Miss West also compared the "meanness" of the story—which was all she got out of it—to a rat nibbling in the wainscoting. Edmund Wilson gives an account of the book as eerie and academic and ambiguous beyond the repair of any explanation which he can offer. With a single exception, the other critics who have dealt with James have either ignored *The Sacred Fount* or dismissed it as flat failure.

The exception is Wilson Follett who produced an article upon it in *The New York Times Book Review* for 23 August 1936 which he called "Henry James's Portrait of Henry James." To Mr. Follett I am indebted for eloquent support in my own view that the book contains "319 of his most important, most luminous, and most neglected pages," and that it is the very nexus between his later middle work and his three late great novels which it immediately preceded. The nexus is a nightmare nexus in the sense that it gives a hallucinated, an obsessed, a haunted—perhaps a noxious—parable of life and the artist rather than such a slice of life as was then conventional in the sandwich of the novel.

Mr. Follett goes on to argue that it is not a novel at all, that James could not have regarded it as a novel, that it was, rather, a fictional presentation of James's philosophy of fiction: a kind of stupendous parody, fantastic and farcical, of James himself in contact with a chosen sample of his material. Mr. Follett was here only partly right. *The Sacred Fount* is not a novel as the novel then stood at the turn of the century nor within Mr. Follett's estimation of the form a generation later. But it is certainly a novel, or a use of the novel to a preponderant degree, in the sense that we call the works of Virginia Woolf, of Proust, of Kafka and of Joyce, novels. It would seem that James had not only predicted the course of a good deal of modern fiction but had indeed actually anticipated a good many of its novelties of form. *The Sacred Fount* only once more exemplifies James's own phrase to the effect that the novel "remains still, under the right persuasion, the most independent, the most elastic, the most prodigious of literary forms."

Let us say at once that what is prodigious about *The Sacred Fount* is in the mystery that the book encompasses and acknowledges, lucidly and luminously, but which it never reveals, as novels are expected to reveal mysteries, in terms of a plot or a series of actions. It makes its revelation rather in terms of older forms, the forms of the parable, or the fable, or, indeed, of the "mystery-play." But it does so within the frame and through the specific technique of fiction. Thus we have a fable that is dramatized if you are thinking of Aesop, or a mystery-play made into a narrative of meditation, if you are thinking of *Everyman* or *Dr. Faustus*. The intellectual intention of a fable so framed and so executed would be to find a formula for some central focus of human conduct which could be applied many times as occasion arose. The imaginative intention was to translate the intellectual formula into symbolic form. The total intention would be so to handle affairs that the book would create a meaning for itself apart from what had been foreseen either intellectually or imaginatively. It is in this sense that creation, for the artist, is discovery; and the genius of the artist shows in the skill by which he makes his discovery manifest, so manifest that we come at last to feel it in the mere title. At any rate this is so in James, his titles are gestures which come to mean all that is within.

But other influences than those of the fable and the mystery had operated to produce the peculiar form of *The Sacred Fount*. James had been for twenty years delightedly writing ghost stories, of which the most famous is *The Turn of the Screw*, but of which more characteristic examples may be found in such tales as "Owen Wingrave," "Sir Edmund Orme," "The Friends of the Friends," "The Beast in the Jungle," "Maud-Evelyn," "The Jolly Corner," and "The Altar of the Dead." If we are to understand either the total intention or the form of *The Sacred Fount*, we must have in mind a rough sense of the ghost stories out of which it sprung.

The first thing to emphasize is that by ghost story James did not mean the Psychical Research Society sort of ghost; he had no access to and no imaginative interest in the supernatural; his ghosts were invariably the hallucinated apparitions of the obsessions that governed or threatened, or as we say haunted the men and women whose stories he told. The ghost was the projected form of either a felt burden or an inner need. If the burden could be lifted or the need satisfied the ghost would be laid. But there are some burdens that, once felt, cannot be lifted, as there are some needs that it would be fatal to satisfy; and from these come familiar spirits, ghosts that are quite unlayable and become virtually our other selves. In one guise or another, they are the meaning that pursues us or is beyond us, drawing their shapes and habits from those parts of our imagination which are not occupied by the consciousness but which rather besiege the consciousness in all its dark environs. Thus where the siege is successful, there is an apparition, and the invaded mind becomes deranged, obsessed, or driven, as the case may be, though sometimes, too, it may be ordered, freed, or guided, which is the case when instead of embodying our apparitions we call them insight, intuition, or leading ideas. That there may be combinations of the two kinds, made in the underside of the mind, is a splendid imaginative possibility to the artist bent on expressing all his inarticulable knowledge of life in symbolic form. Whatever the logic of the matter, such was James's practice. In practically everything he wrote after 1900 and in much written before there is either an invoked and embodied ghost or an obsessive image, that is either a hallucinated person or a hallucinated theme, which when we can grasp it gathers up all the meaning in the novel or tale. Do not the wings of the dove, the golden bowl, the notion of embassy fairly and omnivorously haunt his three great novels? Are not the titles the alter egos for the books themselves?

All this is to say that James employed his ghosts, his obsessions, his general intense hauntednesses, to symbolize the deep underlying base for the moral images of possible life seen meshed in actual life to which his imagination was prone and his intellect devoted. For James was an inveterate moralist, and the great difficulty of his modern readers is to realize that morals may require an imaginative and prophetic, a symbolic, mode as well as a prudential or pragmatic mode, just as much in a twentieth-century novel as in the *Divine Comedy* or *Don Quixote*.

One more small emphasis is perhaps prerequisite to make us see James's version of the ghost story as a development of the fable and the mystery into a new and rational imaginative form capable of general use. It should be put with full italic emphasis, that whatever strange or ineluctable matters James's ghosts may represent, and whatever forms they may take, they are invariably given to the reader through some normal person's apprehension of them. They thus make no surrender of the rational imagination, but constitute rather an extension and enrichment of it, reaching imaginatively further and further into the field of actual moral experience. Like Aesop's animals, like Ovid's metamorphoses from man to animal to god, James's ghosts represent the attempt to give objective rational form—knowledgeable form—to all the vast subjective experience of our "other," our hidden, our secret selves which we commonly either deny, gloss over, or try to explain away. James knew as well as any philosopher—and rather better than his brother—that we cannot master our knowledge until we have objectified it, and cannot objectify it until we have found conventions to give it form.

The Sacred Fount is among other things an attempt to establish such a convention, and that is one of the lights in which we shall approach it. But we have other lights which must be turned on first and from quite a way off; and of these the first is the light of the tale called "Owen Wingrave" in which the ghost, though the full symbolic agent of the action, hardly reaches either the condition of an apparition or the condition of a full-fledged obsession, but is rather made powerful because it is posited as an agent that *ought* to appear and *ought* to obsess, both from the point of view of the protagonist and that of his enemies. The story is seen through the eyes of Spencer Coyle, a coach for Sandhurst, and deals with the young and too-soon death of one of his pupils, Owen Wingrave, at the double hands of his family and his own conscience. Owen is the grandson and heir to an old military family, a merciless old family of blood, but at the moment he is expected to go up to Sandhurst he refuses on the ground that war is stupid and Napoleon a scoundrel. His family and his fiancée Kate Julian combine to bring every pressure upon him and when he still refuses threaten to cut him off. As a final measure his coach Spencer Coyle is asked down to Paramore, the Wingrave country place, to add his pressure to theirs. Also present, and for the same reason, is young Lechmere, a companion of Owen's in

Coyle's school. Coyle, however, finds himself in sympathy with Owen rather than with his family, and sees the courage in Owen's act where his family see cowardice. The situation is heavy, embarrassing, and threatens catastrophe for the following day, when Coyle goes up to bed. There is in the house an unused room supposed to be haunted by an ancestor who in a fit of rage had struck and killed his young son and who had then died in that room. Owen's fiancée dares him to sleep in the room and when he says that he already has calls him liar. He then proposes that she lock him in, which she does. Grown compunctious during the night she goes to the room, unlocks it, and discovers him dead on the ancestral spot. "He was all the young soldier on the gained field."

The clue to all we want is in this concluding sentence, and especially in the last phrase: "on the gained field," which for me is indeed the true title of the tale. Owen is the end of his family and by his death has vanquished the family, which James has let us see as harsh and unscrupulous, as well as merciless and bloody, and altogether more violent than secure in its convictions: a family which, till Owen makes his decision, has never seen itself plain. The field which Owen gains is desolate, for the battle which he fought was against himself, against the dead hand of his family within himself. It is to be noticed in this connection that it did Owen no harm to sleep in the haunted room privily, nor any evil either. It was not until his family, through his fiancée who by upbringing was part of his family, knew it that the ghost came fully into the struggle between the mutilating conventions of society and the integrity of the individual. Even then, the ghost is not seen; no one reports a sight of it, and Owen says only that his ancestor's portrait on the staircase "moved" when he passed it. The ghost is nothing but the obsession of inherited conscience which Owen's own conscience, individually achieved, vanquishes. To make clear how closely James underlines the terms of the struggle, the name of the country house where the action occurs should be kept well in mind: Paramore. Paramore or paramour was once the name a knight gave to the lady-love for whom he did battle, but it is now the name given to an illicit love, the object of a degraded passion, which may yet have almost irresistible attractiveness. It is the ghost of Paramore that the death of Owen Wingrave lays.

A simpler tale along similar lines is that of "Sir Edmund Orme." A Mrs. Marden, upon being widowed, is haunted by the jilted lover of her youth, Sir Edmund Orme. The narrator of the tale is also haunted by him from the moment when he finds himself in love with Mrs.Marden's daughter Charlotte, and Charlotte in her turn is haunted when she acknowledges her love for the narrator. And at this moment Mrs. Marden dies. From the course of the story it would seem that the ghost appears so soon as Mrs. Marden or the narrator or Charlotte is in a position to jilt a true love. The act of jilting was for James, throughout his work, an act of moral abasement, for in performing it one damaged one's integrity. Again the clue we want comes at the end of the tale. "Was the sound I heard when Chartie shrieked—the other and still more tragic sound I mean—the despairing cry of the poor lady's death-shock or the articulate sob (it was like a waft from a great storm) of the exorcised and pacified spirit? Possibly the latter, for that was mercifully the last of Sir Edmund Orme."

If we may say that Sir Edmund Orme whether as ghost or as man was an object and guiding principle of human sympathy, I think it can be put that in "The Friends of the Friends" James takes a normal human ghost and makes something monstrous out of it. The ghost here comes near representing one of those hallucinated hysterias, those terrible looming fixations, those deep abortions of the human spirit, which destroy the humanity in which they fester precisely by seeming real when they are only actual—actual in the sense that a mirage is actual; it is experienced. The actuality for the imagined persons concerned is ineluctable, but the representation of it for the reader, through the perception of the narrator, is as James calls it, monstrously lucid.

It is lucid, but out of context with James's own obsession with the lost dead (which we shall come to) it is exasperating. In brief what happens is this. There is a man who had seen the apparition of his mother at the moment of her death and there is a woman who had suffered the apparition of her father at the moment of his death. The man and woman are unknown to each other but known to the narrator who believes that since they have so much in common they should become friends, or even better than friends. The narrator makes many attempts to introduce them but accident always intervenes. Thus in their very frustration they become increasingly aware of each other, a frustration of which the narrator makes an obsession sufficient for all three. The narrator, a middle-aged unattached woman, becomes engaged to the man, and makes what seems a fool-proof appointment for the two to meet at last. The woman writes that although her husband, from whom she has been separated because of his cruelty, has just died, she will come nevertheless. The narrator fears her own jealousy and writes her friend to come later, and so the meeting apparently fails. The narrator discovers two things the next day, first that her friend has visited her fiancé the night before, and second that her friend has died—also the night before. The question is whether it was her live body or her ghost that made the visit. Her fiancé insists that his visitor had been alive, but the narrator persists in believing that it had been her ghost and builds her jealousy of the ghost she has created to a tower of ruin. Her fiancé, she says, gives her only the dregs of tenderness and really loves only the ghost. She breaks off her engagement. Her jilted lover never marries, but dies not long after, which proves the narrator's case to her own satisfaction. He died—or as it were killed himself—"as a response to an irresistible call."

We see here the opposite instance to that of "Owen Wingrave"; we see a person bent on encompassing her own ruin by creating a conscience outside of and inaccessible to her own life. It is an example of how one creates the devil who destroys one, creates him out of the first obsession that comes to hand. It was the narrator, not the man who died, who responded to an irresistible call.

Much the same thing happened to the hero of "Maud-Evelyn" but with a greater encroachment of the obsessed illusion upon reality. A young couple about to marry brood upon the past so that it grows and grows: they did with the past, says James, what they would have wanted of the future they never, otherwise, had.

The young man, Marmaduke, believing falsely that his Lavinia has jilted him, goes off to Switzerland and there falls in with an elderly American couple, the Dedricks, who take him up so completely that they pretend he is married to their dead daughter. Marmaduke falls in with their obsession and gradually, so he tells Lavinia, "realizes" his courtship, wedding, married life, and his widowing, and dies, shortly after the death of the Dedricks, leaving everything to Lavinia. His early brooding upon the past has led him to make a temple of death, using the Dedricks' true obsession with the death of their daughter to fill out his own false obsession. Of such is the vacuous privity of those so vain as to think that life, not death, has bereaved them; there was nothing James so much liked as to punish a cad, and no way he so enjoyed doing it as by invoking a ghost.

Yet what was perhaps James's most poignant instance had no mere ghost but a deeper apparition, an apparition which as we shall come to see represented a failure in the flow of the sacred fount. This is the tale of "The Beast in the Jungle." Here again we have a young couple, John Marcher and May Bartram, apparently about to marry, and with every reason to do so. What prevents is that Marcher has the sense of something prodigious in store for him. "Something or other lay in wait for him, amid the twists and turns of the months and the years, like a crouching beast in the jungle" either to slay or to be slain. So for many years Marcher waits, using May Bartram in full egotism, never loving her, as she does him, for herself, until at last she dies. As she dies she almost tells him what he has done to her, but refrains. Later, in the graveyard, seeing one actually bereaved, whose look cut like a blade, he knows what all his sense of the prodigious has come to. He was the one man in the world to whom nothing had happened. So, out of the jungle of life, the beast leaps, and he falls on her grave. The man who had found nothing good enough for his anticipation, which is the man as the perfect cad, finds that he has been haunted all his life by the nothingness within him. Here again we have the man who denies himself for what he takes to be the sake of his self creating his own most fitting damnation.

Let us now examine two tales—our last before coming to *The Sacred Fount*, itself—in which, as in "Owen Wingrave," the direction is towards salvation rather than death or damnation. I say the "direction towards" rather "the accomplishment of," for one of the tales is "The Altar of the Dead," and here the altar is the tale itself, one of the most beautiful as it is one of the most needful that man has ever raised in the desert of his need. It can be thought of with "Lycidas" and "In Memoriam" and "Adonais," and without their particularity of reference. It serves no individual, but all the dead.

But it is through an individual that the service is performed, as in James's theory of the art of fiction all services must be performed. The individual is George Stransom, whose fiancée had died after their wedding date had been fixed, and who had been left thereafter permanently bereaved, but most so on the anniversary of her death. He had at first no arranged observance of the anniversary; it was merely that on that day he felt the mistress of his house as most absent. But gradually he formed the habit of numbering his dead—the deaths of his friends—and made a religion of remembering them, for the outward show of which he set candles burning, one for each, at an altar in a Catholic church. For one of the dead only he refused to light a candle, an old friend, Acton Hague, who had betrayed him. Many persons he knew dead better than he had known them alive; dead women, he says "had looks that survived—had them as great poets had quoted lines"; and he almost wished that certain of his friends might die and, earning their candles, come more intimately into his mind; but for Acton Hague he had nothing but the rankling wish to forget.

It was, however, made impossible for him to forget his friend and he was not allowed to reach his own death until he was ready to remember him, completely, candle and all, with the others. Haunting his altar in the church, there is a woman devoted to her dead as he to his. He discovers her dead to have been Acton Hague, whom, though he had betrayed her, she has forgiven. She tries to persuade Stransom to forgive and remember, and when he will not, they both break off the service of the altar—which has come to be the service of each other. Stransom falls ill, and on his recovery returns to the church knowing that there is one more candle still to be lighted before his life can be completed. "It was in the quiet sense of having saved his souls that his deep strange instinct rejoiced. This was no dim theological rescue, no boon of a contingent world; they were saved better than faith or works could save them, saved for the warm world they had shrunk from dying to, for actuality, for continuity, for the certainty of human remembrance."

Being so saved, it is the dead themselves that cause Stransom, in the end, at the verge of his own death, to insist on granting the woman's request, that the last place in the blaze of light be filled; for how otherwise could he himself be remembered? For these things take place among the living; it is only by the living that the dead can be remembered. Acton Hague's candle is his own; or his own is Acton Hague's. James shows himself here, in his addiction to the dead, as the deep and inveterate humanist. He strove to make human, to bring back to the center, that passage of experience furthest from the human in the normal life, which is the experience, not of dying which is a mere personal termination, but of the dead. The sense of the state of the dead was, as he put it in the preface to this tale, "but a part of the sense of the state of the living," and it was that community which had to be felt, and it had to be felt against "the general black truth that London was a terrible place to die in; doubtless not so much moreover by conscious cruelty or perversity as under the awful doom of general dishumanisation."

If in "The Altar of the Dead" James made a fable of the dead who must be kept alive for the sake of the living, in "The Jolly Corner" he made a fable of the living who must be slain for the sake of the living, which if at first it sounds like nonsense can easily enough be cleared up. I mean that James saw that there are within most of us those partly living other selves, those unused possibilities out of the past, those unfollowed temptations of character, which if not struck down will overwhelm and engulf the living self. The psychiatrist usually deals with such struggles in our day under his own abstracting terms just as the church formerly dealt with them in the guise of exorcism, the casting out of devils. Yet as the adventures themselves are imaginative, and constitute the chief romance of desperation as they make up also the tragedy of vain hope, the artist has a right to practice his own form of exorcism, which is exorcism through the objective representation of some normal person's perception of the particular horror concerned. "The Jolly Corner" is an attempt at such an imaginative exorcism.

But what is to be exorcised must first be seen and judged. Spencer Brydon, at fifty-six, returns to New York City after thirty-three years as a sporting gentleman in Europe in order to see to his affairs. As he picks up knowledge of the tenements he owns he also resumes something of his intimacy with Alice Staverton. It seems to him, now on the great scene of business, that he might have been a good businessman and perhaps ought to have been so even at the cost of not ever having won his sense which he shares with Alice, of "Europe"—the whole cultivated great world. What raises this temptation as much as anything is the Jolly Corner, the house in which he was born and grew up, and in which as he visits it he feels "the impalpable ashes of his long-extinct youth, afloat in the very air like microscopic motes," and the house which, upon the moment of his return, is about to be pulled down after having been kept in order for him these many years by a caretaker, Mrs. Muldoon, who goes in an hour a day but who wouldn't, she says, go in after dark. With the image of the house always in the foreground, Brydon intensely speculates, as James puts it, upon what he would have been had he stayed in New York. He shares his speculations with Alice Staverton during the afternoon and early evening, and late at night takes up the habit of visiting the house. Alice finally tells him that she has twice dreamed of that other fellow, that alter ego which had never actually bloomed. The knowledge of her dreams promotes his own sense of possibility, and he begins to stalk the big and dangerous game of his unrealized self late every night, protecting himself by telling the people at his hotel that he was going to his club and the people at the club that he was going to his hotel.

Thus he would be a terror to his own ghost, hunting it, driving it to bay. After a few futile nights, the game turns, and he begins to feel that his alter ego is pursuing *him*, and he feels at best that he has become reduced to the state of holding on while slipping, sliding, down some awful incline, and he feels at worst the imminent danger of flight. One night he finds on an upper floor a door that is closed which he has left open, and flees part way down. His discretion prevents him from opening the door, lest he find what he is after. "Great builded voids, great crowded still-nesses put on, often, in the heart of cities, for the small hours, a sort of sinister mask, and it was of this large collective negation that Brydon presently became conscious." Deeply demoralized, he goes back to see, through his dread, if the door is now open, resolved if it is to go out the window. The door is still closed, and he goes down to leave the house and finds the inner vestibule open where he had left it closed. He has now to go on whether for liberation or for supreme defeat. As he hesitates in the dawn light there *is* his alter ego, hands raised over its face, with two fingers shot away from one hand. The hands drop, and there is revealed the face of a stranger. Evil, odious, blatant, vulgar, the figure advances for aggression—a rage of personality before which his own collapses. He wakes a few hours later, his head in Alice's lap; she had, she says, dreamed the stranger at the moment of its apparition exactly as Brydon had seen him, mutilated spirit and imperfect hand and all, and had accepted it as different because it was her imagination had made it so. Thus by seeing, through her eyes as well as his own, precisely what he might have been but couldn't be, Brydon was liberated from even the temptation of ever becoming anything but himself. He had struck the sacred fount.

But he had struck it, like the other men and women in these fables of hallucination, a little too pat, a little too much by the author's mere contrivance, his combination of exhortation and coincidence, quite to fit our taste for the represented verisimilitude. That is the trouble with the fable as a fictional form; however eloquent it may be, however just and penetrating, however ex-emplary and applicable, it is always a little too much about the other fellow, until one acts it out for oneself. It leans a little too much upon our willingness to accept its intention and neglects to show us enough, to make manifest enough, the precarious balance of inward stresses upon which it rests. In a fable it is only the poetry of the passages of commentary that rise to mastery, never the drama or the narrative, which is not to belittle the poetry, but to say why it is that even the most poetic fable is supreme only by the way, in passing, in preparation for something else. If I may make the distinction, I would say that the fable cannot master experience by containing it as the drama and the novel can, but gives us rather an imaginative formula which we can fill out from our own resources as occasion and the quality of our imaginative will permit.

For James the fable and the novel worked together, and also against each other, sharpening his mind, quickening his sensibility, developing his grasp of the coordinating powers of overt form, from about 1880, when he wrote the *Portrait of a Lady*, to 1900, when he wrote *The Sacred Fount*, which served as the final preparation for his great later work precisely by merging, to a degree that most of his successors have failed of, the external form of the fable (the kind of significance that may be formulated in a few sentences), the mediate or psychological form of the plot (the kind of significance that comes by the anticipation, suspension, and delivery of action) and the substantive or poetic form which belongs especially to the novel (the kind of significance which is embedded in the detail and context of the language itself). I do not say that *The Sacred Fount* was the first attempt James made of his late skills, for such books as *What Maisie Knew*, *The Awkward Age*, and *The Spoils of Poynton* all preceded it by a few years, but in none of these is there the intensity either of intention or of illumination which *The Sacred Fount* for the first time shows. He had previously seen his methods and felt his themes, but he had not attempted to put them together until suddenly, in *The Sacred Fount*, the influence of his ghost stories, his "mysteries," his pure fables, afforded the nexus between his themes and his methods; and that is why his ghost stories have been dealt with here at such length. They furnish us an angle of approach similar to that which James must more or less have used himself when he came at last again to try for a full picture, a full story, a full drama, with the added dimension of as full a hallucination of life as he could manage to see.

How shall we describe this added dimension if not as the sense of mystery felt? It is what you know without ever quite being able to say. The closer you come the more you know it is there, and even what it must be, but you never see it plain, never put it behind you. Its greatest reality lies in its inaccessibility. Its only actuality is in the represented experience of its pursuit. It is before you, ever recessive, ever imminent, ever precarious, represented ever, if at all, as what we may call the *prehensility* of the imagination itself in the face of mystery.

What is prehensile is what is able to grasp, take hold of, and by extension what is able to grasp sensitively, intimately in the sense of closely, like the monkey's tail on the branch, or the fingers on the ladder rung when the foot slips. As applied to the imagination then, the prehensile quality is the quality of being in direct, absolute, and undifferentiated contact with the substance of interest. It can be thought of at one end as the quality of raw experience and at the other end as the sphinx quality of experience. It may be either pure response or pure knowledge. Either aspect of such experience is common in actual life, focal in religious life, and the central object in works of imagination. It is the door knob held or turned; it is the quality of experience which comes with unmitigated attention. Unmitigated attention may be easy in the bloodstream, in love, before the face looking in at the window; but in the life of the mind it is the hardest condition to come by. In one respect it is a freed condition secured by absolute surrender of the will; and in another respect it is an imprisoned condition imposed by the utter absorption of the will. The point is that all that is intermediate in the ordinary run of things is made immediate; which is what we mean when we say that breathing becomes breathless, hope becomes terror, or time stands still, but without any cessation, in any of these cases, of life, faith, or motion, and with an access of inward, of mutual verisimilitude. That—the heightened sense of being, of self-proving identity, of the authority of experience—that is what the prehensile imagination grasps.

No wonder then, if I am right in describing the quality of imagination at work, that in *The Sacred Fount* there is a relish of detail, a passion of attentiveness, a specific pride of free achievement, which together give a tone of independent, unassailable mastery to all but the last pages of the book. Nothing else of his creative work shows such a tone for more than a few pages; only in the critical Prefaces is the tone of assurance at all comparable. Perhaps only in these two works did James feel wholly at home, finding his creative will both surrendered and absorbed. That the coupled ease was no accident but congenital, of the very blood of James's work, will I hope be made plain as we get at the substance of *The Sacred Fount* and estimate its archetypical value.

One sense of its substance partakes of one of the most familiar of all pressing mysteries. It is the mystery of the power that passes among us, depleting or restoring us, in friendship, in love, and even in more public relations. There is not one of us who has not felt, suddenly in the midst of the indifferent ease of intimacy, the sense of having been battened upon to the point of exhaustion by his friend, his lover, or the ominous stranger; and there is not one of us, either, who has not felt the opposite, that he has taken fresh vitality, drained all the season's sap from the other fellow. It is in our lonely moments, in which we feel ourselves, as the case may be, either most nearly whole or most nearly nothing, that we feel the pressure of this mystery most nearly; and as James dwelt so much in his lonely moments it is only surprising that he did not sooner fasten all he could muster of his prehensile imagination upon the beautiful, the critical job of making that mystery manifest.

Manifest, in *The Sacred Fount,* it immediately becomes, merely by accelerating the pace and projecting a critical awareness of the ordinary experience of human intimacy; and it is even called an apologue or parable and given a rough form of words quite early in the book, on page 29.* Whether you batten or are

*New York: Charles Scribner's Sons, 1901—Ed.

battened upon, you tap the sacred fount. "But the sacred fount," James goes on, "is like the greedy man's description of the turkey as an 'awkward' dinner dish. It may be sometimes too much for a single share, but it's not enough to go round."

That is the nub or germ or seminal principle of the book upon which, if you grant its initial validity, all the rest hangs; for it is a principle of growth which no novelist who saw it could help taking up, and in this book the hero, the presiding consciousness, is a novelist. Appearing anonymously, but in no other way beyond our powers of identification, we may follow Follett and for convenience call the narrator—him whose sense of things makes up the story—James himself, but in doing so we only give ourselves a handle to a door which later will open of its own accord. For the narrator could be any novelist, and the novelist could in the long run and in the same predicament be any man.

James, then, finds himself, in the first chapter, on the station platform on the way down to Newmarch for a weekend house party which, in the last chapter, he is about to leave, rather before the others. The elapsed time is no more than a day and a half and the measured time—the represented time—is very near, saving the digestive hours of sleep, equal to the elapsed time. Yet this short time, because of the intensity and the singleness of the action, is elastic and recessive and progressive, and goes through nearly all the temporal paces which may be envisaged to make a nexus between the inward and personal time and the outward and impersonal clock time. Neither Proust nor Mann made more use of either the proliferation, the inner doubling, or the intermittences of time than James in this book; an affair in which James had what is still the great operative advantage that he kept as close as fiction can well keep to the three unities of time and place and action—so close that in retrospect the book seems to have represented, and exhausted, but a single moment, all the rest being supports or extensions of it, though which moment it is we should be hard put to it to say.

Perhaps, provisionally, we can say it is the moment named on page five when James asks himself how Grace Brissenden, who had been plain so long, becomes pretty so late. At any rate the rest of the book is but a combination of a free development of that question and an increasingly intensive attempt to answer it. It is not, of course, a question about Grace Brissenden only, for her transformation directly involves that of others. Her husband Guy, for example, actually years younger than she, has grown visibly older. If the Brissendens were the only people concerned, it might be a mere matter of the exhaustive process of marriage, enormously hastened by passion and James's prophetic imagination. But there are others. There is Gilbert Long, who like Grace, has grown suddenly young, and who is found in Grace's company. And there is May Server, who like Guy suddenly shows as exhausted and limp and old, and who is found in Guy's company, drawn together by the fellow feeling of the naked. The one thing James is at first clear about is that these changes are the result of the power not oneself that made for passion, and that power is felt as an unseen impalpable scent, the scent of the maculate, the peculiar, so deeply craving to be known that, known, nothing else can be attended to. Thus May Server, being exhausted, is seen as immanently a vampire, and the senility of Guy Brissenden is felt as having been gained not honestly but by cheating of some deep hidden sort. Similarly, Mrs. Brissenden and Gilbert Long are felt as facing each other, full to bloating almost, and craving to be drained of their dishonest, because unconscious, gains.

Something like this is the predicament in which James feels his four characters when he begins to pump them, both directly and through the aid of Ford Obert, a painter, who is only less given to scrutiny than James, and who has his own conversations with the four victims, which he reports to James for rebuilding. The credibility of these conversations is secured by an appeal to that extraordinary and ambiguous force of the ego in all of us, which in order to feel itself deeply must needs also spread itself thin on the surface—a force everywhere attested to by the tenacity of interest with which people listen when you talk about *them*. So precarious and so necessitous is the self that it craves to the point of jealousy any and every reassurance however much it may come to mere vulgar gossip or blatant formulas about character. James takes full advantage of this vanity of the self, but takes no less

advantage, too, of that pride of the self which keeps Mrs. Brissenden and Mrs. Server from ever giving themselves quite away no
matter how tenaciously and relentlessly he tries to make them. It
is indeed their resistance that gives James his deepest clues. It is as
they try to hide that James knows where to look.

Let us put what James looks for and what he finds on its
most obvious plane, not in order to leave it there, but to give
ourselves, as it gave James, something to go on with. What ought
to have happened, according to James's figure about the sacred
fount giving too much for a single share but not enough to go
round, would be something like this (and I follow Follett's account). Mrs. Brissenden has drained Brissenden. Brissenden seeks
replenishment from May Server, draining her so far as he can.
Mrs. Brissenden pours out her bounty on Long, without ex-
hausting herself. Long pours out on May Server. Thus two have
been emptied and re-filled, and two have been filled and re-
emptied, all movements having been by the law of gravity in a
downward direction. The circle should be completed and the
status quo ante restored. James has just about finished this picture,
on evidence unimpeachably gained from his four persons, to his
own satisfaction as a novelist, when the whole thing breaks down.

The novelist had come too close to perfecting life in his
fiction for the peace of Mrs. Brissenden's nerves. Dealing so completely with her vanity—with all their vanities—she begins to
fear for the citadel of her pride. She therefore resorts to a subter-
fuge supported by a lie, and goes so far, as life almost always
goes, as to make the lie actual. Life, in James the novelist's view,
always lives its lies with the most complete and befuddling sincerity possible. Mrs. Brissenden comes running to James at midnight and with all the eloquence of guilt protests that she is at one
with her husband, and has never been anything else. Brissenden is
thus taken away from May Server, and Gilbert Long is credited
with having associated himself with some other woman, perhaps
Lady John (another guest of the house), perhaps someone else
unnamed. James believes none of this, but nevertheless admits
himself vanquished by Mrs. Brissenden and states that he will be

leaving early. The novelist can do no more with these monsters he has created; life has taken them over.

For Wilson Follett this is all. James has written his parable of the novelist who works at his vision only to find that at the moment of its clarification life barges in and muddies the stream; and perhaps that is as far as one should go. Certainly James has repeatedly throughout his career accused life of spoiling art, and certainly he has insisted that it is only art that can "do" for life all that life cannot do for itself, give it, in the particular instance, the intelligence and meaning and completeness of form. The moral of art for James was always that it took a hint from clumsy, stupid life and made of it the beautiful intelligent instance. Things come to pass, whether for good or for evil, that in life only ought to happen; which is to say that art is prophetic where life, on the same prompting, is defeated or inconclusive. That is a good deal to believe, and to believe it demands more of one than most artists demand. How much James did demand it is clear in the following passage.

> There was a general shade in all the lower reaches
> —a fine clear dusk in garden and grove, a thin suffusion
> of twilight out of which the greater things, the high
> tree-tops and pinnacles, the long crests of motionless
> wood and chimnied roof, rose into golden air. The last
> calls of birds sounded extraordinarily loud; they were
> like the timed, serious splashes, in wide, still waters, of
> divers not expecting to rise again. I scarce know what
> odd consciousness I had of roaming at close of day in
> the grounds of some castle of enchantment. I had
> positively encountered nothing to compare with this
> since the days of fairy-tales and of the childish imagi-
> nations of the impossible. *Then* I used to circle round
> enchanted castles, for then I moved in a world in
> which the strange 'came true.' It was the coming true
> that was the proof of the enchantment, which, more-
> over, was naturally never so great as when such coming
> was, to such a degree and by the most romantic stroke

> of all, the fruit of one's own wizardry. I was positively
> —so had the wheel revolved—proud of my work. I had
> thought it all out, and to have thought it was, wonder-
> fully, to have brought it.

If we stop at this point we shall have made James—the James
who is the narrator of *The Sacred Fount*—content and justified
with his work as a novelist; but James did not stop there, nor did
his justification; he went on directly:

> Yet I recall how I even then knew on the spot that there
> was something supreme I should have failed to bring
> unless I had happened suddenly to become aware of
> the very presence of the haunting principle, as it were,
> of my thought. This was the light in which Mrs. Server,
> walking alone now, apparently, in the grey wood and
> pausing at sight of me, showed herself in her clear
> dress at the end of a vista. It was exactly as if she had
> been there by the operation of my intelligence, or even
> by that—in a still happier way—of my feeling.

What this haunting principle of thought, the force beneath
his intelligence, was, will become clear if we pursue it among its
perceptions; not all of them, of course, for that would be to quote
the book, but a few that may seem exemplary. James sees very
soon that Mrs. Server, as a victim, may be conscious of her
abasement, and that her consciousness of it is her tragedy. Thus
he sees her (as he has made her) "a wasted and dishonoured
symbol" of "the possibilities of our common nature." As he talks
to her, forcing her to talk, he slowly reveals himself to the reader
as her conscience, the externalized and figured form of her inner
voice, which if she acknowledges it will break her down unless
she can first find strength, from some new person, with which to
meet it. But she will not acknowledge James, as the voice of her
conscience or otherwise, for she has not enough intelligence to do
so. Conscience is the created other self of the hallucinated intelligence. "If there had been," says James, "a discernment of *my*
discernment," he would have had to take it "as the menace of

some incalculable catastrophe or some public ugliness." And when Lady John begins to discern, calling him a bore for trying to play providence (which is surely another name for conscience), James heads her off, telling her that she has a lucidity in which "the highest purity of motive looks shrivelled and black"; which is his way of suggesting that her clumsy curiosity sees too little to see anything but evil.

Mrs. Brissenden, unlike Lady John, and unlike, too, all the other figures presented, has enough intelligence to see all that James sees; has enough, that is, to begin to create for herself the sense of what James has stood for all along, the sense of criticism, the sense of horrors, the sense of conscience. But where James revels in it as the deep exhilaration of intellectual mastery of things unamenable, she rejects it as the scruple that destroys the very amenableness of things when one does not seek to master them. She tells him he is crazy, a busybody, a creator of horrors that do not exist, and insists that she will have nothing to do with him. But even in her insistence, she acts under his influence; even in denying him, and all he stands for, she has at least to *pretend* to modify her life according to his word. He has forced her to make at least the sign of reparation for the actually irreparable injury done to Mrs. Server and to her own husband. She has been hallucinated—supposing James *is* crazy—into accepting his vision of life against her will and without her knowledge. James had given her the butter and honey of his imagination to eat, so that, if we may borrow the language of Isaiah, she might know to refuse the evil, and choose the good. Thus we see that as novelist James is the hidden conscience of his characters, and as conscience he is himself their sacred fount. For is not conscience indeed that imaginative resource of which, if one has it at all, one has too much for a single share and yet not enough to go round?

Such at any rate seems to have been James's obsession to a varying degree for some twenty years. It is conscience that is the haunting principle of all the ghost stories we have dealt with, and the alter ego that each of them struggles to create or to recognize is but the projected image of conscience, either good conscience, or bad conscience, either succeeding or failing to join imagination and life at a focal moment. From the merely asserted conscience of the characters in the earlier fables, it became the conscience of their creator as well in *The Sacred Fount*; so that we may call that book the last lucid nightmare of James's hallucinated struggle with his conscience as a novelist. For in *The Wings of the Dove*, which was his next book, the novelist and his conscience disappear into the novel, and the sacred fount flows unimpeded through the created characters themselves.

IN THE COUNTRY OF THE BLUE

We are now about to assay the deep bias, the controlling, characteristic tension in the fiction of Henry James as it erupts in those tales where the theme is that of the artist in conflict with society. To erupt is to break out irresistibly from some deep compulsion, whether of disease or disorder, into a major reaction; and that is exactly what happens to James when in the first full maturity of his fifties he began to meditate, to feel borne in upon him, the actual predicament of the artist as a man of integrity in a democratic society. He broke out, he erupted from the very center of his being, and with such violence that to save himself he had need of both that imagination which represents the actual and that which shapes the possible. James made of the theme of the artist a focus for the ultimate theme of human integrity, how it is conceived, how it is destroyed, and how, ideally, it may be regained. For James, imagination was the will of things, and as the will was inescapably moral, so the imagination could not help creating—could not fail rather to re-create—out of the evil of the artist's actual predicament the good of his possible invoked vision. As the artist is only a special case of the man, so his vision is only an emphatic image of the general human vision; that James could make so much of the special case and the emphatic image of the artist comes about because, more than any other novelist of his scope, he was himself completely the artist. By which I mean that he was free to dramatize the artist precisely because he was himself so utterly given up to his profession that he was free of the predicament of the artist the moment he began to write. He felt none of that difficulty about conviction or principle or aim in his work which troubles a lesser writer; both his experience and his values came straight and clear and unquestionable, so much so that he seems to inhabit another world, that other world which has as substance what for us is merely hoped for. James, as an artist, was above all a man of faith. As he said of one of his characters in another connection, he was copious with faith.

But there is a disadvantage in too complete a faith, as well for an artist as for a saint. Complete faith runs to fanaticism or narrowness. The act of faith tends to substitute for understanding of the thing believed in. If your values come to you unquestioned, you risk taking them on principle and of course. Only the steady supplication of doubt, the constant resolution of infirmity, can exercise your values and your principles enough to give them, together, that stretch and scope which is their life. If you dismiss doubt and ignore infirmity, you will restrict the scope that goes with the equivocal and reduce the vitality that goes with richness of texture. So it was with Henry James. His very faith in his powers kept him from using them to their utmost and caused him to emphasize only his chosen, his convicted view. That is why he is not of the very greatest writers, though he is one of the indubitably great artists, and especially in our present focus, the portrait of the artist. That is why, too, as his faith increased he came less and less to make *fictions* of people and more and more to make *fables*, to draw parables, for the ulterior purposes of his faith. He came less and less to tell and more and more to merely say. But— and this is what saves him to us for reading—the habit of the novelist was so pervasive in him that he could no more than breathing help dramatizing his fables or actualizing, to the possible limit of his frame, the story of his parables. Indeed, in his old age, which for him constituted a continuing rebirth, he made of the frame of his fables a new frame for the novel or tale only less than the greatest frames. I refer to *The Ambassadors, The Wings of the Dove, The Golden Bowl*, perhaps to *The Sense of the Past* and *The Ivory Tower*, and certainly to the tales in *The Finer Grain*; for in these works the form of the fable, the point of the parable, are brought to extreme use precisely by being embedded in the sensibility of fiction. These take rise I think in *The Sacred Fount*, which, not a novel at all but a vast shadowy disintegrating parable, disturbing distressing distrait, indeed distraught, remains in the degree of its fascination quite ineluctable. It is the nightmare nexus, in James's literary life, between the struggle to portray the integrity of the artist and the struggle to portray, to discover, the integrity of the self.

This is another way of saying that the tales which exhibit the artist occupy an intermediate position in James's work; and we shall see that they look both ways, to the social novels that preceded them and to the fiction of fate that came after them. They look back to the conditions of life in general and forward to the prophecy of life beyond and under, or at any rate in spite of, the mutilating conditions. I think of Isabel Archer, in *The Portrait of a Lady*, how the conditions of life, particularly the conditions of money and marriage and their miring in manners, slowly dawned on her. You feel that if Isabel can only acknowledge the conditions, if she can see for once what life is like, she will be free to go on, where to go on means to meet more and more conditions. We know that in the process of going on she will lose—indeed she has already lost them—the freshness and promise and candor of youth, which are taken as the ordinary expenses laid out for the general look, whether dimmed or sharpened always somehow maimed and marked, of maturity. So for Isabel Archer and most of the early fiction. On the other hand I think of Milly Theale in *The Wings of the Dove*, whom we see actually killed by the conditions of life, acknowledge them how she will, but who yet so transcends them that her image—the image of the lost dead—brings to Kate Croy and Merton Densher, who had betrayed her in life, an unalterable unutterable knowledge of what life is under its mutilated likeness. Things could, as

Kate told Merton at the end, never again be the same between them; all because of the freshness and candor which had not perished but been discovered in the death of Milly Theale, and the unbroken, unbreakable promise of life which merely for *them*, as they had failed Milly, could not be kept but was to hover over them unavailingly ever afterwards. Milly had her triumph in death; but in *The Ambassadors*, Lambert Strether had his triumph in life, and so Maggie Verver in *The Golden Bowl*, both triumphing precisely over the most mutilating conditions of life that could well have come their way. So again, perhaps with the most beautiful lucidity of all, there is the shabby little bookseller Herbert Dodd in "The Bench of Desolation," whom we see deprived of the last resource of outward dignity—as a character he is all scar tissue—till he has nothing left but his lonely hours upon his seaside bench of desolation. The bench of desolation is where you sit still with your fate—that of which you cannot be deprived. For Herbert Dodd that bench has these many years turned out to be enough, when the return of the lost love of his youth, whom he thought had betrayed him, makes it a bench of triumph as well. The triumph consists for him, as for the others, in the gradual inward mastery of the outward experience, a poetic mastery which makes of the experience conviction.

Between the earlier persons who master life by submitting to its conditions and the later persons who master what lies under the conditions by achieving a conviction of the self—for surely a man's convictions may be said to be the very shape of his self—comes the little, the slightly anomalous race of artists. Why they come between, rather than either as a culmination or a beginning, is plain when we look at their characteristic fate. The man who is completely an artist is incompletely a man, though in his art he may envisage man completely. The meaning of the artist in history, that is in life as he lives it, in the conditions under which he works, is like the meaning of history itself. History, as Niebuhr says, is meaningful, but the meaning is not yet. The history of the artist is prophetic, but the meaning of the prophecy cannot now be known. What happens to the artist, apart from his meaning, is common enough knowledge. If we look at the fables Henry James offers us, we see at once that all these artists are doomed men, as doomed as the characters in Hemingway, but not as in Hemingway by the coming common death. They are doomed either because they cannot meet the conditions of life imposed upon them by society or because society will have none of them no matter how hard they try. That, for James, was the drama of the artist, and he put it in the simple white and black terms of the fable and the fairy story. The artist either gave in to the evil and corruption of society, or society refused a living to the good and incorruptible artist. But let us ask why James chose the artist for the living focus of his drama, when it might as well have been the queen or the kitchen maid as in the fairy tales, or the men and women next door who provide us, unadulterated with any self-interest, such excellent views of our selves. Why, that is, did not James begin with the persons he came to?

We may say that he did not know enough, that he had not matured enough, and perhaps it would be better so to beg the question. But there is a kind of logic which we can apply after the event, which is where logic works best. The artist is *given* as in death-struggle with society, as much so as the thief or the murderer but with the advantage of heroism and nobility as a luminous character in the mere murk of the struggle. That every man and woman, and perhaps more so every child, is also engaged in a death-struggle with society, or at least with his neighbor's society, is not so clear; you would not think of *yourself* as struggling with society, but the artist and his critics have, I regret to say, vied with each other at every opportunity to see which could say so louder, especially since the spread of literacy and education has multiplied artists of all sorts at the same time that changing institutions took away the function of the artist in society. The artist became thus a natural puppet, ready-made, completely understandable, to represent the great central struggle of man as an individual, which is not often, when you consider the stakes, an understandable struggle at all, and to make a drama of which the novelist has to work from the ground up. It is no wonder then that James should consider the struggle of the artist as one of the great primary themes, especially when you add to the picture that he might

incidentally dramatize himself a little—a temptation not beyond
the purest artist—and do his trade a good turn.

But the evidence is not limited to the writings of artists and
critics. There comes particularly pat to the kind of artist of whom
James wrote a passage in de Tocqueville's classic work on the
republic of the United States of America. It was not quite going to
be, he foresaw long before Henry James began writing novels, a
model republic of letters. There is a little chapter in the first book
of the second part called "The Trade of Literature" from which I
extract the following passage:

> Democracy not only infuses a taste for letters among
> the trading classes, but introduces a trading spirit into
> literature. . . . Among democratic nations, a writer
> may flatter himself that he will obtain at a cheap rate a
> meager reputation and a large fortune. For this purpose
> he need not be admired, it is enough that he is liked.
> . . . In democratic periods the public frequently treat
> authors as kings do their courtiers; they enrich and
> they despise them. . . . Democratic literature is always
> infested by a tribe of writers who look upon letters as a
> mere trade; and for some few great authors who adorn
> it, you may reckon thousands of idea-mongers.

The picture is fresh enough for our own day, and we take it with
the more authority because it was frankly prophetic on the part of
a man more than generously disposed towards democracy. It is a
description that James could have made for himself, and which in
fact he did largely make, both in his life of Hawthorne and in the
fiction which we are about to engage. De Tocqueville only re-
minds us of what James well knew, that an author can expect his
readers to know that the race of literary artists is itself composed
of good and bad, of very black and very white practitioners; so
that the nobility of the good writer will go as granted once it is
mentioned, as will the flunkeyism of the bad writer. Thus the
author of a fiction about an artist has all the advantages of coarse
melodrama without losing any of the advantages of high tragedy.
He can merely impute unto his chosen character what virtues or

vices he likes without being under any necessity to show them. In fiction, the stated intent of goodness, of high seriousness, is worthless in every realm of life except that of artist; elsewhere the character must be shown as actual, in the artist the stated intention is enough. We shall see that James fully availed himself of this freedom, redeeming himself only by the eloquence of his statement and the lesson of his parable. These, the eloquence and the lesson, will be what we bring away with us. For it goes without saying that James was never taken in, in his created characters, by the meretricious, and was always deliberately sold by the high serious. In this respect, as perhaps nowhere else in James, the reader always knows exactly where he is at. What happened to the literary personages will vary with the incident and the conditions recorded; but nothing can happen to their chances once they are stated, for their characters are articulated ready-made as soon after their first appearance as possible, like puppets or like gods as you may choose to think.

This is no accident nor any part of James's idiosyncrasy; it is a limiting condition of the artist as a character in fiction to the extent that he is represented in the role of artist. If he drops the role, anything within the power of the author to represent may happen to him as a person; as artist he is only a shrunken and empty simulacrum of himself in his other roles; he may know the meaning, but he cannot share the motion.

This is one of the lessons that, if James's fables are taken literally, they best attest; and literally is very near how James meant his lessons to be taken. But we do not need to stick to James. The character of Stephen Dedalus, both in *A Portrait of the Artist as a Young Man* and in *Ulysses*, certainly works of the greatest richness and scope, comes to us very fully as a young man, but as an artist he comes to us only by the eloquence of Joyce's mere statement. The poem he writes and the diary he keeps, the lecture he gives on Hamlet, come to us quite independent of the created figure of Stephen. Even the great declaration that ends the earlier book, where Stephen resolves that he will "forge in the smithy of [his] soul the uncreated conscience of [his] race," must be taken either as a free lyric spoken by an actor, where something else might have done as well, or as an image in which the whole boy shrinks suddenly into an agonized intention that can never be realized in life or act but only in art itself. It is much the same thing with Herr Aschenbach, the old novelist in Thomas Mann's *Death in Venice*, who is never given to us as a novelist except by imputation. The role of artist is indeed called on for other purposes, to give quickly a background against which the reader will find credible and dramatic the image of old Aschenbach, the famous and dignified novelist, as an outsider, a figure so isolated by his profession of artist that he fairly aches to corrupt himself, to debase himself, both as a man and as an artist. It might almost be put that to the degree that he had become an artist he had ceased existing—as it were, ceased living—so that the desire for life becomes identified with the temptation to corruption. And so it turns out. The only possible resumption of life for him is tainted with corruption, with effeminate infatuation, with deliberate indignity and self-humiliation. But it is too late in the season, the season of his life and the season in Venice, both of which are struck down by pestilence. His adored and beautiful Tadzio is taken away to safety, and Herr Aschenbach resumes his profession, in the act of dying, by in his delirium reenacting the *Phaedo* of Plato. Aschenbach the artist could have no life except in that terrible privation of life which is art.

It is only the obverse of the same coin that André Gide shows us in *The Counterfeiters*, where the novelist reaches life only by a driven and deliberate corruption, a personal disintegration as great as the formal disintegration of the work of art in which it is represented. That Mann and Gide show us corruption as the necessary predilection of the artist, where James and Joyce show us art—that is, integrity of spirit—as the redemption of life, is perhaps due to the seeming fact that neither the German nor the Frenchman have as full and fanatic a conviction of their profession of artists as that suffered at an equal maximum by both James and Joyce.

To get back a little nearer to our particular problem of the portrait of the artist in Henry James—though indeed we have never been far from it—there is another way of expressing the

predicament of the artist as a character in fiction. He comes to life
only as he ceases to be an artist; he comes to life, in a word, only as
he *fails* to be an artist, and he fails when the conditions of life
overcome him at the expense of his art. This becomes a very pretty
problem indeed when the novelist reflects that all this amounts to
saying that the actual source of art, the life of which it is the
meaning, is the artist's undoing. Gide solves the problem, and so
does Mann, by disintegrating the art as well as the life. Joyce,
with no greater honesty but with greater moral insight, represents
the struggle of the man *in society*, not as an outsider but as one
very much at the heart of things, to become an artist. It was not
for nothing that Joyce defined the sentimentalist as one who "is
unwilling to incur the enormous responsibility for a thing done."
Stephen Dedalus is shown to us in the very process of realizing,
for the sake of his art, responsibility for every deed of his life. In
Joyce, the artist, like God, dies every day. He dies into man and is
reborn; the death is necessary to the birth. Henry James had
neither the catholicism of Joyce, the bitter protestantism of Gide,
nor the faustian spirit of Mann at his back; he had rather—and
only—his unquestioned faith in the adequacy of the free intelligence in life and the freed imagination in art. He had thus less
equipment, or at any rate a less articulated philosophy, than the
others, and it is perhaps for that reason that he produced his ideal
artists who failed only in life and succeeded only in art, and his
other artists, equally ideal, who failed in art only because they
insisted on success, financial or social success, in life. The realm
of the ideal is often nearest to those who have nearest to no
philosophy; but so is the realm of the actual, which is the artist's
realm, and James may have been nearer right in what he did with
his facts than the others.

At least we have James's own abundantly eloquent answer
to the charge that he ought never to have exhibited in art creatures
who never existed in life. I give part of the answer as he made it in
the preface to *The Lesson of the Master*.

What does your contention of non-existent conscious
exposures, in the midst of all the stupidity and vulgarity

and hypocrisy, imply but that we have been, nationally, so to speak, graced with no instance of recorded sensibility fine enough to react against these things?—an admission too distressing. What one would accordingly fain do is to baffle any such calamity, to *create* the record, in default of any other enjoyment of it; to imagine, in a word, the honorable, the producible case. What better example than this of the high and helpful public and, as it were, civic use of the imagination?—a faculty for the possible fine employments of which in the interest of morality my esteem grows every hour that I live. How can one consent to make a picture of the preponderant futilities and vulgarities and miseries of life without the impulse to exhibit as well from time to time, in its place, some fine example of the reaction, the opposition or the escape?

In this passage, and in the whole preface from which it is taken, I think James reaches the pinnacle of principle to which he was able to expose the idealism with which he worked; and I have planted my quotations here in the center of this discussion of the portrait of the artist because they raise—especially just after our references to the practice of Joyce and Gide and Mann—considerations of great importance not only to the criticism, the appreciation, of James's fictions but also to the whole general theory of fiction itself—if you like, to the whole theory of art. There are several theories of the value of art which are tenable until you begin to apply them in the interpretation of particular works of art, when as a rule the value of the art shrinks at once to nothing and there is *nothing but* moral value left. No artist and hardly any user of art whose eyes are open can take the slightest interest in any *nothing but* theory of art's value. James's theory is very tempting because, if adopted, it shows how moral value gets into a work of art without leaving you to shudder for the fate of the art. The artist, he says with all the rush and eloquence of immediate experience, the artist *creates* the moral value out of the same material and by the same means with which he creates his other values—out of the actual and by means of imagination. The values are, though distinguishable, inextricable. Some works may show aesthetic values without moral values, and other works very clearly have no aesthetic values and yet shriek to heaven with their moral values, but where you have both orders of value as they are created, together, so they must be felt together, at least so long as the work being enjoyed is enjoyed as art.

Among the consequences which flow from James's statement, if I understand it right, there are two which deserve emphasis for the freedom and the privation they impose on the artist. One has to do with the inclusive nature of moral value in art. As the experience in art must be somehow of the actual and as the record must be somehow of the imaginative, then the artist is free to create evil as well as good without risk of police interference. It is not that his vision of evil may overcome his vision of good, but that, if he is to be an artist of any scope, he must create both, and if the emphasis is on the one in a given work it must have the other as its under or supporting side. It is truly the devil who minds God's business as it is God who gives the devil something to do. But, and this is the second consequence kept for emphasis from James's statement, to have validity whether moral or aesthetic, whatever the artist *creates* (though not what he merely puts in by the way) must show its source in the actual; for it is otherwise either immoral or vapid, and likely both. If the architecture of even the noblest cathedral were not based on the actual it would fall apart, but without a vision beyond the actual it could have never been built at all. Art, in this view, tends toward the ideal but without ever quite transcending the actual from which it sprang. The ideal, in fact, in this restricted sense of the word, is what the artist creates; but the ideal, to have any significant worth, must approach the actual, with the striking effect which needs every meditation we can give it, that the nearer it approaches the actual the more greatly ideal the creation will seem. There is the force of Dante's ideal hell, that it approaches so close to the actual of this life; and there is the relative weakness of James's tales of the literary life, and despite his plea of moral necessity, that though they spring from hints in the actual world the "super-subtle fry" of his authors do not approach near enough to the actual. The fable is always frailer than the image, however more cogent. Thus Joyce's Dubliners who translated the initials IHS of *In Hoc Signo* over the cross, as I Have Suffered, were not blasphemers but better believers for so doing.

The examples are endless; but to our present interest it is the principle that counts, and its relation to the artist, and if we turn to our chosen tales of Henry James we shall find that though as dramas they do not show us very much of the actual, as fables they illuminate the principles by which James was later to anchor his most difficult and precarious ideals safe and firm—poetically valid—in flesh and blood. That is, as these tales occupy an inter-mediate position in the general development of James as works of art, so they represent for us an intermediate state of knowledge, that critical and fascinating state when principles fairly itch for action but have not yet run down into the skill of the hand that acts, that in this case writes. As stories they are stories about stories, and the most fascinating kind of stories, those that for both aesthetic and moral reasons can never quite be written. All the moral value is in the possibility not lived up to, and all the aesthetic value is in the possibility not lived down to. It is the same possibility, looking either way, the possibility of the really superior artist triumphing over society by cutting himself off from every aspect of it except the expressive, or the possibility of this same superior fellow—and I hardly know which version is more tragic—coming to failure and ruin, expressive failure and personal ruin, by hands whose caresses are their most brutalizing blows, the hands of society itself, the society that, in de Tocque-ville's phrases, would like an author rather than admire him, or, worse, would enrich and despise him.

The possibilities are indeed wonderful, and furnish half the conversation at literary parties, where the most enriched authors always turn out the most despised, very often justly. James does not deal with the literary party, whether because the institution had not grown much in his day or because it was open only to satire, which was not his purpose. He deals rather with the English house party and the English dinner party where there is a reputable author present for demolition. The effect is not too

different, and affords the advantages of an outwardly more deco-
rous set of conventions and even for a welcome shift of scenes
from lawn to church, dinner table to parlor, or parlor to smoking
room, smoking room to bedroom; which taken together, as even a
novice at fiction should know, makes the problem of moving
people from place to place and so of setting up new relations or
modifying old ones, relatively easy. So it is that all but one of the
fables we are dealing with make use of the machinery of entertain-
ment for the mechanics of the plot. That is, the artifices that in
actual society do most to prevent communication and obscure
situations, James uses to promote intimacy and to clarify situations. He mastered the means which because of his life—in one
London year he dined out three hundred times—were almost
alone at his disposal; the lesson of which may be that it explains
why so many of James's people are never able to meet each other
openly and yet contrive to put everything between them that is
necessary.

That is exactly the situation in "The Figure in the Carpet,"
where I think we may put it that we know what the puzzle is
precisely to the extent we realize it is insoluble, like the breath of
life. The narrator who is himself a writer and nameless (the
narrators of all these tales are writers and most of them are
nameless) reviews the latest novel of Hugh Vereker in a magazine
called *The Middle*, and shortly afterwards attends a house party
where Vereker is a guest, as is his book, both unopened by any of
the company, though both are the principal subjects of attention.
Someone shows Vereker the review and Vereker says it is very bad;
he had not realized the reviewer is present. When he does so, he
apologizes to the narrator but insists that, nevertheless, like everybody else, he has missed the Figure in the Carpet: the general
intention, the string to his pearls, the passion of his passion. The
narrator tries his best to make up, both by reading Vereker's
works and by tackling him personally. On his failure he passes
the puzzle along to his friend George Corvick, who shares the
problem with his fiancée. They in their turn grow futile and
frenzied—so frenzied that their marriage comes to hang upon
their success. Corvick goes off to Bombay as a correspondent, and

while there wires: Eureka. The narrator and Corvick's finacée, Gwendolen Erme, try to guess what it must be. Corvick stops off on Vereker at Rapallo during his return journey, and writes that Vereker has verified his discovery. Gwendolen marries George on condition that he reveal his secret; he dies on his honeymoon before writing it down. Gwen refuses to tell the narrator what it is, because, says she, it is her life. Vereker dies. Then Gwen, who has remarried to Drayton Deane, a critic, herself dies on the birth of a second child. After a decent but excruciated interval—for in James decency most of all is subject to excrucation—the narrator does his best to discover from Deane what the secret of Vereker's work had been. But Gwendolen had never told him; and the Figure in the Carpet is safe. Nobody knows or can know what it can be. What then was the puzzle? It may be that there was none, or none except to those who wrote—or read—for the passion of the passion; which was certainly not how the narrator, nor any of his friends, either wrote or read. A frenzied curiosity is not passion. Or it may be that the Figure in the Carpet is necessarily ineluctable. Perhaps it only ought to be there; that much, acuteness can discover. In his prefatory remarks, James does nothing to help; but says only that "the question that accordingly comes up, the issue of the affair, can be but whether the very secret of perception hasn't been lost. That is the situation, and 'The Figure in the Carpet' exhibits a small group of well-meaning persons engaged in a test." We can only note that well-meaning persons are notoriously unperceptive, and add that the secret of perception in readers comes very near the secret of creation in artists.

"The Figure in the Carpet" is perhaps a tea-time and tepid whiskey fable, for it is over these beverages that it largely occurs; and so represents, I think, no more than at most can be made out of obsessed gossip. James may have meant more for it—his preface suggests that he did—but it would seem actually, as written, to mean no more than that there is a figure in the carpet if you can imagine it for yourself; it is not there to discover. It is rather like Kafka, manqué, the exasperation of the mystery without the presence of the mystery, or a troubled conscience without any evidence of guilt.

Rather similar but carried further, further for actuality, by the very conventionality of its fantasy—its *glaring* incredibility— is the fable of "The Private Life." Here again the narrator is a writer unnamed, this time on vacation in the Alps in a house full of people connected with the arts. Among the guests are Clare Vawdrey, a writer of genius but a second-rate man; Lord Mellifont, a magnificent public figure but nothing much when not in public; and Blanche Adney, a great actress, for whom Vawdrey is writing a play, and who is quite friendly with the narrator. The second-rateness of Vawdrey and the magnificent public presence of Mellifont gradually become suspect to Blanche and the narrator. Pursuing their curiosity, the narrator sneaks into Vawdrey's room in the evening, while Vawdrey is outside talking to Blanche; there the narrator discovers Vawdrey's other self writing industriously in the dark. Later, by plan, Blanche gets her chance, and while the narrator keeps Vawdrey outside herself makes the acquaintance of the other or "ghost" self and falls in love with him. Meantime the narrator finds the outer self even duller than he had thought: "the world," he reflects, "was vulgar and stupid, and the real man would have been a fool to come out for it when he could gossip and dine by deputy." Lord Mellifont, on the other hand, must be himself an apparition, called into being by a public relation only; by himself he must be nothing, literally nothing. Blanche and the narrator go looking for him on that assumption, and of necessity he appears in front of them; if they had not looked for him, he would have been unable to materialize. "He was all public and had no corresponding private life, just as Clare Vawdrey was all private and had no corresponding public." Of this little piece what does one say but that the ghost story is the most plausible form of the fairy tale; it makes psychological penetration ominous because not verifiable. Who would care to verify a ghost, especially two ghosts who have the unity only of opposites? Life, the actuality, lies somewhere between; and it is a relief to think that your dull man of genius keeps a brilliant ghost in his workroom, just as it is a malicious delight to figure that your brilliant public man is utterly resourceless without a public.

"The Private Life" is a fantastic statement, so far as it has a

84   STUDIES IN HENRY JAMES

serious side, of the inviolable privacy of the man of genius. "The
Death of the Lion" makes a plea for the protection of that privacy,
and for much more, on the ground that if you successfully violate
it, your genius, if he have no deputy self to gossip and dine, perishes
from exposure. The narrator, again a young, detached writer and
journalist with a strong sense of allegiance to the great, is sent to
write up Neil Paraday at the moment he achieves, at the age of
fifty, after a long illness, with his new book, the public success of
being made a subject of a leader in *The Empire*. An interviewer
for thirty-seven syndicated papers arrives just after Paraday has
read the narrator the manuscript plan—a plan finished and perfect
in itself—of his next and greatest book. The narrator takes over
the interviewer, and goes on to take over as much protective
custody of Paraday as possible. But Paraday, with his success, is
nevertheless taken up by the unreading, by those who hate literature in the guise of adoring writers, especially by a Mrs. Wimbush
who has the fortune of a great brewery. Paraday a little excuses his
not throwing Mrs. Wimbush out of doors on the ground that he
can get material for his writing out of her. The narrator, however,
has a single success in keeping off an American girl with an
autograph album to fill, but who really loves Paraday's work,
understands that reading is greater than personality, and agrees to
seek the author, as the narrator tells her to, "in his works even as
God in Nature." Neil Paraday had been made, as the narrator
says, a contemporary. "That was what had happened: the poor
man was to be squeezed into his horrible age. I felt as if he had
been overtaken on the crest of the hill and brought back to the
city. A little more and he would have dipped down the short cut
to posterity and escaped." To be a contemporary was to be a lion
and lions of the contemporary necessarily die soon. Thus Paraday
soon *wants* to become ill again; he knew what was happening to
him, but he could not help surrendering to it. "He filled his
lungs, for the most part, with the comedy of his queer fate: the
tragedy was in the spectacles through which I chose to look. He
was conscious of inconvenience, and above all of a great renounce-
ment; but how could he have heard a mere dirge in the bells of his
accession?"

What happens is inevitable from the title and from what has already been said. Paraday is seduced into going to a house party at Mrs. Wimbush's country place which is called Prestidge—a surface quality obtained, if you remember your etymology, by sleight of hand. There is to be a great foreign Princess there, and many others, all to hear him read his precious manuscript plan. He falls sick and, dying, instructs the narrator to print it as his last work, small but perfect. However, Mrs. Wimbush has lent it to a guest who in turn has lent it to another, and so on, none of them by any chance reading it; so that it is lost. Before our lion actually dies, he has become a burden, for the next two in Mrs. Wimbush's series of lions come before he is out of the way; and it is in the identity of the new beasts that we see the true estimation in which Mrs. Wimbush—in which society—holds literature. The new beasts are two popular successes, Guy Walsingham, who is a woman, and Dora Forbes, who is a man with red mustaches. Their publishers think it necessary that they take opposite sexes in their pen names. But the narrator says rather that they are writers of some third sex: the success-sex, no doubt, which can alone cope with the assaults of an adulating society.

Here we see the figure of a great writer preyed upon; the lion is brought down by the brutality of a society which could have no use for him except as quarry. In "The Next Time" we have the contrary fable, that of the writer who struggles desperately to make society his prey, but fails because he cannot help remaining the harmless, the isolated monarch of his extreme imaginative ardent self. Society, seen as his prey, has no trouble at all in keeping out of his way. Ray Limbert's only successful step was the initial step of a "bad" marriage to a good wife, who has a mother and bears children who require support. He has a sister-in-law who is a successful popular novelist, where he himself is incontestably a great writer. He gave the narrator (again a literary man) "one of the rarest emotions of the literary life, the sense of an activity in which I could critically rest." However, it was necessary for him to earn his living, and after failing at journalism, the narrator gets him the post of editor with a year's contract at complete liberty. As an editor, Ray Limbert resolves to contribute serially a deliberately bad novel in the hope of achieving success, and requires of his friends that they do not read the installments for shame. His difficulty there was that he was one of those "people who can't be vulgar for trying." He loses his post as editor, partly because of the authors whom he had printed but mostly because of his own novel, which so far from being popular or obvious was "charming with all his charm and powerful with all his power: it was an unscrupulous, an unsparing, a shameless merciless masterpiece. . . . The perversity of the effort, even though heroic, had been frustrated by the purity of the gift." As the narrator finished his reading he looked out the window for a sight of the summer dawn, his eyes "compassionately and admiringly filled. The eastern sky, over the London housetops, had a wonderful tragic crimson. That was the colour of his magnificent mistake." It was a mistake which Ray Limbert—by the terms of the fable—repeated, always believing that the next time he would do the trick. All the narrator could say was "that genius was a fatal disturber or that the unhappy man had no effectual *flair*. When he went abroad to gather garlic he came home with heliotrope." Finally he forgot "the next time." "He had merely waked up one morning again in the country of the blue and had stayed there with a good conscience and a great idea," and died, writing.

"In the country of the blue" is a very lonely place to be, for it is very nearly empty except for the self, and is gained only by something like a religious retreat, by an approximation of birth or death or birth-in-death. James tried for it in fiction I think but once, in "The Great Good Place," here mentioned but in passing, where there is an adumbration rather than an account given of the retreat of the author George Dane, made for the recovery of genius, "which he had been in danger of losing"; he had returned to himself after eight hours to find his room "disencumbered, different, twice as large. It was all right." Yet there was some constant recourse for James to the country of the blue; it was where he would have had his projected great authors live, and it was where, as we shall see he reported, he sometimes lived himself.

But before we look at that sight, let us look at the tale which of all that James wrote best prepares us for it, "The Lesson of the Master." This is probably the finest, surely the clearest, most brilliant, and most eloquent of all James's pleading fables of the literary life. It has greater scope than the others, itself rings with greatness, and is more nearly dramatic in character, more nearly joins the issue of the ideal and the actual. Unlike the other tales in our present list it is related in the third person from the point of view of the most implicated person in it, Paul Overt. The relations between that distinguished young talent and the Master, Henry St. George, who has for years done less than his best work, are exhibited in terms of Marian Fancourt, of an interest and an intelligence in the arts hardly less than her beauty, as a nexus for the conflict of loyalties between the master and the disciple. All three meet for the first time on a country weekend at Summersoft. Both men are taken with Marian Fancourt. Overt respects St. George vastly, and when St. George tells him that he is good and must be better, referring to his own inadequacy, he responds by a kind of preliminary submission. In London Overt falls in love with Marian, St. George more or less making way for him. For each the two others are the poles of attraction. Overt visits St. George in his study after a party, and for most of thirteen pages St. George exhorts him magnificently to give up everything, marriage, money, children, social position—all the things to which St. George himself had succumbed—for the sake of his art. Overt takes the master pretty much at his word and goes abroad for two years writing his best thing yet under great privation of all personal life. While he is abroad St. George's wife dies, and Overt returns to find St. George and Marian on the verge of marriage, and so feels brutally cheated. It turns out that St. George has married Marian partly to save Overt from succumbing to the false gods, to save him from having everything but the great thing.

The great thing is: "The sense of having done the best—the sense which is the real life of the artist and the absence of which is his death, of having drawn from his intellectual instrument the finest music that nature had hidden in it, of having played it as it

88 STUDIES IN HENRY JAMES

should be played." When Overt complains that he is not to be
allowed the common passions and affections of men, St. George
answers that art is passion enough. When the whole ascetic position is explained—for it is no less than ascetic in that it draws the
artist as mostly not a man—Overt sums it up by crying that it
leaves the artist condemned to be "a mere disfranchised monk"
who "can produce his effect only by giving up personal happiness.
What an arraignment of art!" And St. George takes him up: "Ah,
you don't imagine that I'm defending art? 'Arraignment'—I
should think so! Happy the societies in which it hasn't made its
appearance, for from the moment it comes they have a consuming
ache, they have an uncurable corruption, in their breast. Most
assuredly is the artist in a false position! But I thought we were
taking him for granted." It was when Overt found Marian married
to St. George that he realized *what* he had been taking for granted.
One *hardly* knows whether society or the artist is worse flayed
here; but one knows, and there is only the need one feels for a
grace note in James's concluding remark that "the Master was
essentially right and that Nature had dedicated him to intellectual,
not to personal passion."

The portrait of the artist in Henry James is now almost
complete: the man fully an artist is the man, short of the saint,
most wholly deprived. This is the picture natural to the man still
in revolt, to the man who still identifies the central struggle of life
in society as the mere struggle of that aspect of his life of which he
makes his profession, and who has not yet realized, but is on the
verge of doing so, that all the professions possible in life are
mutually inclusive. One's own profession is but the looking glass
and the image of the others; and the artist is he who being by
nature best fitted to see the image clear is damned only if he does
not. If he sees, his vision disappears in his work, which is the
country of the blue. That is why the only possible portrait to
paint of the artist will be a portrait of him as a failure. Otherwise
there will be only the portrait of the man. That is why James
portrayed the artist chiefly during his intermediate dubious period, and why in his full maturity, like St. George, but in a

different richer sense, took the artist for granted and portrayed men and women bent not on a privation but a fullness of being.

There remains still to record only James's portrait of himself as the artist in the man mature, and for that there are two passages to quote, of which one is from a letter written at the age of seventy to Henry Adams urging him to cultivate the interest of his consciousness. "You see I still, in presence of life (or of what you deny to be such), have reactions—as many as possible—and the book I sent you is proof of them. It's, I suppose, because I am that queer monster, the artist, an obstinate finality, an inexhaustible sensibility. Hence the reactions—appearances, memories, many things, go on playing upon it with consequences that I note and 'enjoy' (grim word!) noting. It all takes doing—and I *do*. I believe I shall do yet again—it is still an act of life."

That is the man in life as artist. The other passage, with which we end the chapter, is taken from some penciled notes written some time in his last years on a New Year's eve, near midnight, during a time of inspiration. Lubbock prints the whole of the notes in the Introduction to his edition of the Letters,* saying that "There is no moment of all his days in which it is now possible to approach him more clearly." I quote only the last paragraph. The shape, the life, the being of a novel having shown itself clear, the exaltation is so great that James is left once again with just the story of a story to tell, this time of himself.

> Thus just these first little wavings of the oh so tremulously passionate little old wand (now!) make for me, I feel, a sort of promise of richness and beauty and variety; a sort of portent of the happy presence of the elements. The good days of last August and even my broken September and my better October come back to me with their gage of divine possibilities, and I welcome these to my arms, I press them with unutterable tenderness. I seem to emerge from these recent bad

The Letters of Henry James, ed. Percy Lubbock (New York: Scribner's, 1920)—Ed.

days—the fruit of blind accident—and the prospect
clears and flushes, and my poor blest old Genius pats
me so admirably and lovingly on the back that I turn, I
screw round, and bend my lips to passionately, in my
gratitude, kiss its hands.

The feeling in this passage is not uncommon; most of us have
been terrified at its counterpart; but the ability to surrender to
the expression of it is rare, and is what brought James himself,
for the moment of expression, into the blue.

HENRY JAMES

On the level of the ideal—on the level of art—American fiction achieved in the novels and short stories of Henry James a kind of reality different from both the literal record of a Howells and the philosophical naturalism of a Zola. This reality was his response to the human predicament of his generation, which James felt with unusual acuteness because of the virtual formlessness of his education—the predicament of the sensitive mind during what may be called the interregnum between the effective dominance of the old Christian-classical ideal through old European institutions and the rise to rule of the succeeding ideal, whatever history comes to call it. To express that predicament in fiction no education could have been more fitting than his, for it excluded him from assenting to the energies of social expansion, of technology, of the deterministic sciences, and of modern finance and business. Unconscious assent to these forces, over and above any rebellion against their moral values, caused most active minds in his day to conceal the fact of interregnum. James's mind reacted only to the shadows of those forces as revealed in human emotion and in social behavior and convention. With his abiding sense of the indestructible life, he expressed the decay and sterility of a society pretending to live on conventions and institutions but lacking the force of underlying convictions. He described what he saw, and he created what lay under what he saw.

They tell a story of Henry James which cannot be verified as to fact, but one which is so true and just in spirit that we may take it as the scriptural text for this chapter. Once, in the nineties, while James was staying in an English country house, the only child of a neighbor died of a sudden illness; and although James had quarreled with the neighbor and they had not been on speaking terms he announced to his host that he would attend the funeral of the little boy. His host argued that, in the small church in the small village, it would be conspicuously unseemly for him to go—the bereaved parents could only take it as an affront; but James was obstinate. When he returned, his host asked him how on earth he could have brought himself to go, and to sit, as he had, in the pew directly behind the mourners. James brushed all argument aside and, with that intensity in his eyes which made his face seem naked, stated firmly: "Where emotion is, there am I!"

All his life long, and in all but his slightest work, James struggled to use the conventions of society, and to abuse them when necessary, to bring himself directly upon the emotion that lay under the conventions, coiling and recoiling, ready to break through. So to bring himself, and so to see, was for him action in life and creation in art. "Where emotion is, there am I!" If he could find the emotion he could for himself realize life, and if he could create the reality of the emotion in his art, in terms of actual characters and situations, he could make his art—in James Joyce's phrase at the end of *A Portrait of the Artist As a Young Man*— the uncreated conscience of his race. The story of that struggle to realize life as emotion and to create it as art is the abiding story of Henry James, as near as we can come to the Figure in his Carpet.

With the events of his life we have here little to do except see how their conditions, both those imposed upon him and those which he imposed upon himself, led him to an increasing devotion to that struggle, and to the final decision at full maturity that in the very passion of pleading for full life in others, for him life had to be sacrificed to art. As he sometimes put it, his own life had to disappear into his art just to the degree that he was a successful artist. The conditions imposed upon him were freedom of sensibility and conscience and the emotional insecurity that is apt to accompany that freedom. His was a minimum financial security and the curious need to prove one's own value that in responsive natures sometimes goes with that security. His also was so wide a variety of social and educational exposures, which had in common only their informality, that he was left the most social man in the world but without a society or an institution that could exact his allegiance. His, further, was an accidental injury by a slip or a fall in early manhood which seems to have left him with the sense of a physical uprootedness and isolation that only aggravated, as it fed upon, his emotional isolation. Like Abélard who, after his injury, raised the first chapel to the Holy Ghost, James made a sacred rage of his art as the only spirit he could fully serve.*

2

Henry James was born in New York City, April 15, 1843, the second son of Henry James, Sr.—a peripatetic philosopher and dissenting theologian of considerable means, a friend of Emerson and Carlyle, and a great believer in a universal but wholly informal society. It was he who on his deathbed directed that the only words spoken at his funeral should be: "Here lies a man, who has thought all his life that the ceremonies attending both marriage and death were all damned nonsense." To his sons William and Henry he gave a kind of infant baptism after his own heart by taking them abroad before they could speak and dipping them generously in the font of Europe: a rite which was

*Although Blackmur suggests that what James called his "obscure hurt" was an emasculating injury, James's biographer, Leon Edel, states that "the evidence points clearly to a back injury" (*The Untried Years*, New York: Avon, 1978, p. 183)—Ed.

to mark them both with particular strength and weakness for life.
After Europe in 1843 and 1844, the family alternated between
Albany and New York. The children were sent to at least three
schools before 1855, when in June they went to Europe for a
three-year educational experiment at Geneva, London, Paris, and
Boulogne. The year 1858–1859 was passed at Newport, Rhode
Island; 1859–1860, at Geneva and Bonn. Thus the boys learned
languages and manners and fragments of many systems of formal
education; but more important were the incalculable effects of
years of exposure to the sights and sounds and tones of "other"
worlds than that in which by birth they might have been expected
to grow up. Part of their father's intention was to give them, by
keeping them safe from any particular soil, the richest and most
varied human soil to grow in. When he had given them as much
of Europe as possible, he removed them to what was at that time
the least American of all towns, and for two years they lived again
at Newport. There they came under the influence of a young man
who was to become the least American of all American painters,
John La Farge. Then, in 1862, Henry James made his one attempt
at formal education, in the Harvard Law School, a venture which
seems to have had no effect on him at all. It was at this time that
he sustained his injury and was kept out of the Civil War, the
great historical action of his time.

The young James then turned to literature, at first uncertainly
and as a "possible" occupation but within four or five years
firmly and fully as a profession. His earliest story appeared in the
Atlantic Monthly in 1865, when he was twenty-two, and he published stories, sketches, and critical reviews frequently thereafter
in that magazine, in *The Nation*, and elsewhere. In the fiction and
sketches the writing was easy to the point of facility, romantic in
tone except where it was humorous, and distinguished chiefly by its
competence; in the criticism, it was high-toned and even captious.
It showed the influences of Dickens and Hawthorne, Washington
Irving and perhaps a little Balzac, in short the dominant literary
influences of his time. The American scene, as characterized by
Boston and New York, kept him alive but did not provoke reaction
or experiment in his writing.

In 1869 he went abroad again, this time to literary as well as social Europe, and for ten or twelve years paid visits to America rather than to Europe. Abroad he alternated between London and Paris, London and Italy. London was to live in, Paris was to learn in, Italy to love; America had become chiefly something for his literary and social sensibility to react on. London gave him the support of an institutionalized society which made for security and position. Italy gave him color and form and warmth, and the ideal satisfaction of all his romantic nostalgia for those qualities. But Paris gave him his profession; for there he met Turgenev, whom he called the "beautiful genius," and Flaubert, whom he found vulgar in person but perfect in writing. It was in Paris that he learned that the novel was an art and that art was the mastering, all-exacting profession that alone made life tolerable by making it intelligible. He learned also that the art of literature, like the art of painting or of music, was an international art, however locally rooted it might have to be in inspiration, and for himself he made the decision that his inspiration might well be as international as the art. It was a decision for which his education had prepared him, just as was his decision to live in London but to keep up his American and French connections. Perhaps it was the very informality of his education that made him grasp for safety at the formalism of English society and the form of the French novel of Flaubert and the Russian novel of Turgenev who was himself a result of the French influence. Formalism and form were for him the means of understanding the formlessness which was life itself; but he never confused the two, though he sometimes made the mistake of refusing to see the life, either in America or in the novels of "disorderly" writers like Dostoevsky and Zola, if the form was not within the habit of his perception.

The effect of these years of discipleship and decision was triple. They transformed James from one more American writer working at his trade to an addicted artist working to perfect the form of his chosen art. They gave him his three themes: the international theme, the theme of the artist in conflict with society, and the theme of the pilgrim in search of society. And through his work, the form of the novel in England and America was developed to a new maturity and variety and responsibility. In 1881, with the publication of *The Portrait of a Lady*, the European novel as a form became part of the resources of the English language, and James himself a great novelist, for in that novel his three major themes were for the first time combined in a single objective form.

These years ended the first long period in James's literary life with a high climax, at the same time that they ended the actually international aspect of his personal life. Perhaps his father's death in 1882 helped diminish his sense of personal American connection. Perhaps his loss of popularity after *The Portrait of a Lady*, which was the last book to sell really well in his own lifetime, forced him into the more private reality of his English connection. Perhaps he had merely finally made up his mind. At any rate, he remained in England without visiting America until 1904 (when he made the tour which is recorded in part in *The American Scene*), and in the nineties he established himself in the nearest he ever had to a real home, at Lamb House, Rye, in Sussex.

The "middle period," from 1882 to 1897, when he published *The Spoils of Poynton*, was one of experimentation, refinement of medium, exacerbation of sensibility, and extreme sophistication of perception. Nothing written during that period reached the stature of *The Portrait of a Lady*; much of it was water in sand that only rearranged the grains, though much of it was exquisitely molded. It was then that he earned his reputation for finickiness, difficulty beyond the necessities, unreality, and remoteness. His disappointment was so great that, during the latter part of this period, he succumbed to the temptation to write deliberately "popular," deliberately "well-made" plays, none of which did well, and one of which, at its London performance, brought him the humiliation of personal hisses when he appeared on the stage at the call for author. Yet he had finally mastered the art that was to make it possible for him to write, in the third period, from 1897 to 1904, first-rate novels and tales, among them the series of three great novels, *The Ambassadors*, *The Wings of the Dove*, and *The*

Golden Bowl. Perhaps his failure in his one effort at treason to his high calling when he turned to drama, and the personal humiliation of that failure, jolted him back with new strength by reaction to his old conception of the novel; perhaps he had merely needed the long time of experiment for secret incubation; in any case, preparation was necessary for maturity of technique and, more important, for maturity of sensibility.

The fourth period began with a visit to America in 1904 and 1905 and might well have prepared him, had he lived longer or had the First World War not intervened, for the still greater art of which we can see the signs in the volume of stories called *The Finer Grain*, collected in 1910. These years were spent in the revision of his novels and tales for the New York Edition, in the volume on *The American Scene* (1907), and in the writing of several volumes of memoirs. After 1910 two experimental novels were begun but never finished, *The Ivory Tower* and *The Sense of the Past.* War and sickness prevented their completion and they were published as he left them after his death in the winter of 1916. At his life's end he had a number of friends but none close, many acquaintances but none important to him, and considerable influence on the younger writers of his time, though nothing commensurate to the influence he was later to exert when the luxury of his sensibility and the rigors of his form became increasingly necessary to a larger number of readers and writers. Howells, Bennett, Wells, Ford Madox Ford, Conrad, and Edith Wharton gained by his example, and the last three avowedly made use of his method—Conrad notably in *Chance* and *Under Western Eyes*, Ford in *The Good Soldier* and his remarkable tetralogy about the war, of which the first volume was *Some Do Not*, and Mrs. Wharton in all but her early work. Of the later generation, Virginia Woolf and Dorothy Richardson would have been impossible without him, as less directly Faulkner and Hemingway and Graham Greene would also have been impossible without the maturity to which he had brought their craft. But essentially he died, as he had lived, lonely both in art and in life, a very special case indeed.

3

Yet he is no more special than Swift or Donne or Proust. He is merely one of those writers in whom succeeding ages find differing values and to whom each age assigns a different rank; nor is it likely that within a particular age he will ever escape violently opposed opinions as to the character of what he wrote. He is thus a perpetual anomaly. How he came to be so, why he must remain so and for what literary good and ill, it is the purpose of this chapter to inquire. For in the stresses and oppositions and active conflicts that make him anomalous, we see what he stood for and we measure the varying stature of what he did.

He stood for that universal human society which is held to underlie any and all existing forms of society; and what he did was to attempt to express the supremacy of universal society over the very narrow existing society he fed on for material. What he stood for was deep in him, a shaping part of his nature; but for what he did he was ill equipped with the conventional kind of sensibility, though excellently equipped with the passion—the suffering readiness and tenacity—of extraordinary sensibility. He was therefore driven to excesses of substitution and renunciation and refinement (in experience and morals and style) beyond warrant of any other successful author's use. Yet in these very excesses lay the virtue of his fundamental insight. Given the broad poverty and intense riches of his known world, it was his insight that forced upon him his excesses. He had to go out of the world to judge the world.

That necessity, the privations which caused it, and its consequent excesses were almost family traits. They show in William as well as in Henry, and pretty much combine in their father. Each of the three suffered in youth a central damage from an experience of the immanence of overwhelming evil and its menace to the self, a damage which was never repaired and never forgotten, so that life always remained perilous. But each was able to balance his experience of evil by an experience of something like religious conversion. None of these conversions except that of the father were on Christian terms; none left its subject attached perma-

nently to any particular form of religion or to any particular form
of society. Each of them was left rather with the sense of access to
the very center of society itself. William James gives an account of
his own conversion anonymously in *The Varieties of Religious
Experience*; Henry gives his, in adumbration, in the story called
"The Jolly Corner," and in a manuscript note of a New Year's
visitation of his Genius which Lubbock prints in his edition of
James's *Letters*. But the version which the elder Henry James gives
will do for all three. The last book he himself published, *Society
the Redeemed Form of Man*, suggests the works of his two sons as
well. There the old man, thirty years after the event, said that in
his own religious conversion he had been "lifted by a sudden
miracle into felt harmony with universal man, and filled to the
brim with the sentiment of indestructible life." Such experiences
left all three with what the younger Henry was to call in his old
age that "obstinate finality" which had made him an artist in
spite of all privations.

If the nature of those privations remained always vague, like
an obscure and spreading hurt, and if the experience of conversion was always vague, a force from outside that compelled him
to go on beyond and in spite of the hurt, nevertheless the result in
Henry James's written works is as clear as need be. There is everywhere in it the presence of a deep, almost instinctive, incentive
to create the indestructible life which, to his vision, must lie at the
heart of the actual life that has been hurt. He began at once
to cultivate what his father had planted in him, the habit of
response across any barrier—the more barrier the more response.
His peculiar education had given him the straight look, acute ear,
keen touch, and receptive mind. In his writing life, that mind
received so much and reacted so constantly that it became itself a
primary and trustworthy sense. This is the hallmark of the homemade mind, and it serves pretty well for home affairs, but in the
affairs of the wide world it drives its victims partly to makeshift
and partly to reliance upon naked humanity. To the elder James,
such a mind was enough, because he never had any real intent to
do more than goad and gad the society he lived in. To William
James it was not enough, but he was partly able to make up his

losses by the systematic study of physiology and philosophy. To Henry James it was not enough either, and he was driven all his life long, without ever acknowledging it, to make substitutes pass for the real thing. It was perhaps that necessity that made him an artist. At any rate the eloquence and passion with which he made the substitutes, rather than the act of substitution, pass for the actual, were what gave his writing stature, a kind of contingent or inner reality. Not until war came in 1914 did he see that the true forces of society had all the time been leading to a final treachery to the values its conventions could no longer defend. He had seen it in his art, but not in his life. His immediate response was to throw himself into the war and to become a British subject. The British gave him the Order of Merit; but his response had been lifelong and was already recorded time after time in book after book.

There, in his "International" books, he set the two kinds of society he knew against each other for balance and contrast and mutual criticism. There are two kinds of society which demand writing like this of James: the society of Europe where the vital impulse has so far run out that all its meanings are expressed by the deliberate play of conventions and their refinements; and, second, the society of America where the original convictions and driving impulse have not yet matured in conventions adequate to express them on high levels. James belonged by birth and primary exposure to the second (New York and New England so far as he could deal with them by instinct), and he had a vision—alternately ideal and critical, alternately discouraged and disillusioned—of the first in the Europe of France and Italy and particularly England. Each gave him the means of dealing with the other; each kept the other from seeming the only society on earth; and together they gave him, at his best, great formality and passionate substance.

The International Theme, in short, was what his education had led to. It was the machinery at hand, and in the lack of anything else it had to provide momentum for everything else. Unlike most writers of his time, but a precursor of many who came to maturity after the First World War, he was barred from the help of religion and history, and a perverse critic might say barred even from the help of literature. He could not use religion because he knew nothing of the Christian Church, hardly even so much of its language as remains alive in the speech of those outside it. He did not know what had happened either to the institutions or the practice of religion; he had only the core of religion within him, and it got into his work only by indirection. He could not have written, like his brother, *The Varieties of Religious Experience*, because he was so obstinately a central form, beneath all varieties, of the religious experience itself. He was an example of what happens to a religious man when institutional religion is taken away. What happens to Maggie Verver in *The Golden Bowl*, to Milly Theale in *The Wings of the Dove*, to Isabel Archer in *The Portrait of a Lady*, to George Stransom in "The Altar of the Dead," are examples of religious experience outside a creed, just as what happens to John Marcher in "The Beast in the Jungle" is an example of the privation of religious experience, and just, too, as what happens to the governess in "The Turn of the Screw" is an example of what happens when positive evil inverts religious experience. James would have been wholly unable to relate any of these affairs in formal Christian terms; where for once, in "The Altar of the Dead," he tried to invoke the experience of the Catholic Church, he saved his story to actuality only by the eloquence of his hero's emotion.

As with religion, so with history, only the other way around. If religion was in James an inner primal piety, history was a felt objective residue. He took his history in a single jump from the living man to the ancestral Adam. He was contemporary to an extreme. He took his tradition almost entirely on its face value; yet because he knew so much must have been behind that face, he actually felt more continuity, more unity, than had ever been really there. In that feeling lay the intensity of his sense of history. He lacked historical imagination because his mind lacked historical content; he had never been inside any history but his own; but he had the sense of history because he saw all around him in Europe how he himself came at its end, and all around him in America how he came at its beginning. He felt in himself, so far

as history went, the power to represent the flash between the two
eternities.

The strangest privation in James, and one that troubled him
even less than the others—though it has caused much trouble for
many readers—was the privation of his relation to the whole body
of literature. He was, as Santayana ironically said of himself,
"an ignorant man, almost a poet." It was because he knew so
little great literature in quantity that to many he seemed exces-
sively literary in manner; there were not enough professional
barriers between himself and the printed page to prevent his mere
unredeemed idiosyncrasy from now and then taking over. He
knew well enough the things read around the house as a boy—
Dickens and Scott and Hawthorne; he knew even better his chosen
masters, Balzac and Turgenev and Flaubert; but it is not an
exaggeration to say that he had no organized command of any of
the possible general traditions of literature a writer living in his
time might have taken up. There is very little evidence of reading
in his letters, except for the books of his friends; and when his
brother complained that he ought to read more, he answered that
he had no time. His critical writing, even when it was not frank
book reviewing, was almost entirely contemporary, of narrow
range and narrower sympathies; it is worth reading chiefly as an
illumination of his own mind and writing. Only when he tackled
the technical problems—by the very narrowness of his solutions
of which, in his own work, he so greatly stretched the scope and
responsibilities of the novel as a form—was he critically at home
and master in his house.

He was indeed virtually an ignorant man, actually a poet;
but he had, besides that sense of the human which he shared with
his father and brother, only the two natural weapons of a direct
eye and an expert knowledge of surfaces. He had thus everywhere
to depend more on his method than—in Plato's sense—on his
madness. Only by resources of method which he had often to
develop and sometimes to invent could he get his poetry into the
objective form of novel or tale; for example, put another way, his
use of dialogue is an example of development from illustration to
substance; his use of an active consciousness interposed between

the story and the reader, as in *The Ambassadors*, is almost an invention. He had to find means to get around the problems which trouble most novelists—as war and lust, love and God, troubled Tolstoy—in order to get at the problems that troubled him. Between him and the world he knew he had to interpose the story of the story, the passion of the passion, the problem of the problem; otherwise he could not aesthetically possess the story, the passion, the problem.

So central were morals to James, even though he was a dissenter to the forms in which morals are abused, that there was not ever quite enough for him in any part of the world either to fall back on or to go forward with. It was so in his own mind; his convictions never matured as ideas, but as images or metaphors, as aesthetic creations, always to be created afresh. As he never went backward into the full Christian tradition, but tapped his sense of what underlay it, so he never went back into the whole force of love, only into so much of it as could be conceived morally. It is for reasons such as these that, though he aimed always at the full picture, the full drama, James had to resort successively to the lesser forms of the allegory, the fable, the ghost story, and at the end, where he was nearest his target, to a kind of cross between the drama and the fairy story; for this is the journey James made between "A Passionate Pilgrim" and "The Madonna of the Future," through "The Turn of the Screw" and *The Sacred Fount*, to *The Golden Bowl* and "The Bench of Desolation," where the last two are almost pure Cinderella and Ugly Duckling dramatized and made haunting for every reader who can see himself in their terms. This is the reverse of what happens in novels wholly dramatized. Whereas great drama seems to rest on the driving power of myth, the thing deeply believed and subject to change and criticism only in externals, the fairy tale seems to rest on an insight anxious to prove itself ideal and therefore dependent on externals for access to essentials. In the fairy tale the skeleton is on the outside, sometimes so much so that there is nothing else, while in the drama the skeleton is always fleshed. This is what Edith Wharton meant when she asked James why he left out of his novels all the fringes of what really happened to his people; to which James answered that he didn't know that he had. James leaves the reader relatively everything to put in; all his density and richness develop in the details of his chosen skeleton. The big things are all fairy tale, with that threat of sudden dark illumination at the edge of which the fairy tale, even more than the fable or the ghost story, so often hovers. The bones that articulate the skeleton can be named. Candor, innocence, aloneness, the pure intelligence on one side, and mendacity, unspecified corruption, crowdedness, and a kind of cunning rapacity on the other are given an equally high value; but are given always at a point where each is about to break down, in the contest with actual life, either into renunciation (which to James as to Emily Dickinson was a "piercing" virtue) or into some deep and ambiguous kind of capitulation of good to evil and evil to good—as in the end of *The Wings of the Dove* or of *The Golden Bowl*, where the capitulations are mutual, affirmative, abysmal, shifting. At that point of capitulation, the dramatized fairy tale becomes the instrument and substance—form united with content—of revelation and judgment. This was the prodigy James made of the novel.

4

If this account of privations and defects is any way correct, James's accomplishment in the art of fiction was certainly a prodigy. No writer in the England or America of his time surpassed him, whether with or relatively without his defects, and his peers—Stevenson and Hardy and Moore and Meredith, Mark Twain and Melville and Howells—played in different fields. He had the extraordinary luck to come on a whole baggage of themes and conventions and situations in the same process by which he himself lived, and the luck, too, that made them suited to replenish each other in his chosen forms of the fable and the fairy story; he had had the luck to find a garden which he could cultivate, and did. He deliberately undertook, and invoked for himself, the profession, the role, the vocation of what he called "that obstinate finality" of the artist. As a profession, art gave occupation to his habit of omnivorous curiosity and to his knowledge of surfaces, and it made the sacrifice of other forms of life acceptable for the sake of good practice. As a role, it gave him both an inner independence and the protection of an outer identity no matter what sacrifices and failures might come his way. As a vocation, it overrode or made negative all sacrifices and failures whatever with the conviction of purpose, and so put him in unassailable relation with that universal man and that indestructible life which he felt under any society, no matter what any society in existence might think of his feelings about it. Art was his pride of energy. So much so that the profession and role of artist—both for themselves and as foils and ideal contrasts to other professions and roles—provided the major obsession for his fictions, as did the obsession of the International Theme, of which it was only another, and equivalent, version.

Where the International Theme showed the American against the European, whether as a pilgrim or victim, the theme of the artist showed the writer or painter or actress against the world. The underlying theme which he used perhaps first in *Daisy Miller* (1879), but first clearly in *Washington Square* (1881), and at the last made his chief overt theme, was that of the innocent, loyal, candid spirit at the mercy of the world but reacting to it with high intelligence and spiritual strength, precisely with the artist's perception of what for good and ill it actually was. These stories of young American girls smirched or driven out of society by the cruel stupidity of its conventions alternated with stories of artists who were also smirched or driven out. In James's imagination the two themes became identical. Perhaps this is again a sign of the interregnum in the thinking of modern man: that the artist should suddenly come to have exorbitant value as subject matter—should seem a hero or a traitor to his proper heroic role—and should seem so to the artist himself and not merely to his biographer. In this James is not alone; he is followed by Mann and Proust and Gide and Pirandello and Joyce, to all of whom the artist became the type of hero most precious; but James was first and most copious and most intransigent in moralizing the desperate straits through which the artist pursued his role—sometimes as if he had chosen it, as in "The Figure in the Carpet" (1896), sometimes as if he had been condemned to it, as in "The Lesson of the Master" (1892), and sometimes, as in "The Middle Years" (1893), as if he had accepted it.

In all these stories the fate of the artist is somehow the test of society. As a consequence he finds his own value so high that he cannot assent to society as it is, but has a great craving to assent to it as it ought to have been, for he knows that his very being declares, or is prevented from declaring, its possiblities. The degree of self-consciousness in these tales is equal to this conscious sense of self-value, and it is hard to say which overcomes the other. In "The Figure in the Carpet," the author Hugh Vereker has a secret pattern to his work that, when he dies, no amount of fanatic frenetic work can reveal. In "The Middle Years," on the contrary, the dying author leaves such a sure consciousness of his essential value that his disciple, a young doctor, gives up the certainty of a fortune to remain in the presence of the master to whom in his disciple's "young voice" is "the ring of a marriage bell." To them both, without "the madness of art," which both share, life is frustration. In "The Lesson of the Master," the Master urges the disciple to give up everything, marriage, money, children, social position—all the things to which the Master has himself succumbed—for the sake of his art. The artist is not a man, declares the Master, but a disfranchised monk, and the rarity of his art must be his only passion. To this teaching the disciple is true; he makes his retreat, and writes; but when he returns he finds that the Master, having become a widower, has married his girl, "partly" to make sure that the disciple sticks to his art, and has himself given up writing. James ends his fable with the remark that the disciple felt himself dedicated by nature to intellectual, not personal, passion. One hardly knows whether society or the artist is worse flayed in this brilliant story; but one knows certainly that the moral of the fable, and of that final remark, lies in the representation of the artist's life as the fullest possible human profession.

James thus raised his profession to a vocation—a calling from beyond himself by a familiar within himself—which, as he followed it, was a virtually continuous conversion, for strength, for identity, for piety to life, of his whole being. Who will say that it was not an invoked obsessive device, a ruse to transform life otherwise intolerable? But who will say, in the conditions of his life, that he had an alternative? To him the sense of his vocation was a predominant part of his sense of the animating truth, as anyone can see who reads his own invocation to his own genius, quoted by Lubbock in his edition of James's *Letters*. Unlike his friend Henry Adams, who thought that if anything he sat too much in the center of the whole world, James knew himself actually at the periphery, and had therefore to make himself a center in invoked reality. As an individual he felt himself to be so many *disjecta membra poetae*. But by raising his profession to a vocation, he celebrated, like priest and prophet at once, a rite in his own chapel of the true church. He became thus the individual who knew best how little individual he truly was, and was therefore able to overcome the dead weight of all those who merely thought themselves individuals because they wielded power and direction and routine to society by the accident of rank or privilege or money. The difference lay in the presence of the sense of vocation; and the only profession James could by nature see as vocation was that of artist; and he saw the artist as alternately cheated and blest in his vocation regardless of his immense task.

But he went further; the sense of vocation is primary in most of his fiction. He made a dramatic transposition of the artist's sense of vocation and he saw it as motivating rare and precious conduct everywhere. James habitually envisaged people as either with vocation in an extreme devoted sense—Isabel Archer in *The Portrait of a Lady* no less than Miriam Rooth in *The Tragic Muse* or Fleda Vetch in *The Spoils of Poynton* or Lambert Strether in *The Ambassadors*—or as without vocation, as in the foils to the characters just named, and more or less brutally against those who had it. He did not deal with the much greater numbers of people who are merely occupied as confused human animals. That is the difference between a writer like James and writers like his masters, Balzac and Flaubert. Hence perhaps his failure to understand the degree of remove at which the conventions of society actually work out (at some distance from where any of us are sitting) and how much of human energy other than the animal is merely manipulated rather than absorbed by the conventions. His novels have no ordinary people, except as barriers to the extraordinary; his people feel either the passion of the passion, or they feel nothing.

As an instance of the extremity to which James carried his transposition, one might take that great and beautiful tale "The Altar of the Dead" in which the hero devotes his life to the cultivation of the memory of his loved dead and is led finally, at the moment of his own death, to celebrate also the memory of the one dead man he hated, who seems suddenly to have been equal in need and just obligation to all the rest. But perhaps an example more sharply drawn may be exhibited in the bare bones of "Maud-Evelyn." Here a young man named Marmaduke, after being as he mistakenly thinks half jilted, goes off to Switzerland where he falls in with an elderly American couple named Dedrick. The Dedricks had some years since lost their daughter Maud-Evelyn, and now, to salvage their loss, take up the new young man in the role of imaginary son-in-law. The young man so far falls in with the fantasy that the role becomes as good as the thing itself, and he proceeds to realize it, stage by stage, for all it is worth: that is, as a vocation. Thus he passes through courtship, wedding, married life, into widowerhood and mourning till finally the Dedricks— whose fantasy he had authorized in the transformation of his own nature—die at peace. Shortly afterwards he himself dies, leaving, as his one gesture toward his erstwhile life, all his money to the girl to whom he had been originally engaged. Perhaps the theme is like Proust's, that the past, brooded on, grows and grows. What the old couple wanted was to get from the past what they would have wanted of the future. They made a temple of death in order to profane it, to stretch its precincts to cover the living world. To the young man—otherwise, by James's assertion, empty of clear intent—it was a chance to seize on the offered backward pattern with the intensity of vocation, in full belief that he might make out of it a true self. Thus, in this story, obsession with the dead reaches hallucination and hallucination reaches the new reality of art.

5

Further than this James never went, though in "The Friends of the Friends" he went as far, for he was eager to perfect his mastery of substance as well as of form. In that story an ordinary ghost is made into something monstrously human, and presides over one of those deep abortions of the human spirit which are yet, in their catastrophe, but "a response to an irresistible call": that is, are acts performed in the assumption of vocation. Had he gone further James would not have been so much unreadable—as this last example nearly is—as silly. He was content with his handful of dark fables of unassayable devotion, because they complemented and hinted at the filling out of such clear dramatic fables as *Washington Square* (1881) and *The Tragic Muse* (1890). The first of these is a light piece, done on the side, to show the opposite case to that of *The Portrait of a Lady*, which was published the same year. Catherine Sloper is the only one of James's heroines who is all round dull and plain, the only one whose intelligence is not equal to her innocence. Without intelligence, she is unable to reject or to assent to her gradual exile from society at the hands of an egocentric father and a casually mercenary lover; she merely sticks it out. Her story is not there, and neither are the stories of her father and her lover. If anything carries the book along it is the atmosphere suggested in the title, neither of which—atmosphere nor title—have anything except accidentally to do with the theme of the book: which is that human decency, even when unaware of its grounds and its ends, can, if it is taken as a vocation, come cleanly through any soiling assault. It would have taken the passion of a Flaubert for working the riches of ordinary and inarticulate things to have made excellence out of this Madame Bovary in reverse; and perhaps James was trying to do so; but he did not have that skill, and his book remained in the deep sense only an intention.

Miriam Rooth in *The Tragic Muse,* on the other hand, has at least a real struggle because she has the weapons of beauty and intelligence and a vocation as artist to fight with. She makes the center (together with the bright figure of the aesthete Gabriel Nash a little off center for fun) of a brilliant account, in large scale, of the perpetual struggle between the artist of any sort and society of any sort. But there is more gaiety, more business of the great world and the studio without the concrete representation of the underlying perception of and reaction to it, than a novel can stand and still ring true. James himself thought it moved too fast, and certainly the values asserted are far ahead of the values rendered. As a result, the validity, whether for triumph or assault, of Miriam Rooth's or Nick Dormer's vocation is not so much proved as it is by its own self-insistence impugned. In short, it is very much the same sort of relative failure, but at the opposite extreme, as *Washington Square.* But it is often in his relative failures that an artist's drive is most clearly defined; if only because in his purest successes there is the sense of the self-born, self-driven, and self-complete and these qualities escape definition.

What we can see in these novels which relatively fail, and indeed in a full ten of the nineteen novels which he published in his lifetime (as in perhaps a greater proportion of his hundred-odd shorter pieces), is that James's work constitutes a great single anarchic rebellion against society—against the laws of society—in the combined names of decency, innocence, candor, good will, and the passionate heroism of true vocation. His work as a body is the dramatized or pictured exhibition, at those chosen points most familiar to him in his own society, of the revolt implied in the title of his father's book, *Society the Redeemed Form of Man.* Both Jameses were basic dissenters to all except the society that was not yet; and in both cases the rebellion or dissent was merely eccentric or extravagant in life and manners, but central and poetic in work and insight. That is why in these tales of people who renounce or ignore so much of life which to other eyes would have been precious and even necessary to living, the last legitimate cry is still: Live, live all you can! James was compelled to accomplish his rebellion of the ideal through the very conventions he meant to re-create; they were the given medium in which the underlying reality and the invoked ideal could meet and, in dramatic actuality, merge; conventions were what he knew.

The importance of this is worth any amount of reemphasis; for James is only an exaggerated instance of the normal author, and his works are only a special case of what always goes on in the relations between an artist and a society whose values have become chiefly secular without having quite lost the need or the memory of values divinely ordered. His case is representative of literature in America, whenever it has been ambitious, to a degree greater than we care to say; in their necessary addiction to external conventions, Hemingway and Dos Passos, for example, are no less representative than James. But, granting the addiction, we are here concerned with what the conventions were and what happened to them in James's imagination.

With the *haut monde* and the *beau monde,* somewhat of Italy and France, and particularly England, together with their high Bohemias—to none of which did he actually belong—James had the expert familiarity of the observer. He knew the dinner table and drawing room, the country house and tea table, the library and smoking room, the city square and the estate park, the spas and hotels and promenades, and all the means and times and ceremonies for moving from one to another. They were the straps the people he knew swung on, and with which they held against the lurches which proved that their society was a going concern. Similarly, he knew how they got married, or jilted, or cheated; and he knew beautifully how they made cads and swindlers and lackeys of themselves almost as often as they made berths for themselves. To all this he turned first as to the form of a living society. Then he saw, rather, that this was but the mechanical arrangement of a society, that it was but the reflected tradition of values which the society might not otherwise possess and which indeed it often possessed only to soil and sully—though it could not destroy them. Those who ought to have embodied the truth of tradition in living conventions were in fact those who most demeaned it. He saw through the people, but what he saw was still the convention: the ultimate decency between human beings that could be created or ruined, equally, only by convention.

Thus James knew expertly what people's superficial obsessions were. If he did not know what their ordinary day-to-day preoccupations were, nor what, in consequence, they were likely to do, he did know the basic preoccupations of all people without regard to country or manners: he knew at what point of value men or women wanted, regardless, to live or die and what barriers they could put between themselves and affirmation. Hence he had, as a writer, to combine his two knowledges and jump the ignorance that lay between. Like a child, also a moralist, he had to use fables as the means of the jump.

Sometimes, of course, James tried to make his fables carry more than they could bear. We have touched on two examples in "The Figure in the Carpet" and "Maud-Evelyn." "The Great Good Place" is another, in which the heavenly world is seen as resembling an unusually comfortable club. But *What Maisie Knew* (1897) and *The Awkward Age* (1899) are better and fuller examples still, for in each a major use of social convention was attempted, and in each the failure was virtually, but not actually, saved by the bounty of the author's sensibility and the fertility of his technical invention. In the first the question is asked, what will happen to a little girl exposed to the breakdown of marriage in a succession of increasingly shabby divorces and liaisons? James was able to give so much through the innocence of his beautiful little girl's exposed consciousness that his story constantly both winces and cries out because the conventions through which Maisie is compelled to see her situation prevent the rest of the story, the whole story, the true story, from being told. In *The Awkward Age* the primary question is, what will happen to the publicly exposed relations of a set of people when the daughter of the house comes of social age and first takes part in those public relations? It is sometimes said that the relative failure of this book comes about because James restricted his presentation of his answer to a masterly use of scene and dialogue. But that argument would reduce Congreve to the stature of Wilde. The true cause of failure would seem to lie in the inability of all the characters in the book, including its presumably fresh and plastic young heroine, to bring into the conventions to which they restrict themselves the actual emotions and stresses that the conventions are meant to control, but of which they were never, in a living society, meant to be the equivalent.

In short, neither the domestic economy of social conventions nor the vocation of the artist was ever enough to bring out in James a mastery of substance equal to his mastery of form. What he seems to have needed was either an enlargement of the theme of the artist into terms of ordinary life, an enlargement of the social conventions into the International Theme, or a combination, in the press of one composition, of the artist and the international and the ordinary. At any rate, within these three fields lie his great successes, in which are to be included some fifteen or twenty tales as well as six or seven novels. The International Theme in its simplest form is the felt contrast of Europe and America. But it is a very different thing from the internal American contrast between New England and Virginia, and it resembles the contrast between the Old East and the New West only to the limited degree that, during James's lifetime, the Old East had digested and reversed its contrast with Europe. For the prime purpose of the contrast to James was that it furnished him with a reversible dualism which created as well as adjudicated values. It was not just a question of American girls marrying European men and of European women never, or seldom, marrying American men, though that question suggested many others having to do with the relative values of the maternal and the paternal in the conventional great world. Nor was it only the question of why American men went to Europe for culture, except in the secondary question of whether or not they could apply what they got in Europe to the American scene. It was these and much more. It was a dualism of right and wrong, of white and black, home or exile; and like any true dualism, before it becomes lost in an institution, its terms were reversible, without impairment of their reality. Reversed, right and wrong became fresh and stale, white and black became decent and corrupt, home or exile became integrity or destruction. With these reversals in mind, the questions at the heart of the International Theme can be put afresh. What happens to Americans in Europe? What does Europe do to them? bring out of them? give them, by threatening its loss, to struggle for? And, on the contrary, what happens to Europeans under impact of Americans? What new source do they find to make up for the loss which the exposure has laid bare? And so on.

In the beginning the American is conceived as having in him a dead or unborn place, and is, in moral perception if not in moral nature, gray or black; the European, in contrast, is conceived as alive with inherited life as well as his own and is all gold and pearls in moral perception, however black he may be in moral nature. Thus the gain of the European adventure ought, for the American, to be greater than the loss risked: James never quite rid himself of this speculative frame of mind and could supply, at the peak of his writing life, in the novel he cared most for, *The Ambassadors* (1903), an example in which one American gains every possible strength for his own moral nature through immersion in European moral perception. But he became increasingly forced to draw from his chosen examples the opposite conclusion, and in so doing he was only carrying one great step further the conclusion drawn in his best early work. In *The American* (1877) and in *The Portrait of a Lady* (1881) Newman and Isabel Archer are victimized by Europe; Europe is the disillusion for Newman, and for Isabel the evil and treachery, which overcame them; if they are left intact they are also left shrunk; their strength was in the strength to renounce. But in *The Wings of the Dove* (1902) and in *The Golden Bowl* (1904), the two American girls, Milly Theale and Maggie Verver, although victimized by Europe, triumph over it, and convert the Europeans who victimized them, by the positive strength of character and perceptive ability which their experience of treachery only brings out. Neither Milly's death nor Maggie's re-creation of her adulterous marriage is an act of renunciation or disillusion; they are deliberate acts of life fully realized and fully consented to, done because it is necessary to keep intact the conviction that life has values greater than any renunciation can give up or any treachery soil. By these means, in the figure of the American girl, candor, innocence, and loyalty become characteristic though not exclusive American virtues which redress the deep damage done by a blackened Europe. Thus James dramatized a reversal of the values in his International Theme so full as to make the American's necessary journey to Europe a pilgrimage reversed. It was as if in his writing life he had made a series of withdrawals into a waste in which he assumed there must be an oasis, only to find himself strengthened, on each return, to meet the high values which had all along flourished at home.

It might be said that James had taken for his text the verse from the Sermon on the Mount, "For where your treasure is, there will your heart be also," and used it alternately, first just as it is and then with a reversal of the two nouns, so that a man might expect to find his treasure where and when he had discovered his heart. If we ask by what means he had come to be able to do this, an answer which is at least possible suggests itself: by merging the dynamic dualism of his International Theme with the static, if tragic, insight of the theme of the artist in stories of people extraordinary only for their unusual awareness of life and their unusual liberty to maintain their awareness. Putting it more strongly, if less certainly, James by combining his obsessive themes managed to equip his central insight into the indestructible life of man with a genuinely contingent body of morals and living tradition, regardless of the privation of his life, his education, and his times; and further, in so far as he was able to do this, he found released for use the inexhaustible wealth of felt life in quantities and qualities capable of receiving, and filling out durably, the stamp of form.

The stamp of form was itself a prodigy of accomplishment—and we shall come to it directly—but first it ought to be reemphasized how difficult it was for a writer like James to get hold of life in a way amenable to that stamp. Having no adequate tradition to fall back on for morals (values) or ethics (decision or judgment), James had to make the intelligence do for both, had to make it do as the equivalent of order and law in operation; and, not finding enough of intelligence in the world, he had to create it, and in creating it, had to put it in conflict with facts and stupidities it could not face without choice. For to James the height of intelligence was choice; intelligence was taste in action, and the utmost choice taste could make was the choice to live or die. It was by taste that James got hold of, valued, and judged the life to which his intelligence reacted. If this is so, it explains why his readers divide into such hostile camps of repulsion and attraction. Those who are repelled think the result, in the face of actual life, drivel; those who are attracted seem to find that taste and intelligence operate through his various themes and combinations of themes to drag into being a kind of ultimate human decency which expresses all the values a given soul can stand.

To those who recognize that decency in his work, James was full of the terrible basic ambition—but stripped of its ordinary ordeals—to create characters who meet the conditions of society so as to choose to live or choose to die. Thus his characters take on the heroism and the abnegation, as alternative and equivalent roles, of the artist and of the man or woman who ought to have been an artist in life itself. Isabel Archer in *The Portrait of a Lady*, Milly Theale in *The Wings of the Dove*, Maggie Verver in *The Golden Bowl*, and Lambert Strether in *The Ambassadors* are all clear examples of human decency operating through taste and intelligence to confront life heroically and with success. One is divided between thinking that the force of this decency is a transformation of the force of sex, and that it is a new kind of vocation in morals; in either case specially designed for the novelist to represent in the figures of ideally normal human beings; for such, in the four great novels named, he has created his three American girls and his one American man.

6

But the explanation of how James harmonized his substance and his art had better be put on a little lower plane. Just twice in his life was James able to lift his work to major stature, once at the age of thirty-eight in *The Portrait of a Lady* and once again for a five-year period beginning at the age of fifty-eight, when he

produced beside the other three great novels just spoken of, two
characteristic projections of the artist's faith, *The Sacred Fount*
(1901) and *The American Scene* (1907). The first set up the conscience of the artist to act as the conscience of people who did not
have enough for themselves; the second demonstrated the record
of that conscience in action during his American visit—the first
in over twenty years—of 1904. The period before the *Portrait* was
no doubt the normal period of the growth and formation of his
own character as a writer; the novels of that time could almost as
well have been written by someone else, for they were carried
forward by a combination of the existing institution of literature
and the élan of first impressions. Then, suddenly, in his seventh
novel, James added to the institution a momentum or élan which
was his own; the character and fate of Isabel Archer were greater
than both the social and the novelistic conventions through which
she was exhibited. James had combined his themes for the first
time, and for the first time told a story that demanded of him his
full powers. Not until he again combined his themes, in *The
Ambassadors* (1903), did he again reach full power. It is further
notable that the best of the novels that came in between, *The
Spoils of Poynton* (1897), is really only an elongated tale or
nouvelle, like "The Turn of the Screw" or "The Altar of the
Dead," and that it lacked the American or International Theme.
Its story remains a melodramatic fable and never reaches the state
of dramatized fairy tale in which the novels of full power are so
strangely happy. Otherwise, aside from *The Awkward Age, What
Maisie Knew*, and *The Tragic Muse*, which have already been
discussed, there are two experiments in a genre of which James
never became a master, *The Bostonians* and *The Princess Casamassima* (both dated 1886).

On their faces both Balzacian novels as modified by the
general current of French naturalism, they were actually inhibited
from becoming naturalistic by certain elements in James's own
character as a writer, and so were partially transformed into
something else. Each of these novels plunged him into centers of
human conduct and motivation and obsession—into conditions
of behavior—of which he was only superficially aware. In *The*

Bostonians he made his center the infatuation of a grown woman for a young girl, with its havoc in each of them, and its final destruction by a violently conventional "rescue." In *The Princess Casamassima*, the center is the equally disastrous infatuation of the Princess for the little bookbinder's clerk, Hyacinth Robinson, against a general background of conspiratorial, underground, bomb-throwing revolution, ending in the violence of Hyacinth's suicide in the shabbiest, blackest room in London. Being fascinated by such subjects, James tried to make what he could see stand for what he could not; and if his attempt had been on a lesser scale—on something not the scale of a naturalistic novel—he might well have succeeded.

What did happen to his attempt in these two books suggests a general conclusion about all his work: his repeated argument that the artist should be released from the burden of things as they were ordinarily understood to happen, probably came from his ignorance of ordinary things in general. It also suggests a rudimentary principle for the art of fiction; that if you want the surface to stand for the whole you must put in enough specifications to make sure it is the surface of the thing wanted and not merely the surface of the writer's mind. In shorter forms this certainty may be provided by intensity of form or perception, but the full-length novel requires extensiveness of form and perception, and extensiveness requires knowledge and specification all around. Then James's argument against naturalistic detail would be sound; economy of strong specification would persuade the reader to put in, out of his own stock of perception, all else that was required. Then, too, the further argument would have been sounder still, that most of what we know deeply comes to us without ever fitting the specifications we had prepared for it. If we deliberately free ourselves of all specifications except those that lay us open to experience, who knows what of the vast unspecified actual will not press in?

It is this last question that must have lurked under James's practice, and this inviting risk he must often have felt he was taking. In *The Bostonians* and *The Princess Casamassima* he made a misjudgment of what detail he could do without and of what he needed, as a carpenter says of his tools, to do with. It is not that he left out the details that clutter but that he omitted to put in those that would lay his readers, and in effect the novels themselves, open to respond to the pressure of the actual—the special shabby underground menacing actual that presses inchoate at the threshold of the stories without ever getting in; so that the novels have a strangely transformed air of protecting themselves from what they are really about.

In the four great novels this is not so. There the unspecified actual does press in as the general menace of folly, inadequacy, or sheer immanent evil. Whatever it is, it ruins loyalty, prevents love, sullies innocence. It is the morass in which some part of every human being is in a nameless mortal combat, and which is felt as the dumb part of despair, the horror at the nether end of boredom, or the futility no bigger than a man's hand in any perspective of effort looked at; it is the menace of life itself. To measure, to represent, to reenact the force of that menace is one extreme of the moral feat of art; as the other extreme is to reenact the equally nameless good that combats it. To reenact both in full measure requires of James his combined sense of the reversible dualism of Europe and America, the heroism of the artist's vocation, and the two focused in an otherwise ordinary set of characters. In the shorter pieces, intensity of form and relatively limited perception are enough to give the sense of the menacing, altering force without need of any further articulation. It is its intensity that gives the sense of the jungle to "The Beast in the Jungle," of the corner to "The Jolly Corner," of the screw to "The Turn of the Screw," of the dead to "The Altar of the Dead," and of desolation to "The Bench of Desolation." Each of these tales, if you asked for articulation, would fall flat, but when inarticulated, each shows an indestructible habit of growth into at least the hallucination of actual experience.

The one occasion on which James at all successfully tried for full articulation by direct means was in that testamentary novel *The Sacred Fount*. There the nameless narrator records the passage of the force of life through half a dozen people, with himself as the medium whereby they become conscious of the exchange, and, gradually, conscious of the nature of the force exchanged. He is their conscience and their creator because he is their intelligence; he makes them see what they are. In the end they reject his intelligence, and the reader is left with the ambiguous sense either that the author is crazy and had merely invented his perceptions or that he was right but his creations had now taken over the life with which he had endowed them, with a quite human insistence on mutilating and battening on each other as they themselves chose. The halves of the ambiguity shade into each other interminably in that indestructible association of the moral life in which evil is ignorance but actual, and good is knowledge created real.

Such success as *The Sacred Fount* has is by tour de force; but it is the essential tour de force of James's sensibility; it is the represented hallucination of what, as artist and as man, he wanted to do for life; it is the poetic equivalent, the symbol and example, of what, on his own shaking ground, he wanted to stand for. If he could not say what it was, that is because it was so deeply himself that he could only show it in action, like a man in love or deadly fear. But read with good will and with a sense of the title kept turning in the mind, *The Sacred Fount* becomes the clue to the nature of the intent and to the quality of the achieved substance of the novels and tales, and then in turn becomes clear itself. If there is a secret in Henry James and if there is a way in which we can assent to the secret, both may be found in *The Sacred Fount*. It is the secret of why he was obsessed with the story of the story, the sense of the sense, the passion of the passion. He wanted, in all the areas of life he could reach, to be the story, the sense, the passion not just of the life itself but of the conscience he could create for it. So deep and hidden were the springs of conviction within him, and at the same time so sure the credit he gave to his actual perception, that he could not help believing what he created to be the conscience of truth as well as the reality of art. The being was one with the seeming.

7

In such a life work, making so little call on the ordinary means whereby we symbolize the struggle for our relations with God, society, and ourselves, it was necessary for James to make extraordinary demands upon the formal resources of the institution of literature. His essential subject matter compelled him to transform not only the English novel but also the French and Russian novel from something relatively loose and miraculous to something relatively tight and predictable. Neither *The Sacred Fount* nor *The Golden Bowl* could have been written within anything resembling the form of *Madame Bovary* or *Vanity Fair*. His own view of what magnificence his transformation amounted to may be found in the critical prefaces he wrote for the collected edition of his novels and tales. Perhaps the best sense of it is contained in the single phrase: "the coercive charm of form," and perhaps its best aspiration is found at the end of the preface to *The Ambassadors*: "The Novel remains still, under the right persuasion, the most independent, most elastic, most prodigious of literary forms." For, in James's argument, form coerced true freedom upon the novel; form freed the novel for independent prodigies which, without the force of that form, it could not undertake. For his own work, that is what his rules of form did. He developed out of the resources of the old novel, and by invention of new resources, what we now call the James novel.

Since other novelists have used and misused the James novel and since by contagion it has modified the actual practice of many novelists who never read James at all, we had better try to say what the James novel is. It is consistent to its established variety of skeleton forms; it is faithful to its established method of reporting; and it insists on its chosen center of attraction. To do these things it first of all gets rid of the omniscient author; the author is never allowed to intrude directly or in his own person; the story is always some created person's sense of it, or that of some group of persons, so that we see or feel the coercive restriction of someone's conscious experience of the story as the medium through which we ourselves feel it. Secondly, the James novel uses device after device, not merely to invite the reader's ordinary attention, but to command his extraordinary attention. For example, the dialogue in all the later work is as close in structure and in mutual relationships, and as magnetic upon the reader's mind, as an essay in mathematical logic. The scenes between persons are dramatized as substance, not as ornament; true action is in speech and gesture; and thus the dialogue creates a new form of attention, in which we always sail close-hauled or trembling on the tack. As the command to attend is obeyed, the reader learns a new game which, as it seems to partake of actual experience, he can take for truth; and which, as it shows a texture of sustained awareness never experienced in life, he knows to be art. To gain that effect, to make art truth, is the whole object of James's addiction to the forms of fiction; it was the only avenue to truth he could recognize.

Hence he was compelled to be tight, close, firm, restrictive, and extraordinarily conscious in the process of his art; and had to pretend to be so, like any believer, when he was not, because to an unexampled degree he was unconscious of all the other machineries of the mind and of many of the forces to which the mind reacts. He could not think otherwise, as he grew older and lonelier, than that only the most restrictive possible form could stamp his vision of life as recognizable truth and transform the fine conscience of his imagination into recognizable art. That he wrote both novels and tales only less than the very greatest, and that he added permanently to the scope and resources of his art in the process of doing so, was for him only the achieved act of his nature, the "obstinate finality," as he called it, of what he was— an artist. For us, the finality is equally obstinate, but it is also, as he thought the novel was, independent, elastic, prodigious; a version, not the vision, of life; a language, which, as we learn its beauty for his purposes, we can adapt and develop for our own— especially when we are in those moods he has himself created in us—those moods when taste is intelligence, intelligence is conscience, and the eloquence of conscience is heroic truth. Then he is the special case of our own point of view: he is one version of the story of our story, the sense of our sense, the passion of our passion—to be satisfied nowhere else.

James seems to inspire intoxication either of taste or disgust. But these opposite reactions come to the same thing. Born in 1843, designed by his father to be a perceptive luxury in a society whose chief claims to luxury lay along singularly imperceptive lines and whose institutions during his lifetime grew predominantly deterministic, he took to himself the further luxury of expression as a profession. So long as he expressed chiefly, or at any rate superficially, what was taken for granted, he had a fair share of popularity: he was taken as a smart if somewhat over-refined young man. As his expression came under control and exhibited deeper perceptions, he lost most of his small audience. As the quality of his work not only enriched but became characteristic and informed with passionate taste, his work was positively disliked and regarded as a luxury no one could afford.

This was about 1890. Exiled and alienated as well as dispatriated, he was stung to a new and powerful reaction by his failure with the well-made play. He became again a novelist, and in this second life, beginning in 1896, more than any other writer, he was ever consciously himself; it was his self that had grown, and was more fully and formally a luxury of expression than ever, so that fewer and fewer could afford to read him. At the same time, he had become an institution, by no means ignored but not in much resort. There were always those who read him, some as a cult and as a means of escape, others because he added to the stature of their own perception. He visited America, after twenty years, not as a triumph but as a venture in discovery. Then he revised and collected his work, deepening his tone and making a cumulus of his weight, and began a new career, partly in the form of memoirs, partly in what promised to be a new form of fiction of which the only finished examples are the stories in *The Finer Grain* (1910) where he began to show a remote intimacy, through the poetry of his language, with the preoccupations of ordinary men and women. That same year—1910—his brother William, then in England, fell ill and he went with him to help him die in America. On his return to England, his own health weakened and he finished nothing but memoirs and short essays in the remaining five years of his life.

But he was more an institution than ever. On his seventieth birthday he was presented by three hundred friends with his portrait by Sargent. In July, 1915, he became a British subject; in the following New Year Honours, he was awarded the Order of Merit; and in February, 1916, he died, still a luxury of perception and expression. Gradually that luxury has become an institution of increasing resort for those who require to find upon what assumptions, in a society like ours, unconscious of any unity and uncertain even of direction, the basic human convictions can yet grow—whether for life or for the judgment of life in art.

THE LOOSE AND BAGGY MONSTERS OF HENRY JAMES:
Notes on the Underlying Classic Form in the Novel

All that I have to say here springs from the conviction that in the novel, as elsewhere in the literary arts, what is called technical or executive form has as its final purpose to bring into being—to bring into performance, for the writer and for the reader—an instance of the feeling of what life is about. Technical form is our means of getting at, of finding, and then making something of, what we feel the form of life itself is: the tensions, the stresses, the deep relations and the terrible disrelations that inhabit them as they are made to come together in a particular struggle between manners and behavior, between the ideal insight and the actual momentum in which the form of life is found. This is the form that underlies the forms we merely practice, and it is always different—like any shot in the dark—from the technical preconception of it: what you expected when you applied your technical skills in order to find it. It is also different—as anything revealed in a body of its own always is—from what your moral and intellectual preoccupations expected: for morals in action are never the same as morals prescribed; and indeed, this form, when found, refreshes and recharges your morals, remodels and revivifies your intellect. Thus there is a mutual interaction. There is a wooing both ways; what is found is in some respect affected by the tools used, technical, moral, and intellectual; and it is also true that what is found affects, for the instance, the medium in which it emerges, technical, moral, and intellectual. Out of all these in mutual relationship is created what Croce means by theoretic form for feeling, intuition, insight, what I mean by the theoretic form of life itself. This form, whatever you call it, because it persists for new emphasis, because it endures through phase after phase and through different kinds of attention after attention, I call classic: the underlying classic form in which things are held together in a living way, with the sense of life going on.

The classic, let us say, is the life that underlies the life we know: it is the source of our behavior, it informs our behavior, it is what we cope with when we cope with our behavior. A little reflection tells us that the most interesting questions we can raise about the underlying classic form in the novel will be those which inquire into the relations between it and the various forms of the mind with which it is always associated in fact, and which indeed are the only handles by which we take hold of it. This is especially so in a period like our own when works tend to be composed, and are largely read, as if the only conscious labor were the labor of technical form: the labor of the game of the mind, the play of its conventions and the play of its words. That is, we have to inquire what technical mastery has been made to stand for. If we do not ask such questions we are likely to be left with the notion that all that is necessary to heroism, in art or life, is technical skill and have no notion at all what it was—in morals, in intellect, and in what underlay both—that animated into action the art we heroize.

Something like this is the situation into which a good deal of Henry James criticism has lately fallen. To say this is not to make a discovery but a commonplace in the bad sense; it has been said all along, and to little point. My point is that the technical or executive forms of Henry James, when turned into fetishes if not rules, have been largely misunderstood both with regard to themselves and with regard to their mutual relations with other forms. Both the ideal and the substantial origin of classic form has been ignored, on the one hand; and on the other hand, by critics concerned immediately with morals or what is called the liberal imagination, the poetic—the creative—aspects of James's language and the conventions of his forms have been minimized and cheapened to perception. I am not concerned to repair these damages but to meditate on them along several paths of meditation. The paths are well known and our feet fit them, if not our thoughts; we have only to fit our thoughts to the uneven ground.

One path is the parallel path of verse. In verse, we know that the meter does something to the words, even though the meter be the most rigidly prescribed arrangement of syllables. We know also that the rhythm does something to the meter and to the words, something not the same thing but related. Beyond that we know that the meter and rhythm and words do something to both the intellectual structure and the moral perception of the poem. We understand all this because we appreciate the strains separately as well as feel them together: we know that by their joint operation something has been brought into the poem, which is vital to it, and which would otherwise not be there. What we ought to know is that something comparable to this is true of the novel and we should suspect that we need training in appreciation to recognize it: training so that we may see not only what the author consciously intended but also where he struck on something over and above, or other than, what he intended. We must understand that the poetic mind is as much at work in prose as in verse, and we must understand that nobody—not even Dante, not even James Joyce—can be conscious of, or deliberately take care of, all the skills he uses in the moment of composition. The nine muses may be conscious, but they are too many to hear at once. The poor poet—the poor novelist—must be contented to hear what he can, yet must act with the pressure and power of the others in his writing fingers—the pressure and the power he can feel conscious of only as a haunt that has just left him.

No wonder then, if such is his case, he will confuse what he does know and can hear with what he does not know and cannot hear: a confusion sometimes made with great effect. Half the English poets of the seventeenth century thought that if technical mastery of the heroic couplet could be had, then the English epic might be written, when the fact was that the deep form—the underlying classic form—of *Paradise Lost*, not written in couplets at all, heroic or homely, had solved the problem of the epic for Milton: had solved the problem of what new phase of being the epic of Homer, Virgil, Dante had reached in Protestant, Christian, seventeenth-century England. Other powers, other skills of mind and sensibility had entered into the struggle than the poets knew; yet for all we know the argument over metrical form was the efficient agent for the birth of the new deep form. That there have been no Miltons since, counts nothing; there have been no Dantes since Dante; nor should we want any. It is only the path we want to follow.

If the argument about the heroic couplet helped produce Milton, and if the argument about the "very language of men" helped produce Wordsworth, and if the argument about the "heightened form of the best conversation of the time" helped produce Eliot and Yeats—all these along with a good many confusions and ignorances as to what else helped—then I think we might strike it rich for the field of the modern novel if we look at one of the most confused, most arrogant, and most fertile statements ever made—among so many—by Henry James. The statement is often quoted, and it comes in the Preface he wrote to the revised version of *The Tragic Muse*. I suggest that it is there precisely because at the moment of writing James was prodded—his writing fingers were twisted—by the very muses of deep form that he was only hauntedly aware of. Since he was criticizing, not creating, his response was irritated.

The Tragic Muse, I may say, seems to me a failure as a Henry James novel precisely because its form is so nearly only executive form, and not, as James partly allowed, because he did not give the executive form warrant enough to remake the characters. I take this as the unconscious source of James's irritation in the following remarks.

> A picture without composition slights its most precious
> chance for beauty, and is moreover not composed at all
> unless the painter knows *how* that principle of health

and safety, working as an absolutely premeditated art, has prevailed. There may in its absence be life, incontestably, as "The Newcomes" has life, as "Les Trois Mousquetaires," as Tolstoi's "Peace and War," have it; but what do such large loose baggy monsters, with their queer elements of the accidental and the arbitrary, artistically *mean*? We have heard it maintained, we will remember, that such things are "superior to art"; but we understand least of all what *that* may mean, and we look in vain for the artist, the divine explanatory genius, who will come to our aid and tell us. There is life and life, and as waste is only life sacrificed and thereby prevented from "counting," I delight in a deep-breathing economy and an organic form.

It is curious that James should have reversed the order of words in Tolstoy's *War and Peace*, and if we had time when we got done asking what the whole passage stands for we might ask what that reversal stood for. In brief I think it stood for not having read the book, if at all, with good will—for having read it with a kind of rudderless attention. The important thing is that *War and Peace* does have every quality James here prescribes: composition, premeditation, deep-breathing economy and organic form, but has them in a different relation to executive form than any James would accept. Indeed, put beside *War and Peace*, *The Ambassadors*, *The Wings of the Dove*, and *The Golden Bowl* are themselves "large loose baggy monsters" precisely because an excess use was made of James's particular development of executive form, and precisely because, too, of the consequent presence of James's own brand of the accidental and the arbitrary, and because these together make access difficult to James's own "deep-breathing economy and an organic form." It is these last, however, that hold us to James as they hold us to Tolstoy, and it is in them that we must find the "principle of health and safety"—or of deep ill and final danger—which James found in consciously practiced executive form; just as we would have to show in Tolstoy that his practice was virtually tantamount to an admirable executive form, and must indeed have been so used by Tolstoy. In James we have to deepen the level of our interest in the creative process; in Tolstoy we have to show that the deep things of the mind and the sensibility must after all, when they become literature, be exercised as a game, in the delight of the mind's play, like water lights, upon its experience. It is true that Tolstoy, in a worse case than Chaucer, denied any worth to his novels compared to life; and it is true that James insisted that literature stood for everything worth living in a free life: he was himself, he said, that obstinate finality, the artist. But we can afford the excesses of the great—though we must counter with our own smaller excesses of inquiry to which the great were not committed. The "divine explanatory genius" will never appear to tell us why Tolstoy—let alone Dumas and Thackeray—is "superior to art," but it seems to me possible for a talent not divine at all to suggest why both Tolstoy and James made superior forms of art. Here our business is with James; and all we have to keep in mind of Tolstoy—of Cervantes, of Dostoevsky, of Balzac and Flaubert, of Fielding, Smollett, and Scott—is that on the evidence of endurance and recurrence of interest, on the evidence of the always available and availing feeling of stature, such work must have in every significant sense at least its necessary share of "deep-breathing economy" and "organic form." We must assume that if we asked we might find out indications of how that principle worked and we can be certain that we could find in such work what James meant by the principle of composition—which is what is here meant by executive form. The novel has changed, since Cervantes, and has taken on different aspects of the general burden of literature according to the phase of culture and the bent of the writer, but I doubt that since, with Cervantes, it first undertook a major expressive task, it has reached any greater degree of mastery or perfection or possible scope. It is only the criticism of the novel, not formerly needed, that has yet to reach mastery—a lack here sorely felt; and a lack you will feel for yourselves if you will think of the relatively much greater maturity of the criticism of poetry. To go on with the present job requires the assumption of a critical maturity we do not have in fact and which we do in fact need if we are to make full response to the novel.

This is not to say that James needed in fact or in any other way to ask our critical questions or any others than he chose to ask. For a man concerned with consciousness and conscience, and perhaps because of the supremacy of that concern, James had singularly little need of consciousness outside his chosen perspective of vision, and almost no need at all of conscience—in the sense of knowing things together, with or without remorse—in regard to anything but the conventional and technical aspects of his work. But even if he had been as conscious as an oyster of his pearl, or had he had the conscience of a saint over his last sin, he had as an artist only the need to ask those questions of which he needed the answers in order to look workmanlike at his work. If those answers came then the questions must have stood for everything that counted.

It is different with us; we are not at work, we are using work done; and we have a right curiosity to understand what his questions stood for in the dark as well as what they asked for in the open of daily practice. We know, in a way that no individual novelist thinking of his own work can know, that the novel is all of a piece, and that if examples have not the same end in view, they have likely the same source, analogous means, and a common fate. Thus we have to ask at once how it is that the three novels *The Ambassadors, The Wings of the Dove*, and *The Golden Bowl* should be at the same time modeled on the well-made social play, exercises in the indirect perception of human character and action, direct to the point of the intolerable expressions of the general human predicament, and, finally, symbolic patterns—themselves in their own action—of the permanent struggle between the human condition and human aspirations; how it is, in short, that the most conventional, the most abstract, approach possible should yet exemplify one of the closest scrutinies—the closest forms—ever made of life itself. We have the shudder of beauty—of the many reduced to one, as Pythagoras says; we have the shudder of beauty—the condition of more than usual emotion and more than usual order—as Coleridge says; we have the shudder of beauty—in a unity of response felt as achieved without any feeling that the substance unified has been cheated in the theoretic form in which the unity is expressed. This is the praise of the late novels of Henry James. It may be we cannot say how it happened; if we can possibly say merely *what* happened we shall have made the judgment to go with the praise.

You will remember the well-made play-like structure of these novels—one of the ways in which they differ from all other novels of similar stature. In *The Ambassadors* the hero, Lambert Strether, is sent to Paris by a widow with whom he has "prospects," to rescue her son from an immoral life. Once in Paris, Strether has a classic recognition: Europe is not immoral, it is life itself, and the widow's morality is blatant and empty. Then follows a reversal of roles, equally classic with the recognition: the young man insists on giving up his mistress, who is a great lady, and returning, a cad for riches and a glutton for money, to his mother's America, while, on the contrary, Strether, having discovered life at last in Paris in middle age insists on remaining at the cost of his "prospects" with the widow, and at the worse cost of all security in life. As he has made his recognition and achieved his reversal too late in life the denouement is that he has to renounce all that has come his way in the person of Maria Gostrey, the American expatriate who picked him up at the moment of landing. Thus Strether turns out to have been less an ambassador than a pilgrim: the goods he has achieved are spiritual, to be signified best by the badge of a new face, even a new look in the shoulders seen from behind.

In *The Wings of the Dove*, an American millionairess, Milly Theale, doomed to early death, makes her pilgrimage to Europe to see and live the most she can before she dies. She falls in with an engaged couple who cannot marry for lack of money; they— particularly the girl, Kate Croy—conceive the idea of marrying the young man to Milly Theale so that after inheriting her money at her death they can marry into power and ease. Milly's pilgrimage is broken by her recognition, which is forced upon her, of the plot to get her money in the disguise of love. She dismisses the young man, dies, but leaves him her money nevertheless. The young man, recognizing what he has done in terms of Milly Theale, suffers if not a reversal a deep change of role and finds himself compelled, like Strether, to renounce the worldly goods he has gained. He is left seeing things with new eyes forever.

In *The Golden Bowl* there is a similar but more complex predicament. Adam Verver, a multi-millionaire, and his daughter Maggie make their pilgrimage to Europe innocent as lambs in their riches and their love of each other. Maggie marries Prince Amerigo who requires money and power to preserve himself. Her father marries the Prince's 'true love,' the American expatriate Charlotte Stant, who requires to preserve herself money and—not power—but further relations with the prince. In due time—in the second act—Maggie discovers that her husband and her step-mother have been improving and expanding their relations. After her recognition scene, in what might be called the third act, she too reverses her role; out of her changed goodness and innocence —no less good and no less changed—she draws the power to make something tragically good and ultimately innocent of the two marriages. The sacrifice that she makes is that she renounces the old ground of her beseeching—the aspiration of her innocence, candor, and energy, the innocence of her money—and stands on the new and terrible ground of the conditions of life itself.

It is interesting to observe—and I think it can equally be observed of most great European novels—that the Aristotelian terms recognition and reversal of roles apply sharply to the major motions of the plot and that complication or intrigue applies firmly to the minor motions. But instead of the journey of *hubris* or overweening pride, we have the journey of the pilgrim, the searcher, the finder. And instead of catharsis—the purging in pity and terror—we follow rather the Christian pattern of rebirth, the fresh start, the change of life or heart—arising from the pity and terror of human conditions met and seen—with the end not in death but in the living analogue of death, sacrifice, and renunciation. So it is in James; and so it is in Tolstoy with the difference that sacrifice may take the form of death as with Anna in *Anna Karenina*, subsidence into the run of things as with Levin in that book or with Pierre in *War and Peace*, or disappearance into the heroic unknown as with Vronsky in *Anna Karenina*. In James the end is always a heightened awareness amounting to an exemplary

conscience for life itself, accomplished by the expense, the sacrifice, the renunciation of life as lived in the very conditions on
which the consciousness and the conscience are meant to prevail.
James's novels leave us with the terrible exemplars of conscience
seen coping with the worst excruciations of which their consciousnesses are capable. The order in the three late novels is
interesting, and it is the order of composition if not of publication.
Strether, in *The Ambassadors*, is the exemplar of the life of senses.
Kate Croy, in *The Wings of the Dove*, is our lady of philosophy or
practical wisdom shown as the exemplar of all that is torn and
dismayed, but still persistent in that role. Maggie Verver, in *The
Golden Bowl*, is perhaps as near the exemplar as James could
come to our lady of theology or divine wisdom; she is James's
creation nearest to Dante's Beatrice, stern and full of charity, the
rock itself but all compassion, in the end knowing all but absorbing all she knows into her predetermined self, not exactly
lovable but herself love. Not that James would have admitted any
of these conceptions except the first.

For in the first, which is Strether as the life of senses, that is
exactly what James's own language shows: Strether's consciousness and his conscience are applied to render an indirect view of
the beauty and the excruciation of the life of the senses: he assents
to it, he knows it, but he is only an exemplar of knowledge and
assent: he himself is not finally up to that life. This James clearly
must have meant. But what he meant by Kate Croy in *The Wings
of the Dove* must remain uncertain and I think ought to remain
uncertain. Kate as construed from the notes James left behind,
notes which may be read in Matthiessen and Murdock's book,*
was meant originally to be the villainness in a standard social
melodrama, and she never entirely loses that role—which explains
both her resoluteness and her strange, occasional overriding blind
commitment to action. But it explains neither her beauty—she is
physically the most beautiful of all James's women by a sur-
passing margin—nor her instructed humanity, her sense of what

---

The Notebooks of Henry James, ed. F. O. Matthiessen and Kenneth B. Murdock
(New York: Oxford University Press, 1947)—Ed.

is what, and the necessity, in the given conditions, of her fall from that beauty and that humanity. Somehow Kate the beauty, the girl on the make who will be nothing if she makes nothing of what other people are, somehow Kate is the destructive persistent element of practical philosophy which criticizes, and places, and makes intelligible, and disposes of the overweening image of moral beauty which is Milly Theale, princess in her own American right and heiress of the ages. Kate is criticism which does not destroy but modulates: under her impact we see the nominal heroine of the novel, Milly Theale, for what she is, an aspiration impossible of realization; she is that temptation seen on the high places which is the worst temptation, once seen the most corrupting, appealing with the best impossible appeal to the worst in our natures. That is not what a man wants to do with his image of moral beauty, but it is what the imaginative man, when he sees his image in terms of the actual conditions of life, sometimes must in honesty do. The wings of the dove are still clean and silvery, but the sheepfold is fouler than ever; for the dove has created its dirt.

Maggie Verver as Beatrice—the Queen or at least the Princess of all forms of knowledge walking in human flesh—is perhaps a more tremendous image than James could quite create. It is hard to turn a lamb into a sovereign even among the lions—even, that is, among those predatory creatures of necessity who are best equipped to know that the lamb of innocence exists. That is why, no doubt, James gives Maggie and her father the added strength of their limitless millions: making the godly surrogates of Caesar. The possibility is haunting, and breathless, that such a combination might be effective; but it is not enough, for on some other level of belief—the level Dante and Shakespeare had—the conviction of unity is lacking. Maggie has the kind of imperiousness that goes with the deepest waywardness, the waywardness that is the movement of life itself; but she has no capacity for exerting the imperium itself except in aspiration. There is too much fear in her: she feels too much of her new knowledge as chill; she is too much there to be preyed on; she is too much an ideal ever to take on full power. But she does a great deal just the same; if by her goodness and innocence she cannot make other people good, she can yet by that goodness breed their wrong. By her goodness she is able to put her husband and his mistress (who is also her step-mother) between Scylla and Charybdis: between "the danger of doing too much and the danger of not having any longer the confidence or the nerve . . . to do enough." And that, she says, "that's how I make them do what I like!" When her confidante Mrs. Assingham tells her, after hearing this, that she is amazing, that she is terrible, Maggie makes her great answer. No, she says; she can bear anything for love, not for love of her father, not for love of her husband, just for love. What we see is Maggie learning in the abyss of a London stage drawing room two of the lessons Dostoevsky found in the enormous abyss of *The Brothers Karamazov*: that most men find beauty in Sodom and that love in action is a harsh and terrible thing. But Maggie can accept neither the beauty of Sodom nor the action in love. Thus Mrs. Assingham is right when she tells her husband "we shall have to lie for her till we're black in the face." Her goodness and her love is all of a piece; the broken golden bowl which she can barely hold together with all her force is herself; it is flawless only to those who would protect her and defraud her, who would at once plunder and deceive her, all in the name of love and admiration of her goodness.

Maggie is all of a piece in another sense as well. When early in the book Mrs. Assingham tells the Prince—that image of Old Europe, the Italy of life and crime—that he has all the senses that make a man good, he answers her, answers Maggie, answers the reader whoever he may be; answers in an image which is a major strain in the underlying moving form of the book. No, he says, the moral sense I have not got. "I mean always as you others consider it. I've of course something that in our poor dear backward old Rome sufficiently passes for it. But it's no more like yours than the tortuous stone staircase—half-ruined into the bargain!—in some castle of our quattrocento is like the 'lightning elevator' in one of Mr. Verver's fifteen-storey buildings. Your moral sense works by steam—it sends you up like a rocket. Ours is slow and steep and unlighted, with so many of the steps missing that—well, that it's as short in almost any case to turn round and come down again." Maggie and Milly, and Strether too, work by the terrible amazing steam of their own innocence and candor and courage. They go up like rockets and somehow work great havoc on those who are led, or forced, to go up with them.

In the havoc as it moves and shapes and heaves is the underlying form of the book: the form in which is apprehended the conditions of life. The strongest shape and the sharpest motion—the deepest heaving qualm—James is able to create out of that havoc is the shaping in heaving motion of a conscience out of consciousness. The structure and the gradual emergence of that conscience seem to me the overt and visible acknowledgment of the underlying form. Conscience is the bite of things known together, in remorse and in incentive; conscience is that unification of the sense of things which is moral beauty; conscience comes at many moments but especially, in James, in those deeply arrested moments when the will is united with the imagination in withdrawal.

It is on such moments that each of our three novels ends. In *The Golden Bowl* the Prince tells Maggie "I see nothing but you." That means he is united with his conscience. "And the truth of it had with this force after a moment so strangely lifted his eyes that as for pity and dread of them she buried her own in his breast." The moment was gone. At the end of *The Wings of the Dove* our lady of philosophy Kate Croy and her lover Merton Densher feel stretch over them the dove's wings of the dead Milly Theale. "She turned to the door, and her headshake was now the end. 'We shall never again be as we were.'" Beauty and a shade had passed between.

So it was too with Strether in *The Ambassadors* and there are thoughts in his mind toward the end of that book, applied to the wonderful mistress of the caddish young man he had come to Paris to rescue, but fitting exactly the situation in other books as well. "It was actually moreover as if he didn't think of her at all, as if he could think of nothing but the passion, mature, abysmal, pitiful, she represented, and the possibilities she betrayed." These were the powers the image of moral beauty—of conscience—had attempted to transform. It is the perennial job of uprooted imagination, of conscience, choosing from beauty and knowledge, to raise such an image; but it may not transgress actuality without destruction; the images must not be mistaken for reality though the heart craves it. As Dante says (*Purg.* XXI: 133–36):

Or puoi la quantitate *comprender dell'amar ch'a te mi* *scalda,* *quando dismento nostra vanitate,* *trattando l'ombre come cosa* *salda*	Now may you comprehend the measure of the love that warms me toward you, when I forget our nothingness, and treat images as solid things.

The poor shade of the poet Statius had tried to embrace Virgil, and these were Virgil's words in answer. There the shadow was the only actual. It is interesting to use an insight from Dante here, because in his construction of conscience and moral beauty, James is himself making a late gesture in the aesthetic-moral tradition of the Christian world which Dante did so much to bring into poetry. With both men, it was only a hair's breadth, a mere change of phase, between the spiritual and the sensual, the ideal and the actual; and this is because there was in them both the overwhelming presence of felt, of aesthetic, reality as it fastened like a grapple upon individual souls and bodies.

Also to think of Dante here may remind us again of the great intellectual spiritual form in which James worked: the form of conversion, rebirth, the new life. That is the experience of Strether seen against the actual world, and in that world—"in the strict human order." Not a tragedy in the old sense—that is in its end—its tragedy lies in its center: in the conditions of life which no conversion, no rebirth, no turning, ever leaves behind—not even in saints till they have gone to heaven. The tragic tension lies partly between what is reborn and what is left over, and partly between the extremes toward which conversion always runs and the reality which contains the extremes.

The extremes with which Henry James was obsessed had largely to do with the personal human relations and almost nothing at all to do with public relations except as they conditioned, marred, or made private relations. It may be said that James wooed into being—by seeing what was there and then going on to create what might be there in consciousness and conscience—a whole territory of human relations hitherto untouched or unarticulated. I do not say not experienced, only unarticulated. So excessive is this reach into relation, there is no escape possible for the creatures caught in it except by a deepening or thickening of that relation until, since it cannot be kept up, it must be sacrificed. That is to say, its ideal force becomes so great that its mere actual shade becomes intolerable. So it was with Strether; he denied Marie de Vionnet and Maria Gostrey wholly in order to be 'right' with the ideal which the actual experience of them had elicited in his mind. But the denial was a gesture of this ideal, and it could have been otherwise, could in another soul have been the gesture of assent; for the beauty and the knowledge were still there, and the reality, which contains both the ideal and the actual, and so much more, stands, in its immensity, behind.

Behind is a good place. If we think of what is behind, and feel what we think, which is what James did, we will understand all the better the desperation out of which Strether created his image of moral beauty, the virtuous connection, and how it stood up, no matter what, as conscience. Otherwise, like Strether at his low point, we "mightn't see anyone any more at all." As it is we see with Maria Gostrey: "It isn't so much your *being* 'right'—it's your horrible sharp eye for what makes you so."

We have gotten, as we meant to, rather far away from the mere executive form—gotten into what that form merely articulates and joints and manipulates and takes into itself, itself being charged and modified thereby; but it has been there all along, that form, and we can now look at at least one facet of it with double vision: to see what it is and to see at the same time what happens to it—like what happens to a meter—in use. There are many possibilities—all those executive habits of the artist James

names in his Prefaces, some of them never named before; and all
those other devices, rhetorical and imagistic which James uses
without naming—but for my purpose, which is to show how a
technical device criticizes the substance it puts in motion and how
the substance modifies the device, there is none so handy or so apt
as James's use of the conventional figure of the confidante, a figure
common to European drama, but developed to the highest degree
of conventionality in the French theater James knew best.

Each of the three novels has examples, and in each the uses to
which they are put are somewhat different. In the theater the
confidante is used to let the audience know what it otherwise
would not; she blurts out secrets; carries messages; cites facts; acts
like a chorus; and is otherwise generally employed for comic relief
or to represent the passage of time. Generally speaking, the confidante is stupid, or has the kind of brightness that goes with
gossip, cunning, and malice. In these three novels the case is
different: each confidante has a kind of bottom or residual human
stupidity and each is everlastingly given to gossip; but the gossip
has a creative purpose—to add substance to the story—and the
stupidity is there to give slowness and weight and alternative
forms to the perceptions and responses which they create. This is
the gossiping stupidity for which there is no name in any living
language, but which the Sanskrit calls *Moha*, the vital, fundamental stupidity of the human race by which it represents, to the
human view, the cow, or as we would say the sheep. It is what the
man has been caught in when he gives you a sheepish look; he
was caught a little short of the possibility he was trying to cope
with. It is this role—so much more fundamental than the conventional original—that James's confidante is given to play; and
saying so much it should be evident that she will qualify as well
as report action, she will give it substance, and gain substance by
it, as well as precipitate it.

The simplest form of confidante in our three novels is that
taken by Susan Stringham in *The Wings of the Dove*. Susie is
Milly Theale's paid companion; it is she who makes out of Milly
a Princess and overdeclares her value, volubly and credibly, until
there is a general conspiracy to accept as operative truth the ideal

THE LOOSE AND BAGGY MONSTERS OF HENRY JAMES 141

she puts up: she gives human and fabulous names—a fairy god-mother sort of name—to the attributes in Milly which James could not at first directly present; but she is not otherwise a part of the story. In *The Golden Bowl* Fanny Assingham and her husband Colonel Bob have nothing at all of the fairy godparent about them, but have rather just the opposite function: to make the most intolerable, grasping, greedy, predatory behavior socially and humanly acceptable at the same time that they make out between them that the behavior *is* predatory and *is* intolerable. They fulfill in short the old role of truth-telling, lie-making clowns at the drawing room level. They are the comic relief, but it is a curiously ugly, unredeemable sort of penetrating, revelatory comedy that they practice. Fanny with a refinement of perception —wrong or right—past belief and with an only barely credible polish of diction, and Colonel Bob with the good-hearted cynicism appropriate to the best clubs, dig into the tenderest perfidy and the most charitable frauds they can find, and when they cannot find they create. These are the people, wonderfully rendered in voice and gesture and texture of situation, who stand for all the intrigue that passes for human motive before human motive is created. Colonel Bob assumes that any such substitute will pass muster if let alone; by such as him, the world would get by. Fanny makes a very different but congruous assumption: that no motive inspected—and inspect them she must—could ever get by unless inspected, protected, edited, rearranged, and covered up. Her great sign of the truth is that it shall be worth lying for; and her great warrant for lying is that a lie may create a truth. To her, a mistake only proves her policy right, and a real blunder only asks for redoubled effort. It is people like the Assinghams that ensure the service of the gods of this world; they are that rhetoric of manners that masquerades as decency to cover the plea of guilty or in-adequate action. They create the scandal they would excuse. What they make in the world is hopelessness, futility, emptiness; but they make these tolerable by making them a game; yet without them nobody could get along, least of all the Ververs, Charlotte, and the Prince, the truly innocent and the truly wicked, for without the Assinghams they would have no meeting ground.

Maria Gostrey, in *The Ambassadors*, shares the gossip and the creativeness of the Assinghams, but with the difference that she is the go-between who has something in common with both things she goes between, and that her creativeness is not a substitute and seldom a mistake, for she is, rather, when she pushes herself, clairvoyant. That she pushes herself often makes her a part of the story and part of the emotion that holds the story together. The gift of clairvoyance, the gift of seeing so into the center of things as to become a part of them, and of doing so merely by nature and the skill of a lifetime, gives her powers quite opposite to those of the Assinghams. Instead of hopelessness she creates hope, instead of futility possible use, instead of emptiness fullness; and she never makes tolerable that which ought to remain intolerable. That is why she becomes, in the deep sense, a part of the story, and why the story lifts her from a means to a substance. If it were not that a device ought not to be called so, I would say that this instance of the conventional device of the confidante was also an instance of classic form.

There remains the middle ground of what is nowadays called the mind or the intellect to inquire into: the conceptual, dogmatic, tendentious part of the whole mind: the part inhabited and made frantic by one's ideology. Although there has been a good deal of talk to the effect that James was defective in this quarter, I think all that talk will vaporize on the instant if the question underlying the talk is differently put. Not what ideas did James have, but with what ideas—abroad then and now—is James's imaginative response to life related? It will be these ideas that will illuminate and partake of his underlying form. In short we want to get at the ideas in James's mind that were related to his whole work; and in James these occupy a precarious but precious place. He is not a Dante or a Thomas Mann; his humanism is under cover, part of his way of seeing, part of his "deep-breathing economy" and "organic form."

But it had got twisted by his time and by the superstitions of his time; for although he was 'against' his time he had necessarily to collaborate with it—from the very honesty of his inward eye for the actual, no one more so. I do not know that the nature of this collaboration can be made plain, but a few generalizations may be risked. They have to do with the tendency toward expressionism in art and social thinking, which stem from what is meant by art for art's sake, and they have to do with the emergence of a new concept of the individual as isolated and detached from society in everything but responsiveness, which is a concept that springs, I think, from those changes in society that are related to the facts of population growth and the mass-form of society.

There is a sense in which art for art's sake as we have had it since the *Parnassiens* is itself a reflection of the shift in the bases and the growth in size of any given modern society. As the bourgeois base turns into the industrial base—as the great population engulfs the "great society"—we get on the one hand something called pure poetry with a set of feelings in the poets who write it which has something to do with the impulse to escape (to deny, to cut away) and the conviction of isolation (the condition of the incommunicable, the purely expressive, the fatally private —the sense of operating at a self-created parallel to the new society). At the same time, on the other hand, we get a belief in that monster the pure individual, whose impulse is to take life as a game, and whose ambition is to make the individual *feeling* of life the supreme heroism; so that the tropes of one's own mind become the only real parallel to life. In both cases—in pure art and in the pure individual—we pretend that it was like this in the past just behind our past.

No doubt this is so of some past, but not where it is looked for, in the Great Europe. It is more likely so in some of the over-populated periods in Egyptian or Byzantine history, or in the Rome of the second century: each of which ended in the culture of the fellaheen, where the individual was purified to extinction, from which only Rome has so far recovered. What we overlook in our pretense to a tradition is the difference between a population-burst accompanied by the disappearance of knowledge and the shrinking of the means of subsistence, which is what the past shows us (Egypt, China, India, Rome), and a great continuing population growth accompanied by the division of culture and the specialization of knowledge, along with the tremendous multiplication of the means of subsistence and of war—all of which has been our experience. What we see is the disappearance of the old establishment of culture—culture safe from the ravages of economy—and we do not know whether another culture is emerging from the massive dark, or, if it is, whether we like it. Whatever has disappeared or is emerging is doing so without loss of vitality except in the cultural establishment (now everywhere a prey to the economy) and with otherwise what seems a gain in vitality. What has above all survived in our new mass society is the sense of the pure individual—by himself, or herself, heir to all the ages. Because of the loss of the cultural establishment we have put a tremendous burden on the pure individual consciousness. It seems to us that in order to hang on to the pure individual we must burden his consciousness beyond any previous known measure. We make him in our art, especially the art of literature, assume the weight of the whole cultural establishment—above all that part of it which has to do with behavior, manners, human relations: with insight, with conformity and rebellion, and with the creation or ability to create absorbing human motives. For all this the artist has to find, by instinct since his culture does not sufficiently help him, what I called to begin with the underlying classic form in which things are held together in a living way, with the sense of life going on.

Sometimes this burden of consciousness seems to obscure, if not to replace, the individuals we create, whether in ourselves or in our arts. At any rate, this burden of consciousness is what has happened to our culture. There is no longer any establishment, no longer any formula, and we like to say only vestigial forms, to call on outside ourselves. There is only the succession of created consciousnesses—each of which is an attempt to incorporate, to give body to, to incarnate so much as it is possible to experience, to feel it, the life of the times, including the culture no matter what has happened to it—and including also of course all those other things which never were in any culture, but which press on us just the same.

These generalizations seem to me one of the useful backgrounds against which to look at the novels of Henry James. As background it reflects light on the extremes to which he pushed the limits of his created individual consciousnesses, so much less varied than those of Gide, Proust, Mann, Kafka, and Joyce, but no less intense, no less desperately grasping after life, and the form of life, for and in the name of the individual. In that light we can but understand what Strether, in *The Ambassadors*, is up to when he says *Live all you can!* We can understand also how Mme. de Vionnet, the young man's splendid mistress, is up to the same thing under what are fundamentally the same conditions. We understand how much there is to see—to see unaided by ourselves—how much there is to intensify into form—in the simplest relation between human beings.

James at fifty-eight, when he wrote *The Ambassadors*, had experienced and therefore could dramatize the disestablishment of culture and the shift in the bases of society, and he could do so all the better because he did not, and probably could not, have understood them intellectually or historically. He was concerned with the actuality he found and with the forms under the actuality. He was himself an example of disestablishment and a forerunner of what we may expect to find a prevalent form of disinherited sensibility, the new 'intellectual proletariat,' and he had therefore only to write out of himself against the society which 'intellectually' or by common assumption he thought still existed, in order to create an extreme type of transitional image of the future time. Not unnaturally his original audience—barring the young who were ahead of themselves—thought he had created sterile fantasies; the richer his subjects grew and the deeper he got into them, the more his sales fell off. His own experience of 'America' and of 'Europe,' where America had apparently moved faster than Europe toward the mass society, toward the disinheritance but not the disappearance of the individual, had moved him ahead of his contemporaries; had moved him to the 1930s when he began to be read seriously, and the '40s when he got to be the rage, and now to the '50s when he seems, so to speak, an exaggerated and highly sensitized form of the commonplace of our experience: the sensitized deep form.

If Strether is our example of 1902 looking ahead, what Strether would feel now would seem like the music of Adrian Leverkühn in Mann's *Doctor Faustus*: a heightening but not a disintegration of his feelings of 1902; and it would be a heightening, as in Mann's novel, by parody and critique, because like Leverkühn he would have had so much more of the same thing behind him, and so much more of the same burden put upon him, than he had in the earlier time. Our theoretic new Strether would have found out how much more had to be re-established in a form greater than its own than he had then felt; how much more, by necessity and by choice, must be reborn into actuality out of its hidden form. But the difference between the two Strethers would be by bulk and by kind, not by quality, by scope and not by reach. The reach is into the dark places where the Muses are, and all the rest is the work we do to bring into the performance of our own language the underlying classic form in which they speak.

THE GOLDEN BOWL

(Grove Press)

In his three novels, *The Ambassadors, The Wings of the Dove,* and *The Golden Bowl,* written one a year as he approached the age of sixty, Henry James made a spiritual trilogy which, with each succeeding volume, approached nearer and nearer the condition of poetry. This is one way of stating James's achievement as a novelist and one way of qualifying the stature of his imagination. I mean that the authority and the mystery—the riches and the waste places—of these novels tend increasingly to lie in the poetry of his language, but that the poetry is the poetry of the soul in action. These novels, then, constitute poetic dramas of the inner life of the soul at the height of its struggle, for good and for evil, with the outer world in which it must live and to which it must respond, the world which it must deny, or renounce, or accept. It is by such means that the soul seems, in these novels, to do something to actual life and is itself changed by them through a shifting equilibrium in which a very little soul may by its spiritual intensity balance a great deal of life. Something of this sort is what is meant when we refer to the novel as a way of looking at life, or, better, it is what we might mean if we said that the novel provided us with a theoretic form for life. The novel gives the imaginative parts of our minds a theoretic form for life which will modify or correct the forms which other parts of our minds—all the conceptual and administrative and routine parts—provide; and the novel does this precisely by providing forms in which we can see the soul in action. It is novelists like James who best support this claim.

For it is novelists like James who best show us how in the novel the *craft* of the form—the whole institution of the novel—must intervene between the soul and its actions as the medium absolutely necessary if we are to see anything at all. The more spiritual you are ultimately, the more surely you must be immediately in the senses and the more certain you must be, for both, that you have the aid of mechanical devices and familiar conventions. It is hard for either spiritual things or sensuous things to reach form in themselves (at least in language), and it would seem they are bound to take lodgings in the conventional forms nearest at hand and of the oldest architecture; if successful, they will emerge, as in these novels of James, as new masters of the house, and the house will be beautiful because once again lived in. Each of these novels is a tale of illicit love, two of them about adultery; the one (*The Ambassadors*) the lovely aspiring adultery, the other (*The Golden Bowl*) the hideous intolerable adultery. In each novel the crash of things comes about through the shock by which the illicit love is recognized. In each the act of illicit love is the tragic fault—the *hamartia* of Aristotle—the act which can be explained but cannot be justified. In each the movements of the plot are carefully calculated to insure this recognition and this revelation. This is the plot which derives from the impact of the mechanically well-made play—as in Scribe and Dumas and Brieux, and later as in Maugham and Coward and Philip Barry—upon the novel; and taken in that aspect, James made certain of the existence in English of the well-made novel. But this is not the plot which Aristotle called the soul of the action; it is only the mechanical scaffold, proved strong through long experience and wide current practice in popular writing, which would give support, outer convenience, and mechanical form to movements of the soul otherwise (within James's reach) ineluctable. It is like

Dostoevsky with his series of great novels based upon the mechanical form of the murder mystery.

Perhaps the more ineluctable in itself the real plot is, the more necessary is the preliminary and final existence of the mechanical plot. The imaginative mind must use many modes of seeing in order to come upon a single view and especially so when, as in our age, there is no existing single view to which the imagination gives universal credit and what is universal seems rather what is made fresh. James, at any rate, in writing about his own work emphasized the mechanical aspects of his technique and even created a whole language for its discussion, at the very moment when he was regarding the freshest and most universal of his creations, such as the three novels we have here in mind, and most notably, because most poetic, in *The Golden Bowl*. For there is in each of these novels a plot which does truly constitute the soul of the action, which does truly imitate the conditions and aspirations of human life as seen in the actions of men and women of more than usual worth and risk. Between the operations of the two plots we gain the condition prescribed by Coleridge as the ideal condition of poetry, the condition of "a more than usual state of emotion and a more than usual order." How then shall we describe these true plots?

When we try to describe them, we see at once that James had a many-moded mind, and that there is no simple single formula for any of them. Possibly we can say that the mechanical plot is what the action is about as anecdote and that the true plot reveals the being of the people to whom the action happens and *thus* reveals the action of the soul in its poetic drama. In *The Ambassadors*, Strether finds in the midst of adultery a virtuous connection which makes, though too late for him, life full and free and worth living. In *The Wings of the Dove*, Milly Theale's life stops, when she discovers her young man has deceived her with her best friend, just at the moment when the nature of freedom and fullness of life have become plain to her. In *The Golden Bowl*, Maggie, the little Princess, seizes fast on the freedom and fullness of life in full assent to its cost in treachery and woe—as illustrated, in her case, by the adulterous relation between her husband and her father's young wife. In each novel, the hero or heroine is an almost inconceivably lonely person—so lonely as to be no more than a shade or the dream of a human being—and yet as quick with life as our own flesh cut with a razor or paper's edge. In each novel, too, the hero or heroine, across the gap of loneliness, works permanent ravage and ruin, the shameless punishment and the shameful penance of passion upon itself, on the couples who have been enduring illicit love however lovely or natural or treacherous to the point of mere lust (Venus without Cupid, as Montaigne says) the love had been. Chad Newsome and Marie de Vionnet separate forever (in *The Ambassadors*), Merton Densher and Kate Croy (in *The Wings of the Dove*) are riven by the woe of their very humanity, and Amerigo, the Prince, and Charlotte Verver create a lie between themselves which will separate them ocean-wide forever. Nor do the heroic agents of these separations fare any better. Strether renounces the chance of getting anything for himself out of his embassy, otherwise so successful, to Europe. Milly Theale denies life at the moment she has grasped it. Maggie Verver accepts life with a conviction so violent that it breaks her to pieces and, at the last moment we see her, is unable to look in her husband's eyes at the cost of the life and loyalty her conviction has created there. They are indeed dread shades into which, with their creations in the lives and loves of their victims, they dissolve, leaving only a vital or a mortal pang, vital as beauty, mortal as incentive, when set upon by the evil that springs in the dusk of life.

When set upon by the evil in life it is the good, in James, that in the instance perishes however it may endure in essence or ideal, in the heaven of man's mind. Here I think is the element in James's novels that gives them their fabulous air; we believe in them only as we believe in hellish or heavenly fables, as we might believe in some fabulous form of the uncreated shades of ourselves. These shades have always been the springs of poetry, of individual insight into collective moral experience and created images of moral beauty alike. They trouble our conscience, and indeed are our conscience, not of particular ill doing or omission, but of life itself; and so likewise these troublings teach us ways of love—of

human relatedness—to which even as we see them we are inadequate but to which ever afterwards we aspire.

So it is with these novels of James. Each of the three persons
named—Lambert Strether, Milly Theale, and Maggie Verver—
looms on the consciousness of the other persons as an image of
moral beauty, strikes them as conscience (the agenbite of inwit),
and teaches them a new possible, impossible (James's own phrase)
mode of love in which conscience and moral beauty are joined.
Through these three persons the others learn what they want,
what they are, and what, in the conditions into which they have
warped their actual world, they cannot have. The anguish is as
great as the beauty, the possible as the impossible. Strether and
the two girls suffer as much as the victims of their goodness, their
conscience, and their love; they suffer as shades always must in
the anguish of the actual world, the certainty either of degradation
or extinction, or both. It is of great interest, lastly, that these three
suffer in distinctly different ways but in a rising scale of the value
grasped at, missed only by the hair's breadth of life itself and so
grasped at all the more. They suffer in accord with the plan or
division of nature of Dante, that master who first brought love into
European literature as a primary subject. Lambert Strether suffers
all that is possible to the senses, Milly Theale what is possible
as allegory or created meaning, Maggie Verver is in intention
rather like Beatrice in the *Divine Comedy*, the Lady of Theology,
and suffers the pangs of the highest human love. I will not
say that the one mode of love is in the act superior to the others,
and I am certain that our sense of any one modifies our sense of
the others, but I think if we consider all three modes and the
progression James made of them we will understand how it is
that *The Golden Bowl*, the last, is the most poetic in the sense of
its language as well as its structure, and also the most shadowy.
Whoever attempts creation under the model of Beatrice is in the
very shadows of poetry, and he can expect at most that the
shadows will become a part of the actual world. It is Maggie
Verver herself who might have used Dante's words again, and
whether in addressing her father or her husband. "Now you may
understand the measure of the love that warms me toward you,

when I forget our nothingness and treat shades as solid things."
And it is only with an extra pang that we realize Dante's words
would have been apter still in the mouths of husband and father
addressed to her. The shade was the only actual.

With this much for preface and program let us look at *The
Golden Bowl* for illustration and example of what is meant by a
novel about a shabby adultery which is also a poetic drama of the
soul's action. What does a sweet, lovely, and inordinately rich
young American girl do when she discovers that the Italian prince
she has married was lover to another woman at the time he
married her and is still her lover when, later, she has become her
father's young wife? What does the little American princess of
candor, innocence, and goodness do when she discovers that the
golden bowl of all their happiness is broken—was indeed cracked
secretly to begin with—by the historic and continuing perfidy of
her husband and her stepmother? What, particularly, is this
American girl going to do about an ugly and intolerable situation
when to bring it out in the open under the public standards of the
world would be to ruin her beloved father's life? What, finally,
can she do morally under the standards of actual private experience: what, short of destruction, can she do with a love which
has been soiled, smirched, invaded, and then imprisoned by the
monsters who come out of the human dark at the nightfall of
constancy, loyalty, and candor in human relations? What can the
American girl confronted with the old world, the permanent ugly
world into which all new worlds collapse, do to save herself?

These are the questions the attempts to answer which furnish
the great substance of the book, but they do not come up in
Maggie's terms at the beginning. The beginning is for Prince
Amerigo on the eve and in the early stages of his marriage to
Maggie. Then the book proceeds to the construction of the marriage of his lover Charlotte Stant to Maggie's father on the
theoretic ground that the double marriage would bring freedom
all round. That this freedom would never suit the Ververs is
certain from our first sight of these four persons. The Prince is an
alien: though he thinks in English he speaks it too well—too well
for sincerity, too well to express his thoughts. He is big with

family annals, but too little in himself; hence he needs American money but is unlikely to share American good faith and innocence, though (and he does) he may learn to feel their force. He knows nothing of the white curtain of the polar mind which inhabits Maggie and has no sense of her adventuresomeness which never, or seldom, accepts a specific adventure. Where he is venture capital, she is all long-term obligation. Yet he understands well the nature of the difference between them and what the risk is in their marriage. He puts it that he lacks the moral sense and must therefore depend on them to show him when he's wrong without knowing it; which is exactly, of course, what in the working out of the novel Maggie does show him. He goes on about his lack of the moral sense: "I mean always as you others consider it. I've of course something that in our poor dear backward old Rome sufficiently passes for it. But it's no more like yours than the tortuous stone staircase—half-ruined into the bargain!—in some castle of our *quattrocento* is like the 'lightning elevator' in one of Mr. Verver's fifteen-storey buildings. Your moral sense works by steam—it sends you up like a rocket. Ours is slow and steep and unlighted, with so many of the steps missing that—well, that it's as short in almost any case to turn round and come down again."

The Prince is talking to Mrs. Assingham, the American wife of a retired Colonel, of whom Maggie later says that she doesn't care so much about people being wicked but only about their being fools. But the Prince was nevertheless right about the more flagrantly explosive forms of American and English morality. What he failed to see was that his tortuous morality would be exposed to, and transformed by, the secretly growing, quiet, desolating, convinced force of his wife's morality when it found itself, in peril of its life, opposed like a tide-rip to his own. The tide was stronger than the stream, as it always is until the hour comes, the tide turns, and all flows into the waste sea.

As for our other pair of principal persons, Maggie's father Adam Verver and Charlotte Stance, later Mrs. Verver, it is they who in the end cannot tolerate Maggie's moral beauty, or her conscience, or her new mode of love, at all, but flee across the ocean to American City and the easier force of mere steam-driven morality, mere public conscience, and the milder form of evangelical love. The spiritual violence and the excruciating sacrifice of Maggie's form of love, once understood, are more than they can bear. Charlotte repudiates the love with a violence of her own. She is an Italian Renaissance model of American girl (rather like Kate Croy in *The Wings of the Dove*) all body and money and style, with all the grace that is lithe and none that is luminous: it is in her legs and arms and waist rather than in her eyes. She is no cheap predatory animal, though inhabited by one; she is the most expensive animal on earth, the human animal who at no time forgets that she is one. The Prince thought of her, that "if when she moved off she looked like a huntress, she looked when she came nearer like his notion, perhaps not wholly correct, of a muse." If so, she was a huntress of life and the muse of the philosophy of the senses, which if not adequate are yet consuming occupations, full of intelligent good and equally, because necessary, intelligent evil. The only force she cannot cope with is the good which has grown, from her point of view, fanatic, inhuman, a pure creation out of human losses. That is why she repudiates Maggie's love; under its force the huntress becomes the hunted and the muse becomes stifled.

If she repudiates Maggie's love in fright and despair, her husband, Maggie's father, Adam Verver, protects himself from it by turning silent and moving on—back to American City—the very moment he recognizes it for what it is. He is a businessman who has made unspecified millions in unspecified ways, and as a businessman should be he is prepared to cut his losses rather than, like Maggie, to make a monument out of them. He sees that if he stays—if they all stay—in England he will lose both the possession of his wife and the happiness of his daughter. If he goes he may have some part of his wife; and his daughter, alone with her husband, may in her own way be able to make things right again, with some of her pledges—in the field of morals, conscience, and love—redeemed. At least this interpretation of his acts seems implicit in what James allows us to see of this little, straw-hatted, white-waistcoated old man, a cigar in his mouth, his hands in his pockets, teetering a little on the balls of his feet.

Mr. Verver is a hedonist of a very high order, but when he sees action is necessary he takes it. He loves his daughter greatly but he sees no reason for permitting her love of him to destroy all their lives. Had he been given to Jamesian speech rather than relapsing into the vernacular he would have anticipated Santayana in speaking of his daughter: Fanaticism is when you redouble your effort having forgotten your aim. He *understood* his daughter's new mode of love well enough and it struck him in all conscience as having moral beauty, but he had to protect himself from it. At any rate he cut his losses and took his wife home to American City, full of a sadness that would never issue in fanaticism.

The only other persons of account in this novel—Colonel and Mrs. Assingham—are not given as responding directly to Maggie's force but as giving it critique and interpretation and a ready ear. They otherwise, and particularly Mrs. Assingham, only manipulate the relations between the four principal persons, and they do this on the whole rather blindly and stupidly, as impediments and thickeners with regard to action rather than clarifiers and incentives. Mrs. Assingham makes one exception; she is the early form, rather degraded, of Maggie's great discovery that humbug is necessary in the service of the good; and it is for that reason I think that she is given the anomalous privilege of actually smashing the golden bowl which is the accidental cause of Maggie's full recognition of the steadfast adultery between her husband and her stepmother. To her the bowl represents a cracked idea, to Maggie it represents the happiness of all of them. It is a true illumination, therefore, at the critical hour when the bowl is smashed to see the two women together, the humbug of groomed scandal and the humbug of involved succor, the humbug of social surface and the humbug of personal compassion. Mrs. Assingham would lie to create a false truth, Maggie would lie and does—to everyone but her husband—to preserve her vision of the real truth. The point is, both women are right, and neither form of humbug—or of truth—could get along in this world without the constant aid of the other. That is why confidence is so rare and precious a possession in the relations between people, and why so much has to be ignored for it to persist. Maggie is lost between contrary impulses to know everything and to ignore everything, and the two impulses perhaps nowhere show so plain as in the scene where the bowl is smashed. We have thus both the two kinds of humbug the women practice on others and that in Maggie herself. Among the varieties of humbug the poetic truth slips in, which James meant it to do.

The scene is in two parts. In the first the two women are alone, Mrs. Assingham with the bowl in her hand listening to Maggie's double account of the flaw in the bowl and the flaw in her husband's good faith until, in the conditions, the two flaws become united. Maggie is full of woe growing; Mrs. Assingham, full of the sense that the woe is both futile and unnecessary, moves to a window with a better light in the flush of evening and fills with "an irresistible impulse." If the two flaws are united in thought, then let them be destroyed in a single act.

> And Fanny Assingham, who had been casting about her and whose inspiration decidedly had come, raised the cup in her two hands, raised it positively above her head and from under it solemnly smiled at the Princess as a signal of intention. So for an instant, full of her thought and her act, she held the precious vessel, and then with due note taken of the margin of the polished floor, bare fine and hard in the embrasure of her window, dashed it boldly to the ground where she had the thrill of seeing it lie shattered with the violence of the crash. She had flushed with the force of her effort as Maggie had flushed with wonder at the sight, and this high reflexion in their faces was all that passed between them for a minute more. After which, 'Whatever you meant by it—and I don't want to know *now*—has ceased to exist.' Mrs. Assingham said.

At that moment the Prince comes in asking "And what in the world, my dear, *did* you mean by it?" Mrs. Assingham goes off and we have the second part of the scene with Maggie and the Prince alone confronted by the three pieces of the golden bowl.

Maggie, knowing she would now have to confront the Prince
with her new firm knowledge of his infidelity so long groped after
in shadowy humbug, first picks up the pieces, putting the solid
foot on the mantel and for the moment trying to fit the other two
pieces together in her hands.

> The split determined by the latent crack was so
> sharp and so neat that if there had been anything to
> hold them the bowl might still quite beautifully, a few
> steps away, have passed for uninjured. As there was
> however nothing to hold them but Maggie's hands
> during the few moments the latter were so employed,
> she could only lay the almost equal parts of the vessel
> carefully beside their pedestal and leave them thus
> before her husband's eyes. She had proceeded without
> words, but quite as if with a sought effect—in spite of
> which it had all seemed to her to take a far longer time
> than anything she had ever so quickly accomplished.

I do not know whether the smashing of the bowl or the posing of its
fragments was the more violent act in Maggie's mind. What comes
between—her effort to hold the fragments together in her hands—
has the superior violence of a poetic symbol representing all that is
to follow in the remaining fourth of the novel. Only Maggie's
hands could hold the fragments together, and only two of them,
and momentarily, at that. She has herself become the golden bowl
and has the future task of holding herself together, moment to
moment, and not all of herself at one time. No wonder then she
tries for moral beauty, becomes their troubled conscience, and
strives for a way of love—"the possible, the impossible"—that,
holding herself, will hold them all together. The supremacy of her
effort is the measure of her failure with the possible as it is the
proof of her success with the impossible. The life she could not
create, the shade she could. It is all in the poetry of this scene.

The poetry would not be there if she had not earlier learned—
if at least the reader had not learned—another lesson about the
quarrel of motives which underlay her goodness. During her long

days of suspicion without certainty of Charlotte and the Prince,
she had tortured them to go off together. So by her goodness she
had bred their wrong, and had so put them between Scylla and
Charybdis, between the "danger of their doing too much and that
of their not having any longer the confidence or the nerve, or
whatever you may call it, to do enough." So Maggie to Mrs.
Assingham. "Her tone might by this time have shown a strange-
ness to match her smile; which was still more marked as she
wound up: 'And that's how I make them do what I like!'" And
when Mrs. Assingham tells her she is amazing and terrible, she
answers that she is mild: because she can bear anything for love,
not for her father or her husband but just for love. This is
Maggie's version, by broad day, of what Dostoevsky called the
harsh and terrible thing love is in action. After the smashing
of the golden bowl she could never again—so much greater had
the harsh terror of love become—be so sure of her feelings. Indeed
she says at one place, if I knew how I felt "I should die." She knew
rather what lies had to be told about feelings to protect people
from such deaths even if the lies killed some part of them another
way.

How Maggie learned that—the loss of confidence that lurks
in the woods at twilight—rose in the depths of her own experience
one night at her father's country place when all six of the principal persons in the novel are alone together. Charlotte, the Prince,
Mr. Verver, and Mrs. Assingham are playing bridge. The Colonel
is at the other end of the room. Maggie is watching them, knowing
that she was "more present to the attention of each than the next
card to be played." Here all the evil and all the good, all the
monstrous and all the angelic, in Maggie's vision of life come
together in a series of images and movements and actions, of the
body and of the soul, of the feelings and of the aspirations,
unified in a single but highly complex emotion. Some of the
elements of this emotion may be detached, if only for the quality
of the perception they represent.

Maggie watches for five minutes and all the high decorum
hangs by a hair.

There reigned for her absolutely during these vertiginous moments that fascination of the monstrous,
that temptation of the horribly possible, which we so
often trace by its breaking out suddenly, lest it should
go further, in unexplained retreats and reactions. . . .
She might sound out their doom in a single sentence. . . . After she had faced that blinding light and
felt it turn to blackness she rose from her place, laying
aside her magazine, and moved slowly round the room,
passing near the card-players and pausing an instant
behind the chairs in turn. . . . Her father and her
husband, Mrs. Assingham and Charlotte, had done
nothing but meet her eyes; yet the difference in these
demonstrations made each a separate passage—which
was all the more wonderful since, with the secret behind every face, they had alike tried to look at her
through it and in denial of it. . . . Thus they tacitly
put it upon her to be disposed of, the whole complexity
of their peril, and she promptly saw why: because she
was there, and there just *as* she was, to lift it off them
and take it; to charge herself with it as the scapegoat of
old . . . had been charged with the sins of the people
and had gone forth into the desert to sink under his
burden and die.

These are the first few leaves plucked from the artichoke of
evil. Maggie goes outside on the terrace and, the author of their
play and with the key to their crisis in her hand, watches them
through the window, full of "the horror of finding evil seated all
at its ease where she only dreamed of good," and so watching
triumphs, or nearly so, over the evil; she has still the choice. Then
she walks on, window by window, and sees Charlotte drawn after
her, searching for her to confront her. Watching Charlotte, she
thought of the golden bowl. "The breakage stood not for any
wrought discomposure among the triumphant three—it stood
merely for the dire deformity of her attitude toward them." On
that recognition, her shawl a hood of humility, she is able to deny
that Charlotte has done her any wrong, and to accept from Char-

lotte a kiss on the cheek "that completed the coldness of their conscious perjury." It is in this kiss that the horror and the glory of Maggie's emotion is completed.

It is her goodness and her conscience at work making an emotion which must somehow define itself as a new mode of love in poetry that, so far as the theory of life in this novel is concerned, must be taken as actual, an action of the soul. And so indeed it turns out in the next chapter where Maggie and her father communicate their secret unrests by spying on each other's lips the unspoken words, and end with an embrace, unlike that with Charlotte, in full mutual belief, which "produced for all its intimacy no revulsion and broke into no inconsequence of tears." Yet it would seem to me that as for her father's share in that embrace he lied as much as Charlotte and Maggie had in theirs. For here is how Maggie's declaration of her new mode of love goes. "My idea is this, that when you only love a little you're naturally not jealous—or are only jealous also a little, so that it doesn't matter. But when you love in a deeper and intenser way, then you're in the very same proportion jealous; your jealousy has intensity and, no doubt, ferocity. When however you love in the most abysmal and unutterable way of all—why then you're beyond everything, and nothing can pull you down."

Surely this mode of love grew out of moral beauty and high conscience, but as Maggie applied it, it required the sacrifice of life itself till nothing but the created shade was left. As applied it pulled them down, driving Adam and Charlotte Verver to American City, and driving the Prince to say "Everything's terrible, cara—in the heart of man." The breakdown of these three persons is all the nearer reality because it is protected and sustained by the cover of manners, by the insistence on equilibrium, the preservation of decorum: all under the presidency of Maggie's goodness, the sovereignty of her love, and the tyranny of her conscience. As for Maggie herself, at the end of the novel the Prince says to her "'I see nothing but you.' And the truth of it had with this force after a moment so strangely lighted his eyes that as for pity and dread of them she buried her own in his breast." It was a shade embracing a shade, but in the shades of poetry.

THE WINGS OF THE DOVE

When I was first told, in 1921, to read something of Henry James—just as when I had been told to read something of Thomas Hardy and something of Joseph Conrad—I went to the Cambridge Public Library looking, I think, for *The Portrait of a Lady*. It was out. The day was hot and muggy, so that from the card catalogue I selected as the most cooling title *The Wings of the Dove*, and on the following morning, a Sunday, even hotter and muggier, I began, and by the stifling midnight had finished my first elated reading of that novel. Long before the end I knew a master had laid hands on me. The beauty of the book bore me up; I was both cool and waking; excited and effortless; nothing was any longer worthwhile and everything had become necessary. A little later, there came outside the patter and the cooling of a shower of rain and I was able to go to sleep, both confident and desperate in the force of art.

Such are the advantages and the energies of boyhood. By great luck I had been introduced simply and directly, and had responded in the same way, to what a vast number of people have thought an impossible novel by an impossible author and a vast number of other people have submitted to the stupefying idolatry of both gross and fine over-interpretation. In my boyhood, Henry James had a very few addicts, few readers, and except in a reminiscent way no critics or commentators, at least not in comparison to what happened twenty years later. I knew nothing of the legend of the master and nothing of that account which says that there were three in the James dynasty—I think this is how it goes—James the First, James the Second, and James the Old Pretender. I did not know the Italian contessa who said of James that he was a cheese so ripe—curiously the Italian word is *robusta* —that for the sake of one's nose he had to be kept mainly sealed off under a jar. In short, I was unimpeded.

Thus, I suppose, my appreciation (which as Santayana says some people call criticism) can never be higher than it was then. I can only wish again now, as I wished then, that I had taken a grasping, remembering look at James's living figure when he had been pointed out to me, a child of six, walking down my street at the time of his brother William's death. But I remember nothing but my mother pointing. I can only say that he must have had a "port in air," a presence and a person, with a power within the presence and beyond the person, and must have been so whether visibly or not; for so he is within his books, and most of all, for me —a haunt and a presence—in *The Wings of the Dove*, or the spread of those wings.

Appreciation never heightened—how could it? for I had embraced the shadow of imagination as if it were a solid thing. But of course appreciation deepened, with many readings of the novel itself and of the rest of James's work. As my ignorance became compounded with familiarity and with the contingencies of art and life, there were reservations and recognitions and even enlightenments, and I got to know how to speak of what had so deeply affected me on my first reading with so little knowledge compacting my hungry sensibility. Perhaps I thought and experienced it all to begin with, for thinking is very different from knowing and saying. I did not know, for example, how James had worked on me with the "coercive charm of form," or how I felt, with him, the beautiful incentive of the deep difficulty braved. I think I saw but did not catch the force of the phrase that the relations between Merton Densher and Kate Croy, as they felt the spread of the wings of the dove, was a deep "contention of adverse wills." I did not know how to speak, that is, of that central adversity of the human condition which rises from the "otherness" of every individual from every other individual. It is aliens who make every commerce there is, and every intimacy. Not knowing, but seeing, I could not say how it was that the moral image of the American princess, Milly Theale, could both separate forever Merton Densher and Kate Croy and also give a marred substance of intimacy which would bind them forever together. It is the story of how Milly Theale could do this to Merton Densher and Kate Croy that constitutes *The Wings of the Dove* as a novel, as a psychology of human action and behavior.

To speak ordinarily is to make cries or to take up the time or to echo what once has properly been said. To speak well is to make a poem or a novel, to give form to the cry and a psychology to him who cried, a form and a psychology which can be used again, filled out or erected, as need be, by the reader. That is why when we seem to speak well we speak with voices not our own saying more than we knew we meant, and with a form—a style— into which we seem to have broken through, as into raw air. Henry James gives us such a voice and such a form whenever we need to use them. The voice is that of the psyche speaking and makes a psychology quite as much as Freud does. The form gives resonance to the voice so that it can reach our ears.

Paul Valéry somewhere said that he hoped to meet in limbo the anonymous creator of the sonnet as a form so that he might salute and honor him; for it is form alone that exists, as Mistral says: "only form preserves the work of the mind." Ortega y Gasset, writing on the future of the novel, argued that there was nothing left for the novel to do but to create new psychologies, since he thought other habits of composition had become sterile. It seems to me, looking back on his novels and nouvelles (long stories, short novels), that, for the English languages, Henry James created what these Frenchmen and this Spaniard wanted; and he did so because he was part of the same Western movement of mind as they, and of which we are the same and somewhat wastrel heirs. James made a form for prose fiction as rigid, as integrated, as predictable as the sonnet. Hence, aside from his great genuine influence among those who could modulate and develop the Henry James novel—or deny it in the interests of their own forms (as perhaps D. H. Lawrence did)—there has been a host of sonneteers whose work shows as all the more empty because their talent could not meet more than the external requirements of the form. They could not ally it, as James did, with a new psychology, so their psyches were struck dumb. It is not hard to borrow, as many of them do, from the internally created hidden psychologies of the great novelists where the alliance has been perfected between the form and the life so that life itself seems to have acquired—to have grown into—a durable form. It is what Granville-Barker meant when he said Shakespeare learned about men and women by writing plays about them. And it is also what Malraux (who has written of Psychology and Form) meant when he asserts that the artist begins by imitating, not life, but the work of other artists until at last his own work breaks through into form. One might say that the artist imitates the life of other artists until he has gained his own.

James first reached durable form—and his characteristic theme—in *The Portrait of a Lady* (1881) in which the charming sketch of *An International Episode* (1879) and adumbrated lyric tragedy of *Daisy Miller* (1878), were transformed from a living feast on the work of George Eliot, Dickens, Balzac, and Turgenev into something altogether his own. It is the *Portrait* which shows us what the others are about, and it is the others who grow up into the full fate of Isabel Archer in the *Portrait*. The same could be said for *The Europeans* (1878) and *Washington Square* (1881). One could not imagine that they existed, or their characters (though an exception should be made a little for Catherine Sloper in *Washington Square* because her delicacy is greater than her weariness, and for Daisy Miller because she began it all, the very first of the American princesses) if they were not pendants about the neck of the *Portrait* and Isabel Archer and Ralph Touchett. *The American* (1877) and *Roderick Hudson* (1876), the first brilliant with wit and sincerity and the second fairly somber with promise, do not come into it at all. In both the forms are ragged and the characters are constantly losing their roles with nobody and nothing to pick them up again except the reader out of the conventions of his own life; they are early works which we read now because James wrote them then, and we look in them to see the first hint of what only actually happened later—as Newman of *The American* is perfected as Strether in *The Ambassadors* a quarter of a century afterward: the American only goes home intact, the Ambassador, wholly ravaged, goes home all Europe within him. There are certain tastes in travel which still prefer to travel light, but these should not include those who have read and have liked *The Portrait of a Lady* and Isabel Archer. We see in that young lady, as Carl Van Doren long ago remarked, the dawning knowledge of what life is like and the gradual creation—not at all a construction—of a psychology adequate to meet that dawning even if it destroys her in the process. The difference is easy to state. In *Daisy Miller* that young lady is "at once the most exacting in the world and the least endowed with a sense of indebtedness." Isabel Archer, no less exacting, pays even her own life. Later, in *The Wings of the Dove*, Milly Theale who had no life to pay paid out her own death.

The curiosity is that after *The Portrait of a Lady* James fell into an uncertainty of intention, of form, and of psychology: his tentacles wavered, trying one surface and one substance after another without ever either grasping firmly or being wholly seized up. *The Princess Casamassima* and *The Bostonians*, for example, reached, and touched, the undersides of things in official society and private morals, and *The Tragic Muse* imposed a glittering surface on both in the forms of stage and parliament. But it is clear that none of these absorbed or commanded his talents. None either broke through into form or created a psychology. Besides, he wrote also at this time his stories of the artist and his ghost stories, where though the interest is great and the finish exquisite, the effect—the thing made—is thin, and the magnitude, compared to *The Portrait*, is shrunken like an Argentinian skull. The artist was testing life, the ghosts dissolving life: though both were seeking to tap the force that is under or over-

whelmingly within life. All of them tried and all of them had to
do with his role—in the phrase made many years ago, I forget by
whom—as "the historian of fine consciences" that either might or
ought to exist. It is no wonder that he turned to the drama for
relief and found there a brilliant collapse.

The economy, the essential housekeeping, of James's talent
could not reach the outward concentration of the theater where
the action commands the meaning. He was at home only where the
meaning, closely grasped, specifically interwoven, commanded
the action. This economy he found in his late work where life was
testing the artist and where he enlarged his role of the historian of
fine consciences and became the creator of conscience itself and,
what is even more remarkable in this largely unmotivated world,
the creator of genuine motive as well. In the three great novels
conscience and motive unite. Considered in this way Lambert
Strether in *The Ambassadors*, Maggie Verver in *The Golden
Bowl*, and Milly Theale in *The Wings of the Dove* are conscience
and motive for everybody else taken separately and, taken together,
for the human action as well. Each, naturally, is destroyed.

[Before returning with this in mind to *The Wings of the
Dove*, it may be as well to turn first to these other works: to *The
Aspern Papers*, which one might say is an early, or primitive,
form, to *The Turn of the Screw*, which is a kind of parallel form,
and to *The Spoils of Poynton*, which is a direct preparation for
the great novels. In each a conscience is created which achieves a
deep human action, and from one to another there is a rising level
of intensity and a rising degree of involvement. The heroine is in
each case the seat of the conscience; each acts to the degradation or
destruction of others; and each acts in result of a simple and direct
nature—with the force of naiveté. Naiveté is intelligence at work
for itself alone, but in response to deep principles of being which
only gradually emerge from their hiding in nature. Henry James
was the master of naiveté in the sense that Dante was the master of
disgust, and each author showed his mastery by creating new
forms for his insight—as Dante with Ugolino and James with
Milly Theale, to take only the strongest examples. That James

understood very well what he was up to is clear if we remember his remark that the value of naiveté was very like the value of zero in a number; it depended on the digit that preceded it. His heroines are witness to this in a rising series; and the figure of Miss Tita,* the small one, in *The Aspern Papers* (1888), is, if not the highest, still a very high example of this force. It is her naiveté which is the heart and target of the story. Without her full and unconsidered offer of herself—her meager, shabby, impregnable self—as the rich equivalent of every other value named of literature, romance and habit, there would have been no story, and the pursuit of the "papers" (as one should say, lost love letters of Shelley) would not have had even the mistaken value of the blackguard evil of the avid collector.

For what happens in *The Aspern Papers*? A damned publishing scoundrel—something very near a professional biographer —uses more than every needful fraud and deceit to work himself into the house and almost the confidence of a very old woman who has the relics of a love affair, two generations since, with a very great poet. The old woman—the Juliana, almost the Juliet, of the poems—has with her in her Venetian *palazzo* a niece, Miss Tita, into whose possession upon her aunt's death the papers fall. The papers—the vital papers of a vital love, a very scandal of history—have already cost our anonymous publishing scoundrel (even his *nom de guerre* is never told us, let alone his "real" name) a good deal of what ought to have been his honor and decency, and more money than he could afford besides. He has in effect even, as the least of his basenesses, committed murder, for the old woman dies in the smother of them. He has been the rogue in the fairy tale, a confidence man with a rage to tamper outrageously with the real humanity—the naive conscience—of the middle-aged Cinderella who is Miss Tita. Were it not a fairy tale, a mere moral allegory, we would think him a puerile vampire or emasculated werewolf; and perhaps he was, for in Henry James you can never tell to what baseness his vision of evil descends—it

*"Miss Tina," in the revised version of *The Aspern Papers*.

is for the reader's own abilities to discern, as the tales begin to signify for themselves. I will only say here that our publishing scoundrel moves with energy and vivacity less than human.

At any rate, the pursuit of the papers has cost him a great deal which he has paid with willingness and assiduity, but when he comes to claim them from Miss Tita he finds that instead of plundering her he has brought her alive—the vital image of the vital love the papers had stood for, a very scandal of life itself. She proposes that to gain the papers he should become a relative and, so to speak, become bound by the family restrictions upon them, by the values they themselves were supposed to represent as they were now enacted in her. This, after all, was what he must have been, or ought to have been, seeking. She proposes to him the marriage her conscience had created for him and on the moment destroys in him every power but flight, distraction, and the repudiation of every motive he thought had driven him. At their last interview "she smiled strangely, with an infinite gentleness. She had never doubted that I had left her the day before in horror. How could she, since I had not come back before night to contradict, even as a simple form, such an idea? And now she had the force of soul—Miss Tita with force of soul was a new conception—to smile at me in her humiliation."]*

The Turn of the Screw (1898), which for years has been the puzzlepiece in James for Freudians to play with (it would be more intelligent to apply the drama of the psyche as construed in Jung), is rather a magnificent creation of a bad conscience—a conscience vitally deprived, but vitally desperate to transform its hallucinations into reality. It is by that conscience and its vision of evil that the governess destroys the two children, and having done so escapes into another life. The ghosts she sees are the agents of her conscience, and their malevolence is her motive. In chapter twelve, the very center of the story, the current of evil begins to flow not only from the general outside in, as in the beginning, or just through Quint and Jessel (the ghosts) where it

---

*I have inserted these three paragraphs from the introduction to the Laurel edition (1958) of *The Aspern Papers* and *The Spoils of Poynton*, which is otherwise a slightly reduced version of the introduction to *The Wings of the Dove*—Ed.

had seemed to concentrate for outlet, but also and spontaneously from the souls of the children themselves. Our heroine feels the evil in their unnatural goodness, which she had herself invented, along with the evil, and is therefore prone to feel it as everywhere developing. It is as if innocence is the looking glass for evil. It is only for her to tell *them*, the children, that they are possessed, and so to tell them that they will believe it; and indeed that is what happens. Meanwhile our heroine has begun to show herself quite above any merely primary infatuation, whether with herself or her bachelor employer remote in London. She is now driven by an energy which is suited to this solitary and friendless place and which mustn't be interfered with. She has taken hold; she has pushed along; she has dragged everything; nothing must stop the energy within her, for that energy is creative. So she goes on until she creates "the white face of damnation" and by it succeeds in killing the little boy—but not before he has identified the governess as the Devil. The abyss over which he fell at the moment of death is that of the intolerable consciousness which may often be brought best to us by human cruelty become conscience and motive in a personality driven, possessive, possessed.

Either James's tale is frivolous and the ghosts are "real," or they are actual, the governess's other selves, actual hallucinations by which the moral depravity of the unnaturally "good" parson's daughter is exacerbated and enacted, to the mutilation of one life and the demolition of another. Or it may be that there is a combination of the light-hearted gruesome and the dark-hearted moral apologia, with the second running away with the first, and the first covering up the worse inner cysts of the second. We have in any case the record of the governess's gradual damnation. She reabsorbs her specters, and any respectable servant a hundred and fifty years ago would have known her as a witch and have called on the vicar to exorcise her if not hang her. For us she is as near as the evil conscience can come to creating and enacting the motives of a witch. Yet, either way or both, at the end some part of our heroine, our twenty-year-old girl, should have tumbled after the little boy into the abyss: her ghosts, her other selves, those parts of ourselves.

Our other prefatory example, *The Spoils of Poynton* (1897), contains as many ghosts or specters as *The Turn of the Screw*, and exhibits a witch, in the figure of Mrs. Gereth, as evil in what we call the "sane" world as the poor governess was in the world of her possession. Mrs. Gereth has a houseful of fine furniture (the "spoils" of the title), a son, Owen, and a young girl companion, Fleda Vetch, who loves both the furniture and the son. The son breaks his engagement to Fleda and marries a big horse of a girl, Mona, who has no love for the furniture unless for its price. The contest is for the furniture and through it for Fleda's soul. Almost the witchcraft wins, almost it loses; it depends on the reader's taste, for the story ends in a conflagration in which the house and all its furniture are destroyed. James was still uncertain of his intention.

Who will say it is right or wrong that this novel which belongs to Fleda Vetch's fullness of action should have begun in the consciousness of Mrs. Gereth, or that the scenes all through the first hundred pages should be constructed as drawing room comedy with every real stake ignored or horsed, and with everybody, even Fleda, seen pretty much as a type or a character part? The thing reads like a well-made novel trying to be a well-made play about trifles, about manners with the men and women left out; but with the distinction that rather a cynical fable is about to be unfolded in an atmosphere of sheer brutal brilliance: moral humiliation without moral compassion. Then the story deepens and the stakes begin to show larger at the point when Fleda discovers that Mrs. Gereth has stolen the furniture from her son and crowded it into a small cottage. Then Fleda begins to perceive. She has to fill the conventions, including the stage conventions, with the life and richness of which they had become only the demeaned manners: but somehow not letting go of the furniture, the "things," and the disposition of them, whether in rancor or generosity, since they have become, by the attrition of life, the central symbol of meaning and fate: the spoils of them.

In this contest of adverse wills Fleda is weaker than Mona, than Owen, than Mrs. Gereth. If Mona has no morals and Owen merely craves morals, Mrs. Gereth merely uses morals. That is the effect of turning her interest into disproportionate passion. Mrs. Gereth is one of those personal fanatics who will use morals for her own sake even if she burns for it. She is not a free spirit. Fleda supplies her with value after value and Mrs. Gereth heaps them one after another on her bonfire till she has a general conflagration, and in the end wetted ashes in her mouth. She does not exhaust Fleda so much as abuse her: the values Fleda provides become more and more desperate as she chucks them to her, faggots of love and hope, one after another. If the spirit has a body, the body of Fleda's spirit is pretty well wasted by the time Mrs. Gereth is done with her.

The process of that waste is the whole story of the last fourth of the book, and as we watch it we feel the menace, and then the act: the actual wastage under the open vampirage of unspecified evil: the plain waste of Fleda's otherwise indestructible human goodness. Fleda is smothered under the expansion of Mrs. Gereth's will; she submits like a sick animal to her embrace. In the end, when everything is gone, they have ravaged each other in terms of the spoils, for Mrs. Gereth, too, collapses. Yet Fleda has grown. If you like, Fleda in her intelligence and her free spirit has responded to the awful, attractive force of the spoils by creating a conscience for all the spoils, human and otherwise, for the people and the things. Her created conscience was her spoils—beautiful beyond markers and periods, let alone price; and her spoils have been taken away from her. It is quite fitting and right—it is poetic justice, it is the created justice of the free spirit—that when Fleda is brought by a last temptation to redeem at Poynton, in symbol, some one of its spoils, at the very moment of her coming all the spoils should have been lost or saved in flame.

It is matters like these that achieved magnitude when James broke into form and made a psychology in his three great late novels, and for me especially, in *The Wings of the Dove*, with its hope and its horror, its image of moral beauty and its actual waste of moral devastation—for which, as I should have known since I had been a choir boy, there were archetypal images in the Book of Psalms, though I did not connect them for many years. There is this from the 68th Psalm: "Though ye have lain among the sheepfolds, yet shall ye be as the wings of a dove that is covered with silver wings, and her feathers like gold." And there is this from the 55th Psalm: "The enemy crieth so, and the ungodly cometh on so fast; for they are minded to do me some mischief, so maliciously are they set against me. My heart is disquieted within me, and the fear of death is fallen upon me. Fearfulness and trembling are come upon me, and an horrible dread hath overwhelmed me. And I said, O that I had wings like a dove! for then would I flee away, and be at rest." This last is the voice of the American princess, Milly Theale, and the first is the acknowledgement of her power by those who betrayed her, Kate Croy and her lover, Merton Densher—a beautiful panther of a woman and her sensitive young man. For those who have read the story these lines from the Psalms will re-expand the whole book. For those who have not read it they should make a promise certain to be kept.

The story is simple. Kate Croy and Merton Densher wish to marry but are prevented because of Densher's poverty and because Kate's aunt wishes her to marry money and position. When Milly Theale, a millionaire American princess, appears in London and is discovered to be mortally ill, Kate plots that Densher shall marry Milly, inherit her money when she dies and then marry Kate. Milly learns of the plot, but at her hastened death leaves Densher her money just the same. Densher refuses the money and also refuses to marry Kate. It is a melodrama of renunciation and remorse, of blessings confounding betrayals, of beauty casting too sharp a light to be borne upon the ugliness in which the human spirit struggles. It is also the story of the creation of conscience and the creation of genuine motive in Densher.

There are many other things of importance, but I want to fasten on Densher, for it is only on Densher that the Wings can spread or give the effect of their beat on others. Densher is both the sacrifice offered to the Wings and the test of their power. It is true that the others needed an "ideal" of some sort to reject or abuse, or evade or overcome; only Densher could deeply use Milly without at the same time losing her. Densher comes out not with a bad conscience or a good conscience; the one ought to be for

Kate, the other for the titled adventurer, Lord Mark, who "reveals" the plot to Milly. Densher comes out with created conscience—the very "agenbite of inwit"—and the assertion of conscience is his form of action. He struggles with his own odium and discovers his own self, longing to embrace Kate but unable to do so. This is the stroke of conscience: "As to their final impulse or their final remedy, the need to bury in the dark blindness of each other's arms the knowledge of each other that they couldn't undo," Densher's conscience prevents at the same time that it invites. His weakness is that he is incapable of his own conscience when it is confronted with the conditions of life. This is the course of the last two hundred pages of the novel: the realization and assertion of conscience in the name of, and at the same time destroying, the joy of life. And the conscience is good in every case but Milly.

Kate makes poetic versions of reality, she makes ideals smack of her own needs, and promotes steady action, but her poetics cannot dispel Densher's awkward conscience. Milly, on the contrary, makes disconcerting poetry which gives form to his awkward conscience, and her highest effort is when she tells him, just after he has perceived her to be either divine in trust or inscrutable in mercy, "If I *want* to live I can." This she generates in her spirit and by it she generates spirit in others; it represents pretty nearly all the substance she has. It is this poetics which teaches Densher that loyalty might be another kind of lie, an uncandid profession of motive, and that their fates are mixed. He knew her life was in his hands and that he might kill her.

Thus Kate uses her body because it was the very form of her will. Milly resorts to her spirit and when it fails of aims appropriate to it, she turns her face to the wall. Densher, confronted with both, wrestles waiting in his darkness, building his conscience, forcing Milly toward her death, forcing Kate to a full declaration of herself, of her sublime talent for life no matter what, and forcing himself finally to that assertion of conscience which destroys the incentive of his adventure. It becomes glib, and foul. Densher by his act makes the book a testing of Kate, not of good or bad, but of what she is: of the truth in her. Milly stands, or floats, above all she *dies* behind him: a test of what she

stands for when she is not there. It is so we can see this fully that
Densher is made to wrestle so long between decency and loyalty:
wrestling with Kate's strength in his loins, not his own which she
has taken from him in her embrace; wrestling then with his own
condition, his own abjectness and with the ideal strength of the
girl in white, Milly, who will no longer see him until at the last
feasible moment she makes him the permanent accursed gift of
the strength of her forgiveness. So Densher pays for his conscience
by succumbing to the last temptation of enacted goodness; to go
in for forgiveness under the image of inscrutable mercy.

In taking such views of James's novel several precautions
ought to be taken so that other values will not be overlooked or
forgotten. There are many things in the novel without which the
conscience and the motive would be worthless: things that are
there and that in their own way make an extraordinary amount of
giving and doing and seeing. There is the sequence of the images
of seas, tides, and waves. There is the ever renewable series of
detached lyric reflections on the feel of morals and on the feel of
life under the convulsive distortions afforded by living with people
in any discriminating stage of consciousness at all. And there is in
this novel, beginning exactly in the middle, the image of Venice,
at first attached to Milly, then to Densher, in phase after phase of
what the book is about. I select only these: the Venice of the joy
and the dread of life; the Venice of all evil; and the Venice
profaned and bewildered, in the first sea-storm of autumn, during
Densher's three days of temptation. All these are joined, I think,
in Densher's emergent rock in the gray expanse of straightness;
and together they make a form for the novel where the things are
their own meaning beyond any conscience.

But there is another or final precaution which has to do with
the estimation of the fable of good and evil which is the book's
conceptual form. What does this fable think of its three characters
at the end? We see Kate sitting by the wakened evil of her father
and of her sister's family. Milly is dead and has taken the posthumous action of her absolute goodness and beauty. Densher is
the image of absolute weakness, all that cannot live, but which
judges life not quite up to what it is. In Kate there is some

nobility; she got or will get some of the money and some of the strength. In Densher there is some odium, but he can never again be so weak, for he has found under Milly and in Kate a measure for his weakness.

I think it all depends on the Christmas letter from Milly: the unread vision in the higher dream; it depends, that is, on your reasons why neither Kate nor Densher would open it. Densher was equal only to the idea of it. Kate could learn anything; she was equal to everything but the idea, she could survive everything but the ideal. Densher had to make himself a hero as Milly had to make herself a martyr, but Kate had to make out of herself nothing but the best of what life is. The curiosity is that it is the Kates who are uncommon everywhere; the Millys and Denshers are common enough in type—only the riches, the excesses, are uncommon, and those only perhaps because we are not usually allowed to see them. But Milly is a princess as well as a dove, and she guards Kate always for her sublime talent for life, in the face of which her mere corruption does not matter. Yet the wings spread; there is the vision in the higher dream, and although we do not know what it is, it is nevertheless read in the beauty of the perception.

THE AMERICAN

When Henry James was writing *The American* during 1876 and 1877, in Paris and perhaps in London, he was just getting into his characteristic stride as a novelist. His deep themes were just beginning to emerge, but his familiar habits of composition and sensibility—all that we mean by the style of the man and the style of the writer as they join to animate a body of fiction—remained inarticulate, mere hints of what was to come. That is one reason why this book and his other early fiction are easier to read than the later work. He had not yet found out how much he could do and how much he could command his readers to do. Another reason is that he was writing with a kind of general, or categorical, brilliance, and with a kind of uncommitted insight, where almost anything would do and where almost anything could be left out, in the form which he was later to distinguish as Romance. His distinction is worth paying a good deal of attention to.

It appears in the preface he wrote to *The American* twenty-five years after its original composition in the collected edition of his novels and tales. An author need no more be right about his own work than about the work of other authors, but it is always interesting to see how he gets around what was wrong or incomplete in his insights; it is an instance of how every lie points to, as well as surrounds, the truth, and indeed it is the essence of fiction to do so. If he is also right, so much the better. James was, I think, pretty nearly right about *The American* when he furnished the principle or idea for meditation on it that this was a Romance. Speaking of the large responding imaginations of Scott, of Balzac, of Zola, he says that their currents remain

> therefore extraordinarily rich and mixed, washing us successively with the warm wave of the near and familiar and the tonic shock, as may be, of the far and the strange. (In making which opposition I suggest not that the strange and the far are at all necessarily romantic: they happen to be simply the unknown, which is quite a different matter. The real represents to my perception the things we cannot possibly *not* know, sooner or later, in one way or another; it being but one of the accidents of our hampered state, and one of the incidents of their quantity and number, that particular instances have not yet come our way. The romantic stands, on the other hand, for the things that, with all the facilities in the world, all the wealth and all the courage and all the wit and all the adventure, we never *can* directly know; the things that can reach us only through the beautiful circuit and subterfuge of our thought and our desire.)

A page or two after this parenthesis, he goes on: "What I have recognized then in *The American*, much to my surprise and after long years, is that the experience here represented is the disconnected and uncontrolled experience—uncontrolled by our general sense of 'the way things happen'—which romance alone more or less successfully palms off on us." Then, at the end of the paragraph, James observes that "the way things don't happen may be artfully made to pass for the way things do."

In this the reader helps; for in a good half of his nature every reader wishes to be deceived, to be drugged or altered in his sensibility, into believing what the other half of his nature knows cannot be an image of truth. Not truth and justice but escape and mercy are what he wants, even if in obtaining them he has to spite his experience itself to get them; and if the reader wishes to defend himself he can argue that his society is more romantic, just as it is more immoral, than he is himself, and society, as we well know, is immortal. No wonder, then, he turns to romances, and even less a wonder that the writer of fiction will for a long time, and sometimes for all his life, make romances rather than novels. The frames, forms, and prejudices, the fashions and half the felt needs, that both society and the reader furnish him lead him to do so. In romance all things are possible, the novel requires an ambition very hard to come by and very hard to maintain against the romantic half of his nature. The created reality will always tempt him more than the obstinate and intractable force of reality itself. The created reality is our own, where our experience often seems somehow alien to us, and indeed our worst enemy. We prefer the horrors in imaginary corners and the triumphs and nostalgias in unknown experience. But there remains the fact that reality or experience has a way of intruding on and even taking over the very best made of our own creations. In our love affairs we see this with half an eye, when they get to be marriage, and with the other half of that eye we see it in our romances as they tranform themselves into novels; which is why we call the two so often by the same name. It is for this reason that James kept *The American* in his collected edition; he could write a preface for it in the name of the felt, as well as the created, life which it contained between the romantic members of its frame. As we read *The American* we feel that it gains in authenticity.

We put ourselves into it, and look where we are—alive after all. Christopher Newman could still in a ridiculous way be any one of us, especially if there were a Claire de Cintré to confront us with her beauty and her unavailability in that wicked, other, impossible, and utterly rootless "great world" which can only exist, and must always exist, in the fatality of our own imaginations. We find ourselves playing on the great stage, against implacable enemies, the same roles we actually play in our afternoon naps or on what used to be called our close-stools. We live traumatically in our daydreams, intellectually in allegory, yet nevertheless and somehow within the torn edges of our own predicaments. James himself knew this without the use of our terms, which I hope he might have rejected since he did not wish ever to make that much of a generalization. One can imagine him saying that he was only using the conventions available to him, not always knowing that they were conventions, in order to enact his compulsion to tell a tale. Trauma and allegory would have meant nothing to him, and they must be only a shorthand for us. We all know the continuous brooding, more real than any reality we know, that we do in our daydreams; allegory is the same thing, with the same terrific fruitfulness, in the realm of the intellect, where we brood on the generalized, infinitely concentrated, forms of the daydream. James had the type of mind which began by operating in between the two, but with a tendency toward allegory in the form of convention, proceeded by fastening sharp on the allegory, and ended by using both where the allegory seemed like a fairy tale with all the immediacy and plangency of the daydream. In the earlier books, such as *The American*, what he called Romance took the place of the daydream, and the allegory had a kind of secondary or "natural" power. One sees this if one looks at once at *Daisy Miller*, *The Europeans*, *Washington Square*, and *The American*.

Allegory, to repeat what St. Thomas said of it, is the use of words which signify one thing which in their turn signify something else; and that something else is something you did not expect and something which goes beyond, and is right to do so, what you did expect. So it is with *The American*. Christopher Newman, the American millionaire (whom any of us, such is our legend, might be) and Claire de Cintré, the last Catholic, French daughter of the *Ancien Régime* (whom any of us might wish either to marry or to be) are very simple figures of popular romantic melodrama. It is natural that the American should wish to marry the French girl and it is even more natural that after she had accepted him she should, under the force of her "family," reject him and on the momentum of her broken heart go into a nunnery. Hamlet had told Ophelia no less, and the story is

familiar with Heloise and Abélard. In James's story, as in both
the older stories, there are two victims, not merely the disappointed
hero; and this is what makes the allegory possible. Newman and
Mme. de Cintré begin as puppets in romantic melodrama, but
they go on, as they are seen in action, to seem something else—
something richer which commands more of our attention, while
leaving us room to fill in the detail for ourselves. Two orders of
things—involving history, culture, religion, and honor—come
into conflict, and, because of the entanglement and separation of
the two figures, seem to signify something beyond themselves and
beyond ourselves. It is a lesser scale of Antony and Cleopatra
where the whole of an empire falls into the ruins of their love. In
The American, it is a frame of mind that changes, or as James
puts it, there is a moral somersault.

The pride of an effort at marriage seems somehow to involve
a contrast of cultures and a conflict of morals and a fusion of good
and evil. It is this aspect of romantic allegory that has led so many
readers, professional students of literature, and critics to provide
for James a frame of rationalized and deliberate allegory. Perhaps
they are right to have done so, for this frame, in most of its
forms, provides an immediate access of understanding, and makes
this book, and the others like it, more useful in conversation.
But the critics have been clear-sighted where they ought to have
been blinded, or, in Blake's language, they saw *with* not through
the eye. For the allegory was natural not rational; it sprang
from the significance of the story and of the people. The other
or rationalized account is only good as a kind of preface: as
the understanding which precedes when it does not prevent intimacy, and is afterwards to be taken only as very much on the side.
I mean what is called "the International Theme" and all that can
be construed under the head of America versus Europe. Of course
James helps us to these considerations in the *name* of his hero—
"Christopher," this "Christ–bearing" new man; but what are we
to do with the name of his heroine, Claire de Cintré, née Bellegarde, where the reader may do as he likes with the French?
Again, there is Mrs. Tristram, the agent of all the action, and
Mrs. Bread, who holds what at first seems the final solution. And

then there is Urbain de Bellegarde. All of these can be put together, but only to fall apart; and I rather suspect that the habits of Dickens and Trollope have more to do with it than any intellectual intent in James's mind. (The interested reader can consult the wonderful lists of prospective names that occur here and there in James's Notebooks: we begin to play with names as children and continue as authors.) And I would remind the reader that in this book there is a duel, a cocotte, a bounder, and a Unitarian clergyman from Dorchester, Massachusetts, who may make *another* allegory.

There are many ways of putting meaning into words, and I rather think that in this romantic allegory it is the example of Scott, Dickens, and Balzac that is at work rather than any American bias toward neo-Christian allegory. Later, as soon as *The Portrait of a Lady*, there was also George Eliot, George Sand, and Flaubert, with the elegance of Turgenev besides. James learned from his masters how to write, and he learned from writing about life as it got into art. For when one has learned to write, words work on one and elicit meanings from the psyche which one had not known could go into words at all, so that what seems spontaneous in those who have the gift of the gab, becomes in the genuine writer the exercise of a deep skill which takes all possible training to perform, so that "the way things don't happen may be artfully made to pass for the way they do."

The words in use pull a kind of reality after them. Mrs. Tristram, for example tells Newman "you flatter my patriotism," and something good stands forth in the poor word "flatter." Again, we learn that Newman was not a man wrecked with responsibility or too high a standard. He did not like "obligatory purchase. He had not only a dislike, but a sort of moral mistrust, of uncomfortable thoughts, and it was both uncomfortable and slightly contemptible to feel obliged to square oneself with a standard." Of Mr. Babcock, the Unitarian clergyman, we hear that "He often tried, in odd half-hours of conversation, to infuse into Newman a little of his own spiritual starch, but Newman's personal texture was too loose to admit of stiffening. His mind could no more hold principles than a sieve can hold water." On this we understand better than without it why Newman, when he set himself up in Paris, desired that "The apartments should be light and brilliant and lofty; he had once said that he liked rooms in which you wanted to keep your hat on." Which does not mean that he either kept his hat on or looked as if he did. His hat is indeed distinctly off when in his formal proposal to Mme. de Cintré he says in the midst of many words: "What there is you see before you. I honestly believe I have no hidden vices or nasty tricks. I am kind, kind, kind!" Which will echo in the ears of the familiar reader to the "Old, old, old!" of Milly Theale in *The Wings of the Dove*, and to many other emphatic iterations in others of James's books of the single-syllabled words which contain our deepest metaphors for us to pitch about like pennies. The habit is almost idiosyncratic in James, and when he has another thing to say he takes a different tone and uses other people's methods (in this case that of Balzac): Valentin de Bellegarde speaks of Noémie the cocotte: "She knows her Paris. She is one of fifty thousand, so far as the mere ambition goes; but I am sure that in the way of resolution and capacity she is a rarity. And in one gift—perfect heartlessness—I will warrant she is unsurpassed. She has not as much heart as will go on the point of a needle. That is an immense virtue. Yes, she is one of the celebrities of the future." To return somewhere half between the two tones—to return from an echo of Mme. Marneffe to Mme. de Cintré. She charmed him, "and he handled his charm as if it were a music-box which would stop if one shook it. There can be no better proof of the hankering epicure that is hidden in every man's temperament, waiting for a signal from some divine confederate that he may safely peep out."

Each of the illustrations offered so far lives in its texture and is developed either in scene or reflection as a leitmotif or underthought. But there are other observations that act like suddenly stated sums, bills rendered that can only be paid with the whole being, and these, so to speak, are what the book gradually earns, or leads to as way stations on the road to repentance. There is, for America, Newman's "plain prose version of the legend of El Dorado," and there is sixty pages later, for Europe, the occasion when he hears that Mme. de Cintré has resolved to enter a

Carmelite Convent. He had not, as a Protestant, minded her
Catholicism. "If such superb white flowers as that could bloom in
Catholic soil, the soil was not insalubrious. But it was one thing
to be a Catholic, and another to turn nun—on your hands! There
was something lugubriously comical in the way Newman's
thoroughly contemporaneous optimism was confronted with this
dusky old-world expedient." One thinks, among others, of Mme.
de Vionnet (in *The Ambassadors*) in the dusky shadows of Notre
Dame, altogether the full flower of what Mme. de Cintré was only
the first and not wholly characteristic bloom. And Newman, too,
like Strether in *The Ambassadors*, had his own expedient, I will
not say of the new world but certainly not of the old. Thinking
that for revenge he will reveal the perfidy of the Bellegardes he
calls on a comical duchess of their circle. Her conversation is
lightly scandalous. "A singular feeling came over him—a sudden
sense of the folly of his errand. What under the sun had he to say
to the duchess, after all? Wherein would it profit him to tell her
that the Bellegardes were traitors and that the old lady, into the
bargain was a murderess? He seemed morally to have turned a sort
of somersault, and to find things looking differently in consequence. He felt a sudden stiffening of his will and quickening of
his reserve." In a proper somersault you land upright, and so did
Newman. Like Strether, he entered Notre Dame and sat a long
time. "He thought of the Bellegardes. . . . He gave a groan as he
remembered what he had meant to do; he was annoyed at having
meant to do it; the bottom, suddenly, had fallen out of his
revenge. . . . At last he got up and came out of the darkening
church; not with the elastic step of a man who has won a victory
or taken a resolve, but strolling soberly, like a good-natured man
who is still a little ashamed." In the last paragraph of the book
Mrs. Tristram tells him that the Bellegardes's "confidence, after
counsel taken of each other, was not in their innocence, nor in
their talent for bluffing things off; it was in your remarkable good
nature! You see they were right."

   So both Newman and Mme. de Cintré achieved a conscience
and made a moral revolution; each made a reversal of roles
through contact with the other, and a reversal accompanied by

sacrifice or renunciation. The young woman took the way already provided for those who would leave the world; the young man took the way which is not provided but must be created by the person himself, for there was nothing to receive him when he gave up his revenge. The two make a romantic allegory of which the meaning may be taken as single. Possibly romance is what we know best; and it would not be surprising, we readers of James, if we turned out to have been living a romance without knowing it: that romance which reality rushes to fill. In James, the romance we create gives us a role our reality can play.

WASHINGTON SQUARE
AND
THE EUROPEANS

Neither *Washington Square* nor *The Europeans* need be read for anything but pleasure, and if there are any levels in them deeper than those having to do with the story, they are the levels to which the story leads and constitute the extra pleasure which is the reward of good reading. Unfortunately, today, many of us have to be taught how to read for pleasure: to be instructed in our pleasure, and to let our pleasure instruct us. Whatever Henry James later became, as the author of these novels, or romances, he had no overmastering theme, no vision or psychology of life to reveal, and no great shaping power of artistic form, in the technical sense, which he wished to impose. The last thing he was writing in these books was the Henry James novel in any of the versions of it to which we are now accustomed. He had not reached that narrowing choice or that racking impasse of vision which forces ambition upon a writer. He wrote easily, rather, almost spontaneously, and according to the easier models at hand in the modes of the time. He looked about for a story, found it, and filled it out. He wrote out of his gift, without trying to make too much of it and without making it matter too much. He wrote, so to say, out of the unexamined dictates of his conscience; the talents looked over his shoulder which later were to become the genius that crushingly embraced him. All this he did ably, pleasantly, entertainingly and pretty much in the language and the conventions common to his time.

Pretty much, but not altogether. It does not diminish our pleasure in this early, summer reading to see how his unattended idiosyncrasy could not help already asserting itself. It is like meeting people for the second or third time; the shock of novelty, or the apparent commonplace, has worn off a little and we begin to see that there might be something in these people and to see partly what that something is, or may be. These are people, we say, who will leave their mark long afterward, like random dreams that will later declare their meaning in actions, or refusals to act, that we had not thought to undertake. I do not mean that the child is father to the man, but that in memory or history things sometimes achieve their form in fresh action, and in psychologies that transpire long after they were originally intimated in figure or gesture. Catherine Sloper in *Washington Square* and Gertrude Wentworth in *The Europeans* grow into something else, but without first loss, when we come on Milly Theale and Maggie Verver in *The Wings of the Dove* and *The Golden Bowl*. These are changes of role for the sake of a better meaning and a more fully committed nature. From Catherine Sloper to Milly Theale is an easy motion from a wrenched dismay to a full renunciation, from the gothic shadow of a musty drawing room in New York to the full light that meets deep ill turned to the wall of the palace in Venice. That we should find Gertrude Wentworth inhabiting Maggie Verver is a little harder, and a little more than the normal reversal of the expectations of memory; yet the cool, aloof, nearly arrogant girl of the earlier book is a preparation for the grasping and lacerating conscience of Maggie Verver. But the reader will have less trouble in making the transversion if he will think first of Felix Young in *The Europeans*, with his easy corruptions in the naïve role of adventurer, and then of Prince Amerigo in *The Golden Bowl*, with his hard, ravaging, absolutely vital corruption. One thinks of Henry

James's note on visiting Flaubert, that Flaubert was a deeply corrupted but uncorrupting man. The earlier characters are buoyant upon the conventions of their society even when victimized by them, the later are anarchs fighting for life among the conventions. The earlier are used by their conventions, the later abuse them and charge them, after they are changed, with new warrant. Their fates are similar, renunciation and resolution, but fates damage and mar the shapes of life in the later characters where the earlier are left innocent and quite unsmirched.

To these differences we will return, but here is perhaps the point to emphasize the role in common which James invented for the American girl. There has been much written about it before; it is the attractive role of the American Princess or the Heiress of the Ages. She is a princess without a dominion, an heiress whose fortune doesn't apply, but she is royal and rich up to the point where it matters for herself, and she has every power of taking her lovers into destruction with her at the point where she fails to make her awards pass for enough. I should like to think she does not exist whether as American or otherwise, but I am compelled in the next face I see or around the next corner to believe that she has a virtual and catastrophic existence, as if our girls modeled themselves upon the figures in Henry James. There is an enduring strain of the inhuman in all humans, the strain of that sexuality which can never coalesce, can never swell and burst, and cannot even translate itself into another mode of action, but is an inner dryness that spreads to a desiccated and disarticulated action till the sexual garment sweet is all tatters in dark rooms, cellar rubbish. It is the sort of thing you get when the fairy godmother is the prod in one heartbeat and La Belle Dame sans Merci is the prod in the other. Some of our ancestors saw this better, or more clearly, through their prejudices than we see it through ours; *Daisy Miller* had a scandalous success more than it had a success as a representation of American civic virtue struck down by the conventions of the great but dead world that smother the girl with a Roman fever but enliven the story. It was the fever readers rushed to contract from Daisy, and one wonders whether Lolita is not a great-grandchild of Daisy, a princess under an avuncular regency. These figures are vampires, if indeed they are not werewolves. Listen to Henry James speaking of Daisy Miller.

It is Winterbourne, who never quite fell into the unprepared clutches of Daisy—he was not up to it, but was a good reporter—who is complaining of Daisy's charge that he has been mean to her, "'And what is the evidence you have offered?' asked Winterbourne, rather annoyed at Miss Miller's want of apprehension of the zeal of an admirer who on his way down to Rome had stopped neither at Bologna nor at Florence, simply because of a certain sentimental impatience. He remembered that a cynical compatriot had once told him that American women—the pretty ones, and this gave a largeness to the axiom—were at once the most exacting in the world and the least endowed with a sense of indebtedness."

This is, if you like, a mere cynical observation, an axiom from behind. Here is Winterbourne pursuing his sentimental analogy of a game by joining Daisy when she was in company with her Italian, Giovanelli, the young one. "Daisy on these occasions was never embarrassed or annoyed by his own entrance; but he very presently began to feel that she had no more surprises for him; the unexpected in her behaviour was the only thing to expect. She showed no displeasure at her tête-à-tête with Giovanelli being interrupted; she could chatter as freshly and freely with two gentlemen as with one; there was always, in her conversation, the same odd mixture of audacity and puerility." I quote, of course, to my own purpose, and it may be that my two passages are merely a part of the filling James put into his story to make it last and give room for the action to take place, for it has none of the deeply operative texture of James's later books when he exhibits the prehensile apprehensions of his men and women. It may be so; myself, I think it a characteristic part of what was spontaneous in his special sensibility; it is the circumstantial evidence, the texture of the cloth, the gradual conviction. This princess is without indebtedness; hence her audacity and her puerility.

Daisy Miller was published between *The Europeans* and *Washington Square*, and may be said to look both ways, before and after. Here is a reflection made by Felix Young—the Giovanelli, the *cavaliere avvocato*, the gallant on the naïve make —of *The Europeans*, when he rather thinks that he is in love with three young women at once without power or need to consolidate his choice. "His pleasure came from something they had in common—a part of which was, indeed, that physical delicacy which seemed to make it proper that they should always dress in thin materials and clear colors. But they were delicate in other ways, and it was most agreeable to him to feel that these latter delicacies were appreciable by contact, as it were. He had known, fortunately, many virtuous gentlewomen, but it now appeared to him that in his relations with them (especially when they were unmarried) he had been looking at pictures under glass." One of Felix's three young ladies was Gertrude Wentworth, and it is upon her that his choice settles into marriage, though I do not know that he ever saw her except through a glass darkly. Certainly he never is reported as seeing anything of what James shows us of both the fairy godmother and La Belle Dame sans Merci when she rejects her rightful and established suitor, the reverend and Unitarian Mr. Brand.

Gertrude is a woman the prudent would run from and the passionate distrust but to whom the candidate and the lover of the Muse will always fall prone since there is a dangerous and inhuman virtual reality in her. She listens to Mr. Brand's last reassertion of groundless and vertiginous faith.

> This time his voice was very touching; there was a strong, reproachful force in what he said, and Gertrude could answer nothing. He turned away and stood there, leaning his elbows on the gate and looking at the beautiful sunset. Gertrude left him and took her way home again; but when she reached the middle of the next field she suddenly burst into tears. Her tears seemed to her to have been a long time gathering, and for some moments it was a kind of glee to shed them. But they presently passed away. There was something a little hard about Gertrude; and she never wept again.

Her innocence closed about her, shell upon shell of protective surface, the dryness spreading from within, not only protective of her but fatal to adhere to.

Catherine Sloper in *Washington Square* was more human but had worse luck; her protections at the end only served to hide the inner destruction brought about by an early life of tamperage. For she has been progressively tampered with—by her father, who is horrified by her dumb eloquence and her simpleton nature; by her aunt who wishes to make her the substitute center of all the romances she herself had not had; by her lover, who wishes to plunder her of the riches which it turns out she has not got; and finally by herself in response to all these tamperings, who tampers so deeply that she excludes herself from all ordinary life without even the hint of power surrendered or illumination lost. She lives in a house where the Extracts from the Poets are bound in black with jaundiced gilt and where she herself has a glossy poplin lap. She is, of the lot, the American princess *manqué*, invented by her father and by the society around her. She is taught the geometry of the surfaces of emotion and as a result becomes early an empty bottle. In her emptiness she grows to understand that the emotions that are bent on her have nothing to do with fondness and in the end there is no violence in her, and no room for any, except the violence of her heartbeat, to which she chooses to listen in the increasing vacuum and halting circulation. She has given up everything for the lover who has deceived her and has now deserted her; but at the same time she has given nothing to anybody, anytime, least of all to herself. As the others have tampered with her, so she has learned to tamper with herself. This she sees about her Aunt Penniman, who has, with blunder after blunder, tried to put her into the momentum of society: "A consummate sense of her aunt's meddlesome folly had come over her during the last five minutes, and she was sickened with the thought that Mrs. Penniman had been let loose, as it were, upon her happiness. . . . 'Is it you, then, that has changed him and made him so unnatural?' Catherine cried." And for the rest of her life she cries out to herself, and makes herself unnatural. I take it this is the meaning of the last sentence: "Catherine, meanwhile, in the parlor, picking up her morsel of fancy-work, had seated herself with it again—for life, as it were." This is perhaps not what James thought that he meant. Renunciation, as Emily Dickinson's poem says, is a piercing virtue; one seldom knows its scope, or with what hideous weakness the apparent strength of renunciation is informed.

This is perhaps not what James thought he meant, but this is what his stories of the American princess lead up to all the time. He wrote social comedy—light, witty, brilliant, full of the comic strokes of moral superiority and slashed with the darker strokes of straight perception, showing, now and then, the bare cross-grain of inner disturbance: the springs of action that run counter to all the interests of the self. Here, in *The Europeans*, are a brother and sister who come to America in the hope of making their fortunes by the expense of art and manners; the sister finds herself excluded, the brother finds himself swallowed, for the sister finds herself becoming all manners without force behind them and the brother finds himself with only a salable art to offer. And here, in *Washington Square*, a young girl finds herself exhausted of all her potentialities, both personal and accidental (in her great fortune), before she has time or has developed the skill to test them in any real action. James was not yet aware of the pervasive problem of evil, but he was already aware, at the level of social comedy and instinctive allegory, of the infinitely more dominating problem of the good. I do not say that the good has to take on the tinctures of the evil before it escapes the domain of romance and comedy and becomes the novel or the drama—before it reaches the shapes of the ambitious shaping imagination—but if the example of James is of any use to us, it certainly suggests something of the sort. Goodness seems as much of a calamity as a great man when pressed to action, or to self-knowledge, or to the shapes of ambitious art.

This is one way to look at the sequence and growth of James's art in the novel, and is the most attractive way to let the early art of social comedy instruct us with its pleasures. His stories are reaching for something, or leading to something, and as good a name as any to give the method used is that of natural allegory.

Neither the names of the characters nor the procedures of the stories, their well-made plots and their crashes of conventional situation and institutional values, are allegorical; one does not look for a veiled truth here in that way. The allegory is natural in the sense that it is a natural product of the telling of the story; it is not the machinery of the story but what the machinery of the story makes: things which have their own significance beyond intention, in themselves. This is why we can remember Catherine Sloper and Daisy Miller and, to a lesser degree, the baroness and her brother in *The Europeans*; they are not characters in the round, nor sums in the sociology of suffering, nor affairs of willful symbolism—they are enjoyably their own meaning, and they draw from us our innate and instinctive actions to fill them out. To read them is to pass the time in a delightful way with all our own prejudices on the alert but disengaged. To have been able to write them was the preface to the exacting and commanding fictions into which they grew. It is we Europeans in Washington Square who can bring most to *The Wings of the Dove* and *The Golden Bowl*, where pleasure is made masterful and charm is made strength.

THE PORTRAIT OF A LADY

This is the first of Henry James's books to sound with the ring of greatness, and in these remarks I intend to comment on some of the elements that let it ring. But first we had better put compactly what the novel is about. Isabel Archer is given the chance to do what she can with her life, thanks to her uncle's surprising bequest of some seventy thousand pounds. Everybody tampers with Isabel, and it is hard to say whether her cousin Ralph Touchett, who had arranged the bequest, or the Prince, Gilbert Osmond, who marries her because of it, tampers the more deeply. At any rate, the whole novel shows how people tamper with one another because of motives that pass like money between them. The story of the book is the story of Isabel's increasing awareness of the meaning of the relations between herself and her husband, her husband's ex-mistress Madame Merle, and the young girl Pansy Osmond (who passes as the child of the first Mrs. Osmond but is really Gilbert's daughter by Madame Merle). The money is at the center of these relations. But, surrounding these, there are also Isabel's relations with her three rejected lovers, Caspar Goodwood, Lord Warburton, and Ralph Touchett. Ralph dies, Warburton marries elsewhere; Goodwood, the ever returning signal, she finally understands, though she still rejects him, as the signal of love itself. Minor persons—Henrietta Stackpole, the Countess Gemini, and young Rosier—illuminate but are not part of either set of relations, or of the devastations in which those relations result (and in which, while we read the novel, we seem to live).

That we do not live by novels is plain enough. Novels, rather, are sometimes ways of looking at failures and successes—mainly failures—in human relations. Novels do not supply us with morals but they show us with what morals have to do. So it is with *The Portrait of a Lady*, where we see the American princess, Isabel Archer, brought slowly to recognize as much as she can at the age of twenty-eight of the conditions of life. Then, so far as the novel goes, she disappears into the ruins of ancient Rome, which generalize for us all, and into the particular ruins of her own marriage, which we will generalize for ourselves. What will happen to her haunts us like a memory we cannot quite reenact. We have seen a bright-brash, conceited young girl whose chief attractive power lay in her money, change into a young woman who is luminous rather than bright, human rather than brash, and whose conceit has turned to a suicidal obstinacy. She still has her money but, if we can consent to an exchange of this order, she is now worth her money. We have seen her act with her money as an instrument of destruction, and there is now the forward edge of a vision of money as an instrument of freedom. This is the latent question about money—and about morals, too—in James's novels: will they be instruments of freedom or of destruction? As Henrietta Stackpole says to Caspar Goodwood at the very end of the book: "Just you wait!"

Miss Stackpole with her button eyes meant whatever one wants her to mean; I should like her to have meant something relating to the quality of human judgment as Isabel comes to acquire and to ignore it. I hear Lord Warburton telling her when she is quite fresh in England, "You judge only from the outside—you don't care . . . you only care to amuse yourself"—words which he spoke with a bitterness abrupt and inconsequent in his voice. But I hear more clearly still these words of Madame Merle: "I judge more than I used to," she said to Isabel, "but it seems to me one has earned the right. One can't judge till one's forty; before that we're too eager, too hard, too cruel, and in addition much too ignorant." Madame Merle has more to say, which ends in this way: "I want to see what life makes of you. One thing's certain—it can't spoil you. It may pull you about horribly, but I defy it to break you up."

Madame Merle's own life, whatever the quality of her judgment, had not done so well by her. Her condition is such that she wishes to weep, to howl like a wolf, and she feels the pressure, in the company of Osmond, of "their *common* crimes." As she tells him, "You have made me as bad as yourself." But Madame Merle was false, and Isabel is given as by and large likely to be true. Madame Merle was enslaved by passions she no longer felt; Isabel, in the novel's scheme of things, should be liberated in the passion that as the book ends she has begun to feel, but which she must flee either in acceptance or renunciation—or in some peculiar state where the one doubles for the other: a shifting state, somehow not evasion, in which the sensibilities of James heroes and heroines so often transpire. It is as well that we shall never know how Isabel might come to join her sensibility both in judgment and action. Literature is perhaps not capable of making such answers, except in the form of promises. Rather it brings us only to the threshold of discovery.

We are brought by pedagogy, by education, by training. We see Isabel change, and we see what Isabel sees as she changes and also something of what she cannot or will not or is not yet ready to see—and especially the things she has succeeded in not knowing. That is what pedagogy, education, training are like in the novel. It is for the reader to see under these heads what the heroine experienced in different degrees of aptness and response. (If experience were learned like the alphabet or the integers there would be no novels and life would be over very quickly; we should be thankful in both cases that we are such slow students. Just the same the alphabet and the integers are first helps.) In short, the novelist is offering his heroine the education suitable for her role.

The American princess, whether Isabel Archer or another, always comes to us as innocent as possible, as innocent as the

victim who reigns—yet, precisely because of that innocence, predatory to the fingernails upon all who come within her reach. She
has, to begin with, only what she inherits. Doubtless she has been
somewhere to school but she has never received any training for
her job. In this respect she is not unlike another and once better-
known American production, nature's nobleman. But what will
do quite well for one of nature's noblemen will not do at all for an
American princess. The heiress to all the ages (James's own
phrase) should at least know something about the age she lives in
and perhaps what it has in common with the ages she inherits. It
is not surprising that James's princesses, getting their training
only on the job, come to bad ends, to abdication, death, or deep
frustration. Yet the books these princesses inhabit constitute essays
in training for active rule. It is a training they do not quite catch
up with for themselves, although they often can apply it in
looking at others. In Isabel's case, it sometimes seems she ought to
have applied to herself the language of her mind in looking at
others. Here, for example, is Isabel looking at her rightful lover,
Caspar Goodwood, when he descends on her in Italy.

> Caspar Goodwood stood there—stood and received
> a moment, from head to foot, the bright, dry gaze with
> which she rather withheld than offered a greeting.
> Whether his sense of maturity had kept pace with
> Isabel's we shall perhaps presently ascertain; let me say
> meanwhile that to her critical glance he showed noth-
> ing of the injury of time. Straight, strong and hard,
> there was nothing in his appearance that spoke posi-
> tively either of youth or of age; if he had neither
> innocence nor weakness, so he had no practical philos-
> ophy. His jaw showed the same voluntary cast as in
> earlier days; but a crisis like the present had in it of
> course something grim. He had the air of a man who
> had travelled hard; he said nothing at first, as if he had
> been out of breath. This gave Isabel time to make a re-
> flexion: "Poor fellow, what great things he's capable
> of, and what a pity he should waste so dreadfully his
> splendid force! What a pity too that one can't satisfy
> everybody!"

As it turned out, it was Caspar Goodwood alone of her lovers whom she could neither deal with nor evade, unless by flight; this she was not ready to know, at that moment or when we leave her. For the present she thought she could deal with him merely by again rejecting him on the eve of her marriage to Gilbert Osmond —a marriage and a groom none of her friends approve, except perhaps Madame Merle who had arranged it all. There are moments when the force of marriage—not love but marriage—is greater than the force of the individuals who must endure it. Isabel no doubt thought herself strengthened, when merely bent or deflected, by that force. We know rather better than Isabel and know partly because of one of her own insights into Madame Merle which she had reached at about the time she became engaged. Listening to that lady's long account of herself during their trip to Greece and Egypt, Isabel got the impression they came from different moral and social climes. "She believed then that at bottom she had a different morality. Of course the morality of civilized persons has always much in common; but our young woman had a sense in her of values gone wrong or, as they said in the shops, marked down." Madame Merle was lady-in-waiting to this princess *incognita* (James's phrase) and set up for her a court decadent beyond her understanding and full of things and motives "of which it was not advantageous to hear." We observe that at this point in her education Isabel develops a deliberate deafness, as if deafness were a special form of consciousness, nearly equivalent to what she is learning to hear. I will not say this leaves her more vulnerable, but it certainly leaves her more exposed to fresh assaults she could otherwise have avoided.

Innocence does not act, unless impaired by self-will and self-deceit; that is to say innocence proceeds as a kind of infatuation without an object until it bursts or is punctured. Then, since innocence is irrecoverable, there is, together with the devastation, a necessary accommodation to be made, either a death or a life, an abdication or an assumption—or, as we began by saying, a renunciation or an acceptance. How long Isabel's innocence lasted we do not exactly know. It is present in nearly full force at the end of Chapter XXXV—more than half the length of the novel—

when on the suggestion that a little girl, her step-daughter to be, be asked to leave the room, Isabel responds: "Let her stay, please. . . . I would rather hear nothing that Pansy may not." In the next chapter, three years later in time, the innocence is virtually gone, but its consequences remain mingled with the many-troubled marriage in which we find her. Self-will has been replaced with the effort to achieve a will, and self-deceit has become the deceit of others. The public and the private in her relations have now been reversed. Where so much of her that had been private was now forced into the public, what had been her public ease was now a matter of unremitting private concern. Where previously she had had to bring her life into existence, she had now to conceal the one that had come upon her. She had not only to face a civilized morality where her values were marked down, she had also to act by a morality whose values were not hers at all—as if there were a double morality with different degradations in each. She still expected too much for the one, and she had both the wrong illusions and the wrong disillusions for the other. Nothing was clear except that her husband "spoiled everything for her that he looked at"—an obscure form of intimacy she had certainly not been prepared for. She knew only, and this not too clearly, that without Madame Merle "these things need not have been." If Madame Merle had been the force from behind, little Pansy seemed now to be the only force to draw her on—as if where her own conceited innocence had failed her, the girl could succeed in her obedient naiveté and her naive inner rebellion against the "base, ignoble world," which yet provided the standards and scope if not the springs of compulsive action.

Isabel's first and partial *éclaircissement* comes when after a walk with Pansy among the delicate winter flowers of the Roman Campagna, she "discovered" her husband and Madame Merle in the drawing room.

> The soundlessness of her step gave her time to take in the scene before she interrupted it. Madame Merle was there in her bonnet, and Gilbert Osmond was talking to her; for a minute they were unaware she had come

in. Isabel had often seen that before, certainly; but
what she had not seen, or at least had not noticed, was
that their colloquy had for the moment converted itself
into a sort of familiar silence, from which she instantly
perceived that her entrance would startle them. . . .
The thing made an image, lasting only a moment, like
a sudden flicker of light. Their relative positions, their
absorbed mutual gaze, struck her as something detected.
But it was all over by the time she had fairly seen it.

It was all over so far as her consciousness went, but a larger
form of it had entered what Freud calls the preconscious, thence
to emerge from time to time—as it did that very night when she
had lingered to all hours alone in her salon. It was dark in the big
room. "But even then she stopped again in the middle of the
room and stood there gazing at a remembered vision—that of her
husband and Madame Merle unconsciously and familiarly associated." It is not conscious knowledge, or fresh knowledge, but the
knowledge one did not know that one knew, or but dimly knew,
that bursts upon one, an access of strength; and it bursts from
inside where it has been nurtured with every unconscious skill. So
it is with Isabel as she develops her judgment of her husband into
action. The nurtured knowledge comes clear throughout, as it
were, on the pages of fierce and eloquent polemic, those wonderful creative summaries of his character and sensibility, that are
reported as a kind of constitution for her thoughts between the
apparitions of the image of relations he has with Madame Merle,
and into which we the readers can pour our own possibilities of
coldness and egotism and greed, of worldly dilettantism without
delight, of spiritual caddishness. It is the image that gives the
meditations focus, and the meditations that give the image
meaning.

What more is James telling us when he puts these sentences
into his report of a discussion of Pansy's affairs between Isabel
and Madame Merle? "More clearly than ever before Isabel heard a
cold, mocking voice proceed from she knew not where, in the dim
void that surrounded her, and declare that this bright, strong,
definite worldly woman, this incarnation of the practical, the

personal, the immediate, was a powerful agent in her destiny." A moment or two later, the *éclaircissement* was complete, except for the history, and special treachery of what was illuminated. "She moved quickly indeed, and with reason, for a strange truth was filtering into her soul. Madame Merle's interest was identical with Osmond's: that was enough." The meaning of their history together, and with her, had become plain, though the history itself remained obscure and though it had been affecting her, almost absorbing her, all along.

The discovery that Pansy was daughter to Madame Merle and Osmond joined the history to the meaning. There were all sorts of things, as Osmond's sister Countess Gemini tells her, that Isabel had succeeded in not knowing, but which, as Isabel puts it, had nevertheless *occurred* to her. Now that these things had become available to knowledge as well as to experience, she could complete her judgment of Osmond. She could disobey him, leave him in Rome, and attend her cousin Ralph's death in England; and if she returned to Rome it was with another purpose than she had left it with, and with a new energy, greater in scope and intensity than before, though still with an object not altogether clear. At least she could now play her role if she could find it, and there is no place better than Rome to find a role for a princess without a proper domain. Rome is the city of Annunciation and Incarnation as well as ruins. Some such image awaits *éclaircissement* when we last see Isabel and enter her feelings. If she had renounced, it was for the sake of a later resumption, though it might be that at any given moment she might not know it—as if knowledge, for her, could never be quite *yet!* It is in souls like Isabel's, not invented by Henry James but seen by him in anguished clarity, that flight, as I said above, is the first form either of renunciation or acceptance, where the one may be taken as doubling for the other. We last see Isabel on the verge of such a flight—a flight that might have any and every meaning, whatever its subsequent history—a flight from the man whom she had at last known to be her rightful lover.

I will quote nothing of this; it belongs to the reader's own participation. I will quote instead a few fragments from the long, enlivening analogy to the story of Isabel Archer, the continuing image of Rome's ruins which sit, at any moment ready to rise, throughout that city's immediate life. The experience of cities is no longer intimate, and needs reminding. Here is Isabel, treading upon the daisies, which are like American daisies only in being endemic. "She had long before this taken old Rome into her confidence, for in a world of ruins the ruin of her happiness seemed a less unnatural catastrophe. She rested her weariness upon things that had crumbled for centuries, and yet still were upright. . . . She had become deeply, tenderly acquainted with Rome: it interfused and moderated her passion. But she had grown to think of it chiefly as the place where people had suffered." And again, from another page, one sentence about the Coliseum: "The great enclosure was half in shadow; the western sun brought out the pale red tone of the great blocks of travertine—the latent colour that is the only living element in the immense ruin." It is the latent color of Isabel's vitality we know best as the book ends: a vitality which became, through the money her cousin had gotten for her, an instrument both of freedom and destruction. The money had indeed put wind in her sails, but whether it had made her rich enough to meet the requirements of her imagination is another matter. That there may be no such riches is perhaps what the look in the eyes of this portrait of a lady is saying.

THE TRAGIC MUSE

This is a novel where the theater and the studio are set against the British Foreign Service and the House of Commons. The two sets of institutions have in common only that each is consciously histrionic, with the frightening chance that in each, if success is nearly complete, one's private life, one's uncreated self, may totally disappear into one's public role, or as we more hopefully say, into one's work. The phrases undermine each other, and so I think do the three principal persons who inhabit this book.

Miriam Rooth is all theater. Peter Sherringham, an amateur of the theater, is a career diplomat. Nick Dormer, an amateur painter, is in the beginning of a career as a Member of Parliament. The girl is raw and bold and pert, and her ambition is her only evidence of talent aside from her looks. The two young men are safe in their careers by the right combination of personal ability and social position. Nick perhaps needs the patronage and prospective bequest of a rich and elderly admirer of his dead father, and needs also marriage to Julia Dallow, a young widow who wanted most in life the tumescent emotion of "great affairs and public action" (an emotion none but Shakespeare and Tolstoy have deeply explored). Peter, on the face of it, needs nothing at all: he is on the easy way to pleasant accommodation with, at the end, an embassy in a country that did not at the moment matter. Peter, in short, has no real future except with women. Nick is problematic—one would say of him that he would have done well had he been put on, but unfortunately he had no talent for women. These young men would have gone on according to their mild promise—each with his amateur's commitment to the theater or to painting—had they not together met in Paris the raw, plastic girl who insisted on celebrity and who declared herself devoted to her art, with no fair promise for the one and no measurable conviction for the other; had they not met the tragic muse in a spirit of hope, encouragement, and pedagogy and taken her to the old actress, Mme. Carré, for first judgment and laying on of hands.

There, with practically none of the talent called for, but in the hybrid of her intention and her fear—in the riches of her embarrassment—she made herself austere and terrible, an incarnation of what the two men ever afterward called the tragic muse. It is possible that Miriam would not have made her incarnation and the men would have not seen it, had not Mme. Carré set the tone in some words addressed to Mrs. Rooth, who had hoped Miriam would come to play nothing but "respectable" parts. The words are worth repeating since they affect us all. "You mix things up, *chère madame,* and I have it on my heart to tell you so. I believe it's rather the case with you other English, and I have never been able to learn that either your morality or your talent is the gainer by it. To be too respectable to go where things are done best is, in my opinion, to be very vicious indeed; and to do them badly in order to preserve your virtue is to fall into a grossness more shocking than any other. To do them well is virtue enough, and not to make a mess of it the only respectability. That's hard enough to merit Paradise. Everything else is base humbug! *Voilà, chère madame,* the answer I have for your scruples!" It was these words that charged the body of the young girl, if they could not yet charge her talent, and through her charged the men.

Peter falls in love with her as soon as may be—or at any rate he reaches with her that maximum of extra occupation called infatuation, which is traditionally the right thing to do with an actress. Infatuation is the first hysteria to master us and invites us to our first histrionic effort where we represent our values without regard for our own sincerity or for that of our idol. Peter's response was direct and masterless and in no way in itself desirable. He loved her for his own sake, not hers, and would have swallowed her if he could; yet when he was with her she swallowed him indifferently in the mere voracity of her presence. What he wanted of her was that she give up the stage and marry the foreign service; what she wanted of him was to use him up without acquiring him. Peter saw this well enough. It was a bad future for him that opened out. "The instant he was before her, near her, next her, he found himself a helpless subject of the spell which, so far at least as he was concerned, she put forth by contact and of which the potency was punctual and absolute. . . . At a distance he partly recovered himself . . . but as soon as he entered her presence his life struck him as a thing disconnected from his will. It was as if *he* had been one thing and his behaviour another."

It was not the same thing with Nick. He never fell in love with her; never cared for her; never asked her for anything except that he might paint her portrait. But he felt the force that moved in her, and he translated that force into his own behavior. He gave up politics for art, and lost his Julia as well; for Julia, when she discovered Miriam in his studio, felt her force too, and felt it working in Nick, and repudiated the force and Nick in a single action. Unlike Peter, Nick and his behavior were very nearly one and the same thing. He had, in the presence of Miriam, given up a great deal, but he had renounced nothing of value to him so long as her force worked in him. Like Peter, Nick had reached in the presence of Miriam a maximum of extra occupation, not infatuation but something very like it, the addiction to art. James seemed to think that Nick was in a small way successful in his art, and he worried, toward the end of his preface to the book, that Nick had not turned out as interesting as he was intended to be. But there was, as James saw it, a reason. "Any presentation of the artist *in triumph* must be flat in proportion as it really sticks to its subject —it can only smuggle in relief and variety. For, to put the matter in an image, all we then—in his triumph—see of the charm-compeller is the back he turns to us as he bends over his work." I would say here for Nick, and for the rest of us, that it depends on how you look at him, or at a man or woman in any other profession, whether you see him disappear into his success in that profession. It is a fighting question, but not within the decorum of these remarks. I will only remind the reader of Tolstoy's opening to *Anna Karenina*—all happy marriages are the same, every unhappy marriage different; and of the beginning of the *Ethics*—the Chief Good is that which all things aim at. James *wanted* to see Nick as the successful artist—as indeed he wanted to see himself: finally anonymous, yet all the more, *therefore*, a person. It is this want, this wish, this willed intention that inhabits the whole book, the tone of things by which we recognize what they mean to be. James meant his novel as a novel of art—of the bloom of the expert and the blight of the amateur. As he put it in his preface, "The consistent, the sustained, preserved *tone* of 'The Tragic Muse,' its constant and doubtless rather fine-drawn truth to its particular sought pitch and accent, are, critically speaking, its principal merit—the inner harmony that I perhaps presumptuously permit myself to compare to an unevaporated scent."

The figure may be excessive, but in his prefaces James was nothing if not also excessive, and as a rule he exaggerated something that existed. In the book itself the exaggerations are of a different order and are meant for satire—as when Miriam's mother is given "an upper lip which projected over the under as an ornamental cornice rests upon its support," or when Sherringham thinks of her in the following words.

> She delighted in novels, poems, perversions, misrepresentations, and evasions, and had a capacity for smooth, superfluous falsification which made Sherringham think her sometimes an amusing and sometimes a tedious inventor. But she was not dangerous, even if you believed her; she was not even a warning if you didn't. It was harsh to call her a hypocrite, because you never could have resolved her back into her character:

there was no reverse to her blazonry. She built in the air,
and was not less amiable than she pretended: only that
was pretension too.

Mrs. Rooth does not matter; she is the enemy we rejoice to hear
about, and she has no "serious" function in the novel beyond
that amusement, unless it be as foil and index to the character
of her daughter. Sherringham's thoughts went on: "Mrs. Rooth
abounded in impressive evocations, and yet he saw no link between her facile genius and that of which Miriam gave symp-
toms. The poor lady never could have been accused of successful
deceit, whereas success in this line was exactly what her clever
child went in for. She made even the true seem fictive, while
Miriam's effort was to make the fictive true." Mrs. Rooth did not
matter, but you could not get rid of her.

The whole figure of Gabriel Nash—and this is the great
piece of satire in the book—on the contrary mattered very much,
and if he had not got rid of himself every energy would have been
joined to get rid of him. He falsified in the name of truth,
degraded in the name of purity, made vivid sloth in the name of
hard work, he enslaved in the name of independence, he was the
aesthete in the name of art. He had begun brilliant, the namesake
of incentive and possibility and unaffixed freedom, and indeed of
everything good unless by chance you took it seriously; but he
became bored and boring when commitment showed. His frivolity
was not excess energy or the rise of vital doubt, which are the
frivolity of the great; his frivolity was the only energy and the only
conviction he had, and his only reaction was to tamper, his only
conquest to annoy. He might amuse you with regard to your vices
or the creature comforts of your morality, but you would never let
him near your virtue or your strength. He could amuse your day
off, but if you attended him you might seem to have taken off not
a day but a life.

Nick and Peter had a conversation about him on the occasion
when Peter (and ourselves) first met him, of which I quote a part.
"He's very intelligent," said Nick, "and I should think it might
be interesting to find out what it is that prevents the whole man
from being as good as his parts. I mean in case he isn't so good."

To which Peter: "I see you more than suspect that. May it not simply be that he's an ass?"—"That would be the whole," Nick answered, "—I shall see in time—but it certainly isn't one of the parts. It may be the effect, but it isn't the cause, and it's for the cause that I claim an interest." Nick does see in time; it is when he starts to paint his portrait. When he begins to get his face—fix his character—on canvas, Gabriel Nash disappears from all our knowledge. Nick and Miriam were both by this time committed to the life of art. Nick's commitment had become the regular habit of his life. For Miriam, the excitement of her task had become the humdrum of daily life; her skill was of her second nature. There was nothing more for Gabriel Nash to do in a novel about art once the artists in it were committed by habit and second nature. He had to be there to begin with—as he is ubiquitous in every artistic capital of the world (notably these days in Rome)—but in a Henry James novel about art he was there to be got rid of; and it is not astonishing that in his preface James says nothing about his flashing and flittering portrait.

James says, though, in that preface, a number of things that we ought not to forget, both for their substance and for their tone. And in looking at them we should remember that James wrote his novel in the time of, and his preface in near reminiscence of, Art for Art's Sake, a time when the artist was beginning to emerge as the characteristic hero of fiction: the figure whom we all contain, in a cellar if not in an attic—or if it is a modern house, in the playroom. The subject, he said, had always been with him—"art, that is, as a human complication and a social stumbling-block . . . the conflict between art and 'the world' striking me thus betimes as one of the half-dozen great primary motives." Like Christianity art was scandalous if you took it seriously, and, again like Christianity, the cost of taking it seriously was everything and nothing, with every possible kind of hypocrisy and pretense in between; so that there was an equal chance for satire and devotion. So it turns out; both forms of exaggeration give tone to the book. "The idea of the book being, as I have said, a picture of some of the personal consequences of the art-appetite raised to intensity, swollen to voracity, the heavy emphasis falls where the symbol of some of the complications so begotten might

be made (as I judged, heaven forgive me!) most 'amusing';
amusing, I mean in the blest very modern sense.''

Whether he had himself forgotten it or not, the seed for the
amusement lay in a note he had made several years previously for
a story about an actress who was brought to success by her lover,
an amateur of the stage.

> She goes beyond him, she leaves him looking after her
> and wondering. She begins where he ends—soars away
> and is lost to him. The interest, I say, would be as a
> study of a certain particular *nature d'actrice:* a very
> curious sort of nature to reproduce. The girl I see to be
> very crude, etc. The thing is a confirmation of Mrs.
> Kemble's theory that the dramatic gift is a thing by
> itself—implying of necessity no *general* superiority of
> mind. The strong nature, the personal quality, vanity,
> etc., of the girl; her artistic being, so vivid, yet so purely
> instinctive. Ignorant, illiterate. Rachel.

It was this idea that became Miriam Rooth in all "manageable
vividness,'' the tragic muse herself, all objective and nobody intimate or inside her, but seen by everybody, the actress who captures
us all, and the central figure, for the length of the novel—the
standard or touchstone—by her presence, in the lives of Peter
Sherringham and Nick Dormer. All three have their own stories,
but James's novel is meant to show how the "several actions
beautifully become one.'' To my appreciation the several actions
do become one, as the far off always seems when it becomes
immediate. In memory I cannot detach them one from another,
and I must think of all three if I think of any. That is how a novel
makes the actions of many persons one—the beauty Pythagoras
saw in the reduction of the many to the one—and a new thing too:
by putting them side by side so that they reach into each other for
relation and modification of meaning. It is like seeing people in
an unexpected room, how they themselves alter and join as they
are seen in relation; a new thing. Here they are seen in the relation
of art.

Miriam Rooth is the most interesting of the three and lends
substance as well as motive to what happens to the other two.
Her ambition is a deep animal or psychic drive, so deep there is

no chance that she could have made any other choice than the histrionic career. All she can be taught is how to work; the quality of her work can gain nothing from conscious teaching or conscious attention. She has only a specifically human gift to begin with: the gift which makes any individual, even a crowd, representative to a good camera: what makes the documentary seem so imaginative to the degree that it is let alone, so phony when manipulated or limited to an intended meaning. This is the great gift of our unconscious skills, and constitutes the genuine mark of the artist. Not unnaturally it is often allied to "beauty" (indeed beauty is an unconscious skill). Beauty is by birth, art by genius; it is all the same.

If we consider such matters I think it becomes clear why it is that Miriam almost alone among James heroines never resigned, never gave up, never renounced, whether in submission or to gain extra strength of being. Unlike the others, she would neither have become herself or heightened her value by doing so. She had nothing to give up, on the contrary, which would not have demolished her had she done so. She was an actress and a beauty, the very person who in either role cannot give anything up. There was never any question that she might give up "life" for art or beauty, and it was certain that she could never give up art for life. Peter saw this early and late, and he tried to tell her his vision. "What's rare in you is that you have—as I suspect, at least—no nature of your own. . . . You are always playing something; there are no intervals. It's the absence of intervals, of a *fond* or background, that I don't comprehend. You're an embroidery without a canvas. . . . Your feigning may be honest, in the sense that your only feeling *is* your feigned one." This was early in his knowledge of her; later, when Biddy Dormer asks him if Miriam is false, Sherringham answers her: "She speaks a special language; practically it isn't false, because it renders her thought, and those who know her understand it." Had Miriam given up the theater she would have become a puerility of herself; she remained a scandal—of which only the taint would have survived had she married Peter Sherringham, and what Peter wanted to marry in her would otherwise have disappeared. Miriam demanded to be seen and refused to be known: she was theater.

But Peter had a hard time putting his need out of mind when he returned from his Central American post to find Miriam opening as Juliet and to learn that she had made a marriage (a kind of permanent precaution: "It seemed simpler" she had said to Nick. "It was clear there had to be some one.") to the actor who played Mercutio, Basil Dashwood. Now on the opening night, "The great childish audience, gaping at her points, expanded there before her like a lap to catch flowers." Where the audience was childish and filled, Peter Sherringham was emptied. Who knows what he saw, Miriam or Juliet? "Peter Sherringham, though he saw but a fragment of the performance, read clear, at the last, in the intense light of genius that this fragment shed, that even so, after all, he had been rewarded for his formidable journey. The great trouble of his infatuation subsided, leaving behind it something tolerably deep and pure."

James remains ambiguous as to the depth and purity—unless Peter's marriage to Biddy be a clarification; but there is a passage earlier in the book which may have a bearing. Peter is waiting in Miriam's house for her to come down.

> Familiarity had never yet cured him of a certain tremor of expectation, and even of suspense, in regard to her entrances; a flutter caused by the simple circumstance of her infinite variety. To say she was always acting suggests too much that she was often fatiguing; for her changing face affected this admirer, at least, not as a series of masks, but as a response to perceived differences, an intensity of sensibility, or still more as something cleverly constructive, like the shifting of a scene in a play or a room with many windows. Her incarnations were incalculable, but if her present denied her past and declined responsibility for her future, it made a good thing of the hour and kept the actual very actual.

It is the last sentence that counts. In art, and especially the art of acting, the actual is the indomitable force; in life it is mainly intolerable.

Thus, returning to Peter's *éclaircissement*, seeing Miriam as Juliet, "he felt somehow recalled to reality by the very perfection of the representation." It took him half a Lent to complete his acceptance—to perfect the acknowledgment which ended, in a theater, his "formidable journey." If Pilate asked What is truth? with what word of question could he have asked about the actual and the real? Some ancestral habit prompts the reminder that Pilate's query was in response to Jesus's words: "Every one that is of the truth heareth my voice." To come on, or to achieve, a vision of the actual or the real is a struggle—and a cutting away—of the sensibility and the conscience; and she who presides over the struggle has never had a more blinding or reminding name than the Tragic Muse.

She—the Tragic Muse—will remind us above all of perspective, of the long train of things where the actual undermines our particular perspective of the real and where the real penetrates our heartiest composition of the actual, two scandals we cannot endure.

Peter Sherringham married Biddy Dormer. We do not know that Nick married anyone—we leave him on the dubious possibility that he may paint a standing portrait of Julia Dallow, in which, we cannot help thinking, there will be only half-hidden a discommoding conflict between the actual and the real. But Nick, too, had had his *éclaircissement*, his own unsteadying shock where darkness blinded him to a chosen light. The frivolous question, which is only Pilate's question in its more natural form, suddenly became oppressive. May not one at any moment become disconnected? Sloth of spirit sees every energy down the drain; sloth of ambition sees the *other* fellow's enterprise running on forever, while one's own lags in arrears of false privilege. Nick in the National Gallery looks at Titian and Rubens, Gainsborough and Rembrandt. He did not mind so much his own failure in their own line.

> He found himself calling the whole art literally into
> question. What was it, after all, at the best, and why had
> people given it so high a place? Its weakness, its nar-

rowness appeared to him; tacitly blaspheming, he
looked at several world-famous performances with a
lustreless eye. That is he blasphemed if it were blas-
phemy to say to himself that, with all respect, they were
a poor business, only well enough in their small way.
The force that produced them was not one of the
greatest forces in human affairs; their place was inferior
and their connection with the life of man casual and
slight. They represented so inadequately the idea, and
it was the idea that won the race, that in the long run
came in first. He had incontestably been much closer
to the idea a few months before than he was to-day: it
made up a great deal for the bad side of politics that
they were after all a clumsy system for applying and
propagating the idea.

This is the "immitigable recoil" of the mind before its own
creations, and had Nick been still in politics he could have stared
even at the Speaker with the same lusterless eye that he had just
applied to Titian and Rembrandt. All art is translation, the idea
is always abstraction in discourse; the translation will fail and the
discourse disarticulate itself if the convention or the abstraction
strike a lusterless eye. This, too, is a blind reminder by the Tragic
Muse of the interpenetration of the actual and the real, of the
precariousness of any balance struck, and how a new balance
must be made every instant. But there is another image on which
to end. We see Nick visiting Mr. Carteret at the moment when he
is making his own struggle of decision. There is a ruined abbey
with "huge, short towers. The towers had never been finished,
save as time finishes things, by perpetuating their incompleteness.
There is something right in old monuments that have been wrong
for centuries." That too is the gesture of the Tragic Muse.

THE AMBASSADORS

This is the story of a man who in middle life finds himself in a strange country where he gets to know about goodness and human freedom. Lambert Strether has not so to speak thought about them before. It is as if, while the book lasts, you see that evil is permanent in the world and pretty much the same, but that the good has to be made fresh, and different, each time; which, so far as it is true, is a tragic necessity—especially if like Lambert Strether you try not to know about the particular evil around you but do try to absorb it in a general virtuous pattern. Strether is very slow in coming to his recognitions, not in time—it is only a few months—but in his steps to clairvoyance; he has to be slow, or there would have been no book to write. It is only after we have read the book that we grasp how much has happened in a short time. Then we can see that it was all promised on the first page— in the original American edition—with one word, freedom, on the second page. There is hardly a better testimony to James's power of economy in writing—when he cared to use it—than the opening of *The Ambassadors*, including the plural in the title.

Let us see how the first page goes. Strether, fresh from America, and at the lovely city of Chester rather than at the ugly port of Liverpool, finds that his friend Waymarsh has not arrived and is pleased—or not "disconcerted"—at the absence. Strether has a "secret principle." He wants to be free in his first perceptions —or free of Waymarsh: Waymarsh would bungle the business if he were the first "note" of Europe; he would, Strether is afraid, be Europe enough afterward. Meanwhile he has the note of personal freedom. So: there is a secret principle, there is Waymarsh as friend and impediment, there is a business that can be bungled, there is the "note" of Europe and the note of "Europe"—and there is, if we know James at all, Europe representing or creating personal freedom. We know that Waymarsh will be an obstacle; that he is an old friend, chosen probably for social reasons since they are not reasons of affection, but possibly chosen for business reasons since there is business to be bungled, at any rate not chosen freely. We know that Strether has not seen him for a long time; there will therefore be chances and needs for estimation. There is thus present something richer in their meeting because it has a standard of departure, because it can be prepared for, and because it can be anticipated both rightly and wrongly, in doubt and certainty. We also know that there is an adventure in Strether's coming to Europe. It is a mixed adventure, having to do with business, with the response to Europe, and with the consciousness of personal freedom. Above all we know that Strether is the kind of man who can be disconcerted in his sensibility (the organization of his sentiments and his responses and his conscience) apart from his actions. On the last page of the novel we see the cost with which the promise of the first was kept.

In between comes the story of how Strether fails to rescue from Mme. de Vionnet, a woman of Paris, Chad Newsome, the son of the widow to whom he is engaged. Strether not only fails in his mission, he betrays it, and would have kept Chad in Paris and stayed there himself if he could. As it is, he leaves behind every-thing that he has gained and returns to the America of all that he has lost—an ambassador quite, and permanently, out of office, but become so of his own nature in goodness and freedom. Those who do not like to think of Strether as related only to good men like William Dean Howells and Balzac's Louis Lambert may think of him as related to another good man, Dostoevsky's Prince Myshkin as he is when he returns to Switzerland at the end of *The Idiot*; they are cousins across their cultures.

That Mrs. Pocock—Mrs. Newsome's second ambassador—succeeds in rescuing the young man from the woman of Paris, only marks Strether's refusal to do so (and his other refusals as well) more plainly as vital and, for him, inescapable. We see what he means, and how the meaning is transformed from the actual to the ideal, by his early adjuration to Little Bilham: "Live all you can," which as he repeats it at the end of his remarks in Gloriani's garden becomes: "Do what you like so long as you don't make *my* mistake. For it was a mistake. Live!" When Strether speaks these words his innocence is actual and takes relatively little hold of reality. At the end of the book his innocence has drawn everything to it and become ideal. As for reality, it has become nowhere at all, at all; which is the sadness of Strether and links us to him across its gap.

James gave Strether a phrase for this, too, which he addresses to Mme. de Vionnet: "Men of my age . . . have been noted as liable to strange outbreaks, belated, uncanny clutches at the unusual, the ideal." We see Strether grow to such an outbreak, and these are the stages of his growth. His sensibility is exposed to every good thing that can be called Paris in the spring; his new friends develop his responsiveness as they can and as the weather permits; they protect him from seeing what they are, by becoming a little as he sees them; and they deceive him until he is ready for the truth. At no time does he become used to things; he never becomes inured; instead, his sensibility clears and becomes clair-voyant as we are led further into the confusions of life. As these things happen, we see the decay of Chad, of Waymarsh, of Woollett in Massachusetts: the decay of the mistake of Strether's life. At the same time we see the rise of Mme. de Vionnet, from a conventional menace, to a lady of virtuous attachment, to a woman ravaged and passionate. Her rise happens in close accord to Strether's own rise in his relation to her: from a friend helping, to a conscience

216
216 **STUDIES IN HENRY JAMES**

destroying, to an ideal which the more it is acknowledged is the more certainly never gained. It is what Strether *sees* in Mme. de Vionnet that *happens* to him.

There are of course other things. There is the trickling away of Maria Gostrey—not for herself but for Strether. She was always there and always to be found, yet whenever Strether finds her she is not there for him. There is the apparition of Chad as blackguard and cad, to cancel his first apparition as the new man of the world. Chad, as Strether sees, is the man who knows how to live, but he is perhaps also the man who cannot pay the cost of living except by foisting it off on others. He is at best a sentimentalist without imagination, as Strether is a realist with too much imagination. And there is everywhere about him Paris and everywhere behind him the Woollett of Mrs. Newsome. Perhaps there is a reality of role revealed for Strether when in the cab with Jim Pocock (fresh from Woollett with his wife Sarah) he has one of his summary interludes of futility. He conceives Woollett the reality and Paris the vanity—the vain thing menaced by the real. He then asks himself, after naming all his Paris friends: "Wouldn't it be found to have made more for reality to be silly with these persons than sane with Sarah and Jim?" The question gets bitter as it takes further forms. Looking at Jim, he asks himself would his own marriage to Mrs. Newsome put him as much out of the question as Sarah put Jim? Could he stand the society of American women? Could he stand their invariable activity, their ferocity in quiet, "their fur the smooth side out, the warm side in"?

The vain and the silly have always masked true heroes of the good and the true, the fair and the kind. Strether, that man of the world without a world, is only a special, transitory, and very Jamesian case of the normal in his mighty effort to see for himself —through the "eternal nippers" James so often says he wore, the eyeglasses he took off so that he could put them back on—some share in that heroic role. Heroism may be tender, and eyesight needs to be cleared before it can be resumed. A little more than halfway through the novel, in Book Eighth, Chapter 3, we see Strether for the first time actually recognizing that he has undertaken that role—that the role has undertaken *him*. It is the moment of the change of ambassadors; the scene is a species of *levée* at Mrs. Pocock's hotel (or if not a *levée* a very early salon indeed) and also a gathering when everybody is taking leave. If there had been cards for that reception they would have been marked *p.p.c.*—in order to take leave—though on the face of it it was an arrangement to meet the new plenipotentiary and envoy extraordinary Mrs. Pocock. When Strether comes in, nobody, so to speak, has yet come, only Waymarsh and Mme. de Vionnet; the scene seems crowded because we reach it with multiplied perception.

As for Strether, "he was reached by a voice with a charming sound that made him just falter before crossing the threshold. Mme. de Vionnet was already on the field, and this gave the drama a quicker pace than he felt it as yet—though his suspense had increased—in the power of any act of his own to do." In "the charming sound that made him just falter" is the shock of recognition, but more shock than recognition. We know the "faltering," but of the charm we know only that it is in Mme. de Vionnet's voice. We do not know whether it is Circe or the Siren or Aphrodite who speaks in her, or whether, within the special measure of Strether to apprehend, all three are inextricably blended—to become, as so often in the later James, that agent of the last transformation called Medusa. When, a little later, Mme. de Vionnet says, "We all love Strether; it isn't a merit," she is only dramatizing a sort of reverse possibility: a certainty among certainties producing general uncertainty. In any case, Strether is the object of action in the scene.

It is a piece of pure social drama, superbly executed. Mme. de Vionnet—her coronet so to speak on her head as well as on her card—is there to make sure that Mrs. Pocock has *her* version of what has happened and what the issues are. As a result everybody is red in the face—with Mme. de Vionnet least of all so only because she is more experienced in such things and because she knows what she is up to now. She nails Strether home to her, making him the issue and object of Mrs. Pocock's embassy. Further, to prevent any backsliding on his part toward Mrs. Pocock, she brings Maria Gostrey into it as Strether's private possession: which he perforce, reddening, admits; and as a last stroke she elicits, or wrings, from Strether his consent to visit her at her house. Besides this, she makes play to show Mrs. Pocock that she is in some "good, strong sense" in possession of Chad. On the whole, she womans it outrageously, but unattackably, over Mrs. Pocock about Paris and Europe and "things" quite as if she were unmistakably and everlastingly right.

Mrs. Pocock can only visibly glitter and not let herself go. Strether, between the women, can only see himself given up for ruin. Yet—since his perception of the central confusion is still incomplete—he thinks that Waymarsh is bound to save him, to pick up and patch up his broken pieces and take him home. Waymarsh's occult treachery with Mrs. Newsome seemed to Strether only a deep-dyed old persistent loyalty: a side-wind of loyalty from his big, narrow kindness. Mme. de Vionnet presents her force, and it is great; but, so far as she understands it, Mrs. Pocock stands up to that force. There is nothing to show who will win—or win what: Chad or Strether, both, one, none. And indeed the question is never determined.

Whoever wins, in this novel—in this mode of human relations—wins within a loss. One monster is replaced by another monster, more private, within the bosom; and it is the human loss in getting from one to the other which James's novel measures. If there is a gain it is a gain in identity—a gain by shrinking and by isolation. Consider Strether's last visit with Mme. de Vionnet where human relations are reduced to the ashes of actuality— Book Twelfth, Chapter 1, the preparation for the visit, and Book Twelfth, Chapter 2, the visit itself. These are the chapters of the *clair de lune* and of the odor of blood, of the heartbreak of achieved relation—the deeper the relation the deeper the heartbreak. If you do not think James knew what he was doing, his notebooks and an outline for his publisher prove that he did. We can feel the knowledge wriggle in his hand.

When Strether discovers that Chad and Mme. de Vionnet take weekends together, he discovers that such intimacy is like lying and he is left lonely and cold. And when the next morning he gets a *petit bleu* from Mme. de Vionnet asking him to see her that evening, he does not know but what he might not see her, that

indeed "he mightn't see any one at all any more at all." The
sentiment is familiar; when we feel the shock of it, we recognize
that it has always been with us. It now merely moves from
the menagerie to the *ménage*. The history of that movement is the
history of Strether's embassy. Strether feels the sentiment in the
Parisian post office where he goes to write his answer, his own
petit bleu, so prompt and therefore so final in its delivery. He uses
the public pen at the public table, and we all know how that
aggravates our private sentiments. To James it was easy to say.
Table and pen were "implements that symbolised for Strether's
too interpretative innocence something more acute in manners,
more sinister in morals, more fierce in national life. After he had
put in his paper, he had ranged himself, he was really amused to
think, on the side of the fierce, the sinister, the acute. This lay
generating within him all day, and by evening his irresponsibility,
his impunity, his luxury, had become—there was no other word
for them—immense."

There is a relation between the adjectives of the morning and
the evening nouns, and it is in the relation that their immensity
looms. Strether begins to think of Mme. de Vionnet in her apart-
ment as rather like Mme. Roland on the scaffold. "He knew in
advance he should look back on the perception actually sharpest
with him as on the view of something old, old, old, the oldest
thing he had ever personally touched." It is this "old, old, old"
that is the looming quality in the immensity of fierce irresponsibility, sinister impunity, acute luxury: the immense oldest thing
ever touched, the immeasurable felt as immediate. It is as if
Strether felt the destructive power of his goodness.

Perhaps that is the impossible thing wept for throughout
the wild chapter when Strether is actually with Mme. de Vionnet,
the force of goodness both past and future. Mme. de Vionnet is the
loser in the end; she has lost her daughter, her lover, and Strether.
Here she weeps for everything she had pleaded for the last time
Strether had come to see her (in Book Ninth, Chapter 1). She
weeps because she has changed Strether's life and has taken his
"home" from him. She weeps because to be happy one takes from
others and is still not happy. She weeps because the wretched self

is always there. She weeps because the only safe thing is to give. And she weeps because evidently Strether's goodness is only his way of living. To all which Strether responds by thinking how women are endlessly absorbent and how "to deal with them was to walk on water, and the water rose." He feels that she is afraid of Chad, and that feeling is "a chill in the air to him, it was almost appalling that a creature so fine could be, by mysterious forces, a creature so exploited." She has made Chad what he is, but he is only Chad and of "the strict human order." When he tells her she is afraid for her life, she weeps and wails the more, out of "the passion, mature, abysmal, pitiful, she represented and the possibilities he betrayed." But she tells him straight: "You'd do anything rather than be with us here even if that were possible. You'd do everything for us but be mixed up with us." And in saying so she is right. She had wanted to seem to him sublime, which is the stage beyond even the ideal. "I've wanted you too" are the last words we hear from her. Strether, I think, loses the manners of his soul when "'Ah, but you've *had* me!' he declared at the door, with an emphasis that made an end." I should suppose he was a very bent man when he walked away.

To return to my opening lines, it is what Strether sees in Mme. de Vionnet that happens to him; it is also what happens to her. When we last see Strether alone he is again looking up at Chad's balcony, which is the balcony of his own mind's freedom and goodness. Chad's figure there, instead of Little Bilham's, shows the taint in both freedom and goodness. There is neither for him to hold on to. The good and the free would have to be made all over again but not by Strether. It is Maria Gostrey who at the very end of the book sees this for us as well as for herself—for the everyday and for the long perspective—when "she sighed it at last all comically, all tragically, away." So the comedy of human relations becomes their tragedy when, as with James's central figures, even what is accepted cannot be held on to.

THE GOLDEN BOWL

When thirty years ago very much under the influence of Henry James and T. S. Eliot I misthought myself a novelist, I conceived a rather Jamesey novel with a title taken from Eliot: *The Greater Torment*;* and it seems to me now, rereading *The Golden Bowl* for the fourth time in as many decades, that the phrase from Eliot belongs much more as an illuminating epigraph to a reading of James's novel than to any fiction I might have struggled to write. The Eliot phrase is from the second part of "Ash Wednesday," where the bones of all that we have been sing "with the burden of the grasshopper." I urge the reader of *The Golden Bowl* to read the whole part intimately, and to remember at the same time the fairy tales which inhabited his youth. I do not suggest an identity or a parallel or a gloss; the same fountain springs differently in different sensibilities and from some earlier creation than anything we know directly of. But here are the central lines containing my phrase:

The Greater Torment, an unpublished novel, remains among Blackmur's papers at the Firestone Library, Princeton University—Ed.

The single Rose
Is now the Garden
Where all loves end
Terminate torment
Of love unsatisfied
The greater torment
Of love satisfied.

One says one thing beside another and all sorts of distances waver between, as if in the distances were the reality. One says Maggie Verver and her cracked golden bowl, and thinks of the Prince her husband; and one says these lines from Eliot and thinks of Maggie and the dark embrace with which the book ends. The distances between the two waver and wobble so that both wince, or so it may seem if you care to let it do so.

Caveat Emptor! Some writers have made *The Golden Bowl* a Christian novel, in the sense that Eliot's poem is a Christian poem, and other writers have made it Swedenborgian. I would suppose that James's experience of his Swedenborgian father dictated nothing in his novel at all, and I do not suppose that his novel—this or any other by him—was any more Christian than he could help, seeing that he was brought up in a Christian or post-Christian society. Huxley was a Christian agnostic, though not quite so much so as Thomas Hardy or George Eliot; and Colonel Ingersoll was a Christian atheist,* though not so much so as George Santayana. Our experience of the daily world never fits a particular religion, though our sense of that experience is deeply qualified by our religion even when we have left it behind: the relation between the two is a tension or sometimes a conversion, otherwise an echo. That the two may not become one I will not say; there is certainly a good deal of poetry where they do; but I am sure that of Henry James this is not so. *The Golden Bowl* is a novel of the daily world James partly knew and partly created; and if it goes beyond the human it does not go to God but to the inhuman.

*Robert Green Ingersoll (1833–99), lecturer and promoter of atheism—Ed.

In fact the novel is very much of the daily world; it deals with money and sex and marriage, like Balzac and Stendhal, but without their sense of career and without their issue in overt violence as a means of solution or termination. In James there is at the highest possible pitch the violence that does not come out, which is perhaps why the ends of his great novels involve a surrender, a giving up, a renunciation, and seem so ambiguous an arrest in the lives of their protagonists. But if we do not have open violence we have the fraud and cupidity and treachery and defeated passion that ordinarily prepare an open violence; the evil unseats the good, and the good smirches the evil with necessity. In Shakespeare good and evil make an endless jar; in James, and especially in *The Wings of the Dove* and *The Golden Bowl*, they make an almost purulent infection in each other which somehow seems a single disease. Yet the infection drawn from the good is worse than that drawn from the evil. It is a curious psychology with which James provides us in his late novels. Let us see if we can follow that psychology in the affairs presided over by that American princess of the Good, Maggie Verver.

The tale is simple enough for the Law Reports of ugly divorce cases as they are summarized from hearings and trials in the London *Times*, where one sometimes feels blackguarded as one reads them. The impecunious Italian prince Amerigo, with missing steps in the staircase of his morals, marries Maggie Verver, the daughter of an American millionaire, with morals that shoot to the sky, but maintains his liaison with their common friend, Charlotte Stant. By an arrangement which Maggie thinks she makes, Charlotte is married to her father, the millionaire *proprio*, Adam Verver. Thus Amerigo's mistress becomes his mother-in-law. James makes sure that we know too much, so much that what we ignore—what everybody *must* ignore—becomes the most active part of our perception, like fading light or the swell under a ship. He provides us with a pair of speculatively infatuated gossips, Colonel and Fanny Assingham; they discuss the arrangements between the other two pairs with the obscene delicacy of a traveling American Ladies' club in the front row at the *Folies Bergéres*—the sludge in those activated eyes! It would seem that in this novel James could not let us escape the caddish underpinning of the pimping umbras of society; and this the Colonel and his lady are there to insist on. Their view of things makes the accompaniment for the burden of the story: the history of Maggie's discovery of the relation between her husband and her stepmother and the drama of what she did about it. Her discovery is imperfect, and her action is imperfect though complete: that is, it is disruptive, and without gain of good. She makes everybody—Amerigo, Charlotte, her father, herself—do the wrong things for the right reasons. They say Swift hated the human race, but he never repudiated, as James does, the movement and the intermittences of the heart. Both writers dealt with what was intolerable: the swindle in human relations. Swift, with a lacerated heart and furious indignation, cried out, in the epitaph he wrote for himself, for human liberty; James, at the ends of his novels, for the repudiation of human behavior. I would not say this—no one should say this, otherwise—if it were not for the beauty and the passion of perception with which James leads to his great gestures of repudiation, and if it were not for the humor with which he garnishes the perception; and of course, looking at the affairs of one's acquaintance, one has compulsive sympathy with the position Maggie was led to. The psychology is peculiar: what Maggie did to her father, her friend, her husband, and herself was done in the name of love. But it sounds like the cry of the police, who are interested only in superficial order, Break it up there, break it up, together with the murmur of maternal lamentation when she buries her head in her husband's breast. She sends them packing: her father and his unfaithful wife to American City, her husband and herself to what I would take to be the horrible adultery of incompatible isolation. Whence does this action spring so wrong for right?

I think it springs from the scene of recognition on the terrace of the country house where these four people, together with the Assinghams, are staying alone under the pitiless eyes of the pitying servants. It is in the evening, the Colonel is writing letters, and Maggie watches the other four playing bridge. Francis Fergusson has written admirably and at length of this scene and I have commented on it elsewhere.* I suggest that the scene itself (the second chapter of the fifth Book) explains the whole novel. What Maggie recognizes is that she can destroy them in a single sentence, and that every relation rests on her; instead she goes outside and paces the terrace, looking at their safety through the tall windows. There she completes her recognition: that she cannot and will not give them up, but must master them by her goodness, by love, but by a goodness and love which would nevertheless act as a retribution. I repeat, the scene comments the whole novel and draws into it lines of force from everything that is meant by the cracked golden bowl and everything that is suggested by the pagoda image in the opening chapter of the fourth Book. It is the scene on the terrace that converts both the symbolic actions of the bowl and the image of the pagoda and the actions of love and marriage into actions of the Psyche, that human Psyche who, as Santayana somewhere puts it, after having surrendered everything insists that she has lost nothing. It is one of those lies by which we extend ourselves beyond humanity and degrade the humanity of others.

The instinct for this sort of action in James must have originated in some layer of the psyche much deeper than the imagination. Some might ally it with the instinct for death as in Freud's psychology or with the ideal of Nirvana as in Buddhism, but these would only obliterate the action. In James, the instinct attaches itself to life as directly as a leech or a tick to your arm; it means to do something with life—even with the life that has slipped or been taken away—that will in the end seem to the actor triumphant and an act of love. It was this instinct, perhaps, that was at work in the heart of Catherine Sloper in *Washington Square*; in *The American*, where it drives Mme. de Cintré into a convent instead of the arms of Christopher Newman; in *The Portrait of a Lady*, where we leave Isabelle Archer seeming to enter a convent of her own making. And of course there is "The Altar of the Dead" or "The Beast in the Jungle" or "The Pupil,"

---

*See Blackmur's introduction to the Grove Press edition of *The Golden Bowl*, pp. 158–60—Ed.

or any of a dozen other stories where destructiveness and retribution seem to be attached to and even to engorge love. Once the idea is in hand, it would seem that this instinct is more or less at work in the greater part of what James wrote; but we had better not think this exclusively or omnivorously. It is quite enough to emphasize it where James found himself doing so, in the last three novels (unless you count *The Outcry*) that he finished: *The Ambassadors*, *The Wings of the Dove*, and *The Golden Bowl*. Since they were not written, though they were published, in that order, we cannot say that the emphasis has a rising intensity except adventitiously. In *The Ambassadors*, Lambert Strether, faced with a shabby affair in Paris, loses first the confidence of, and then all relation with, the woman in America he had meant to marry; and his loss comes because Paris had made him see life with a different vision. He then dismisses from his heart and life the two women in Paris, Maria Gostrey and Mme. de Vionnet, who had brought him the most riches he had ever had. I will not say that he loved either of them in accord with the usual modes of love, but Maria Gostrey certainly wished to marry him, and the book (I do not say James) has a wonderful feeling of warm possibilities for Strether and Mme. de Vionnet. His dismissal of them is abrupt and total, and his explanation to Maria Gostrey is that he insists on being the one person who had gotten nothing out of the whole affair. This seems to him a triumph, and the only triumph, this nothing, in a novel which cries out for human liberty and richness of life. Yet when these are possible he prefers their wreckage and goes home to the liberty of isolation and the richness of desuetude.

In *The Wings of the Dove*, Milly Theale dies for a love she could have had for herself had she chosen to live; she could not encompass anything but the surrender of what she most wanted. In dying she perfected the intrigue against her and brought it to nothing. She left wealth to Merton Densher who had plotted with his secret fiancée, Kate Croy, to get the wealth, and turned the bequest into instant retribution. Densher would not take the money, and Kate Croy would not take Densher without the money. Milly by her love and her money had dug a pitfall between them:

they now knew the distance between people and could never recover the nearness. One takes it that in Milly's psychology she had discovered the nearness, and died because she could not tolerate the distance. Neither Eros nor *philia* much agitate the love in the men and women of Henry James, they seem rather only conventional opportunities for fresh failures of human behavior. As for *agape* (the height of Christian love), if Strether and Milly do in any way represent it, by itself *agape* is not enough any more than any conversion is: hence it seems to involve clear suicide or some form of dehumanization.

So it is with Maggie Verver in *The Golden Bowl*. Maggie goes further than Strether or Milly, but it is hardly more than one forced step further, so to speak, a step *through*. She gives a fresh and novel instance of wanting to eat her cake and have it too. Neither nothingness nor renunciation will do for her, while suicide—which in her case would have been a step through into an unselfish act—does not attract her little fingernail. She destroys— it is a kind of murder in the heart, whatever the humility in the throat, or, as James calls it, the hood of humility over her head— she destroys all the values between the two pairs—the Eros and the *philia*—and destroys, I would suppose, all that could make life tolerable and desirable between her husband and herself. There is no beauty in her daily life; so, like Iago, she removes it from possibility—so far as they believe her—from the lives of her father, from Charlotte, and from her husband. She exhibits as if it were riches the poor bare forked spirit of unaccommodated man. Looking into Maggie's eyes one does not see oneself staring back; one sees (in James's own phrase) the Medusa face of life: the face that crumples us into zombies. No wonder Maggie buried her eyes in her husband's breast; at the last moment James reports of her, she could not bear her own triumph over what she held dear. This is the tragedy of those who desert their own values for the sake of the principle (often mistaken for the ideal) which they thought had established the values, but which in the event dumb- founded them. This tragedy is James's invention, and like every tragedy it would not be necessary if it were not for the cheating in people's behavior about life.

There is the tragedy: one is driven to what is not necessary by thinking of necessity. Look at your acquaintance, and see; which is I suppose what James's imagination got late in life into the habit of doing in book after book. There is thus an actualness—a credibility—a staring face around the next corner—both in the report of Maggie's action and in the psychology upon which she bases it. I think it was Ortega y Gasset who said that though a tiger can never be less than a tiger, it is always possible for a man to be less than human. But the excess may be in either direction, and perhaps the worst excess is in the attempt to do without the human as an act of self-privation. If one were really alone in the world, it would not matter; but one is only lonely. Maggie insists on taking the Prince with her into the isolation, walled with privation, which she has created. It is she who hides in his breast, not he in hers, when after a silence he had said: "I see nothing but *you.*" A few moments earlier, thinking "of their freedom to be together there always," the "delay in his return, making her heart beat too fast to go on, was like a sudden blinding light on a wild speculation. She had thrown the dice, but his hand was over the cast." It was thus that "for pity and dread" of what she saw in his eyes she "buried her own in his breast."

Pity and dread; as they are Aristotle's words, the reader may do what he likes with them—may even think of Greek tragedy and *The Golden Bowl* at the same time. But if the reader does so he had better think of Prince Amerigo, not of the Princess Maggie, as the hero of the tragedy. It is his life, not Maggie's, that seen in perspective is tragic and shows a tragic fault, that can be explained but not justified, in the nature of his effort. He did not know that his Roman venality would become a destructive monster in the too candid light of Maggie's American conscience. When we first meet the Prince, meditating and arranging his marriage, he says *sincerely* that he doesn't "lie nor dissemble nor deceive." He had his own sort of loyalty into which not everything in the world entered. But there was something else that disturbed his conviction of the loyalty he had. He didn't, thinking of arrogance and greed, consider that he personally had those vices. "His race, on the other hand, had had them handsomely enough, and he was somehow full of his race." One of the further conclusions he reached about his marriage to Maggie and her father's millions, was perhaps how his race expressed itself in him. "He was allying himself to science, for what was science but the absence of prejudice backed by the presence of money?" The first half of the novel belongs to the Prince so that we see his preparations intimately, but in the second half we have Maggie's view of things, and our knowledge of the Prince is restricted by it. By the author's choice we are never engaged in the Prince's action, and feel of it only its pressing mass—sometimes breaking out in ambiguities and evasions which are crushing gestures. For example, in the next to last chapter, Maggie and the Prince are talking about Charlotte just before seeing her for the last time. This is Maggie's voice. "'It's terrible'—her memories prompted her to speak. 'I see it's *always* terrible for women.' The Prince looked down in his gravity. 'Everything's terrible, cara—in the heart of man. She's making her life,' he said, 'She'll make it.'" And no doubt Charlotte will make her life: precisely because the Prince will not make his; his is made for him; which he sees.

The pity and the dread indeed. Pity for the torment of love unsatisfied, dread for the greater torment of love satisfied, the turmoil and the waste. In Eliot's poem the phrases are part of a prayer for release from these torments. In James's novel the two torments are enacted as ends in themselves, and the greater torment as a supreme end worth any loss and any surrounding waste to attain. From Mme. de Cintré through Isabel Archer, Lambert Strether, and Milly Theale to Maggie Verver, this is the mode of love which James develops. As Yeats says in one of his "Plays for Dancers," God protect us from "this horrible deathless body gliding in the veins of a sudden"—and it is there, a moving coil within us. It is very tempting, it is the next step, and the fascinating thing is it is possible, precisely as possible as the suicide it resembles. Like philosophical anarchy or nihilism—or like the love-death in Wagner's *Tristan and Isolde*—all belonging to James's time—the temptation to annihilation in James's mode of love has only to be named to be at hand. Being not only related to love but, as Maggie asserts it, the very form of love, it rushes to greet you when called. At first embrace it may seem like Raleigh's great lines at the end of "Walsinghame":

> But true Love is a durable fire
> In the mind ever burning;
> Never sick, never old, never dead,
> From it self never turning.

But only at first embrace. Raleigh makes an ideal human to the last syllable, impossible to attain but enriching and demanding every possible effort. In James the syllables are human and beautifully so, but the image of Maggie's mode of love—whatever you call it—is one more instance of that ever-present possibility, man's inhumanity to man. That it may also be, in our circumstances, an approach to charity is what commands us to read the book.

APPENDIX

THE SPOILS OF HENRY JAMES:
A SPECIAL CASE OF THE NORMAL

In a little work of this kind about a man in many ways as large as possible, we cannot expect to see everything, or even to say everything about the relatively little we choose to see. We are bound to make sure though that we begin with some image of the largeness and that at the end of the vista the largeness still looms, not like a monument, but like a man standing, paused in his stride. It will be a man, mind you, thought of wholly as a writer; a figure representative chiefly of his works. If you catch up with him you will recognize him just in the measure that you know his works, and you will never catch up with him unless you do know, pretty extensively and pretty patiently and not at all politely, the body of those works. Your politeness will be kept for that other, struggling man whose good and evil fortune it was to produce the works. Politeness is hard enough, since out of sympathy one wants to be more, and out of disappointment to be less; but patience is harder still. Patience requires both the restraint of complete tolerance and the freedom of complete attention. We are polite in order to endure; patient in order to understand when there is no longer any question of endurance. Mere politeness, like mere cynicism, may cover unfocussed indifference; patience is impossible without focussed attention. No irritations equal polite or cynical attention.

The aptness of these remarks, otherwise only sententious, rises from the fact that Henry James the writer has suffered from a good deal of politeness and a great deal of cynicism, and that Henry James the man—the stammer, the clothes, the fear that rode him—has been dragged in either to justify the cynicism or to make the politeness seem sufficient, or both. The very virtues of the writer have been made to illuminate the defects of the man, and the virtues thereby discounted. The superb fineness of the writer's discrimination, for example, is somehow belittled by being related to a presumed absence of coarseness in the man; and again, what is the height of indifference, his technical mastery is politely admired—like charm at a tea-table—as if enough admiration would guarantee the emptiness of his themes. "All that bother about a houseful of furniture" is the shining indifferent response to *The Spoils of Poynton*, where a more interested response would have been to exclaim "What an extraordinary quality of human value Henry James managed to focus in a houseful of furniture!" I don't say James *wrung* his values out of his subject-matter, as if an orange, or an upholstered chair seat or a face at the window could all be made to express human juice; and I don't say he plastered and painted his raw material over with value, surfaces to chip and stain. No. James saw his values— brutality and horror— and beauty and the strains between these— actually focussed in his materials. These were the spoils—only saved in the light of the novelist's imagination—secured by the unremitting engagement, *and* growth, of his sensibility with the material to which it was prone.

Engagement *and* growth; the notions in these words will provide at least the initial form of an habitual image which when we have expanded it will serve to remind us, all round, of the spoils we get from Henry James. No sensibility was ever more firmly engaged than his with the norm—the daily matters and possibilities—of the human life he knew; and no sensibility, bound to the normal, ever grew so luxuriantly into a series of special cases. We can think of his works as a whole perhaps most profitably as just that one thing, a special case of the normal. If the special is sometimes so immediately and abundantly visible as to seem to exclude sight of the normal, the normal is there just the same, underneath, like the depth of the ocean, perhaps out of soundings, but necessarily what buoys us up. Which is how it always is with the normal; never actually confronting us, it exists either only as we presently rest upon it, or in our special approaches to it, whether in terms of the ideal, as in politics and the Christian faith, or in terms of the besetting flux, as in our daily life and private endeavors, or, again, in some combination of both kinds of terms.

Eliot's close phrase about James—that he had a mind so fine that no mere idea could ever violate it—suggests the kind of combination that he made, and if we remember the early, permeating influence upon him of such writers as Balzac, Flaubert, and Turgenev—writers whom we think of generally as having promoted the mode of naturalism—the suggestion is confirmed. James never rested upon the ideal and never gave in to a thesis in order to establish the normal with which he was concerned. He made his approaches almost entirely through special instances of the life around him; the more special they were the more illuminating they could be made. All that he ever rested upon or gave in to objectively was the craft, the modes, the technique of the novel, the novelette, and the tale; and these he made, in the sense of making them articulate, for himself, gradually, patiently, ardently, as a lifelong labor. Thus we seldom associate James's work with any group of insights, but rather with a permanent development, a new dimension, of sensibility. Only those concerned in their criticism too much with books as the intellection of life will miss the characterizing insights, or value what is missing more than the riches of sensibility actually spread.

It is not that James lacked ideas; no mind is free of that anchorage; but he was not fast to the bottom, with whatever scope; his anchors were all sea-anchors, let go to windward to secure steadiness rather than position. He was more adverb and verb than adjective and noun; more a qualified motion than a formulated name; more a point of view than a proposition. His work realized themes which he had discovered, rather than applied theses which he had fallen back on. His people come slowly on instances of what life is like: they see or show or feel for themselves the figure in the carpet, the turn of the screw, the beast in the jungle, the wings of the dove; they may also incidentally, but never primarily or ultimately, illustrate a pattern or a fate imposed from outside. They represent always possibilities—or impossibilities—the good *and* the evil chance—of the developed, the confronted intelligence.

These are the signs of expectancy for the particular works; they go with the general conditions of what we called above engagement and growth for the work as a whole. Intelligence, in James's characters, develops of its own nature and reaches or fails of its maximum as it withstands or gives in to the experience with which, as it develops, it is confronted. Here is an enclosed, an intensive, moral heroism, all ready to hand and demanding the tight grasp; for in James's general habit, the more you develop your intelligence the more there is you must bear and must struggle with and consequently the more there is of you—there is indeed an integer, an integrity—to break down, collapse, or it may be, *not* break down, *not* collapse, but just transpire or come through, not dulled by stoicism and deprived but everywhere quickened and with a fresh, complete assent of the fully developed, fully confronted intelligence. The struggle into which we see Henry James commit his characters is, in short, the struggle in radically human terms—the very terms of intelligence mustered to its utmost—for the mastery of life. It is the sense of this struggle of the intelligence, once felt, that constitutes the chief attractive force in James's work; it is the tragic tension that brings us home, as it most often brought him, through all the difficulties of manner and discipline, the defects of sympathy and interest, the ardors of style and the rigors of form, to the central strength of his sensibility, where all was, in its special case, plain mastery.

Before we go on to elucidate, if we can, representative examples of that mastery—before we show how and to what effect James worked as he did (which is the purpose of this essay), there are two considerations, one restrictive and the other definitive,

which ought to be put in mind to save us both from overestimating
James's advantage and from underestimating the difficulty of his
task. These considerations are related, twins indeed, of the same
conception: the conception, namely, of the autonomous supremacy
of the arts in the expression and interpretation of the culture of
our times. James admitted no test of the validity of a work of art
superior to the terms in which it was practiced. He both lacked
and never seemed to miss, except for their value as social conventions—as conveniences for imagination—the sense of history and
the sense of religion and the sense of philosophy. The great for
him were great artists and for the most part artists of the nineteenth
century; he shows nowhere any actual addiction—to use one of his
own words—to any writer earlier than Balzac, or, indeed, later than
Turgenev. His actual addiction was to the art itself; to the art he
himself practiced; the art he had, as he well and dearly knew,
himself transformed—as in their turns Turgenev, Flaubert, Balzac
had transformed it before him—the art that he had in truth, and
altogether on his own devoted account, so far refined and articulated as to claim for himself a patent of invention so that it
might be kept free for universal use.

This is to put it, for emphasis, at an extreme. But the seed of
extremity is scattered widely enough in his own words. James did
firmly, and with deep exhilaration, believe that his own use of the
art of fiction ought to be universal, and that it carried with it both
unique and unlimited powers to the full scope of the artist's
authority over his subject-matter, namely, life. The concluding
phrase of the Preface to the novel he thought most nearly successful as a work of art, should be half enough. Thinking back on
The Ambassadors, he was able to affirm for the whole craft what
in the instance he felt for himself, "that the Novel remains still,
under the right persuasion, the most independent, most elastic,
most prodigious of literary forms."

For the other half—for James's notion of what underlay the
prodigy of form—let us take a sentence from the Preface to *The
Spoils of Poynton*. The argument had run to the quarter in which
the author's subject most completely expresses itself. "The careful
ascertainment of how it shall do so," James went on, "and the art

of guiding it with consequent authority—since this sense of
'authority' is for the master-builder the treasure of treasures, or at
least the joy of joys—renews in the modern alchemist something
like the old dream of the secret of life." There is more, here and
elsewhere, but this is enough—especially as James proceeds at
once to deny any extravagance in his statement—this is enough to
emphasize the scope of James's belief in the artist's authority.

It should be marked here that neither the truth nor the
general practicality of James's belief is our present concern; we
are bound only to the fact of that belief and its consequences in
James's writing. Writing, like other forms of action, may or may
not be done with reference to the truth of reality; it is always done
with relation to the actual beliefs of the writer at the moment of
composition—even, it may be added, when those beliefs assume
the weak disguise of disbelief. The point of the fact of James's
belief is that we think of it as gradually responsible for the
perfection of his choice of intelligence and its conflict with un-
intelligence as the prime focus of his themes and the general
motivation of his characters as they take or refuse action. And
this, in turn, brings us directly to the two considerations, restrictive and definitive, which deeply affect our final judgment of the
scope and value of James's work. The argument is not a straight
line but circuitous; we strike it, however directly, at a tangent and
find ourselves not at a point of bearing but in the circuit, which is
to say we find ourselves in a motion of attention which once
undertaken will bring us the full round. What restricts your
action defines, from the observer's point of view, your character;
what defines character restricts the scope of action. The equiva-
lence is near tautology in the logical realm, but is yet disparate in
the realm of quality—the realm that logic actually handles.

It is with that in mind then that we must consider that
James's emphatic insistence on the intelligence as the focus of his
material constituted a radical restriction, a positive deprivation,
at every level of his work, and must also consider that the great
difficulty, for him, and the great virtue, for us, of his work lay in
the fact that he had nothing else in the world but that intelligence
to go on with. In these respects he was so much the advanced,

though unconscious, product of his own times as to be a prophecy
of the times to come; which are our times; and that is why, as we
feel it, we return to him again and again despite the superficial
aversion roused by an idiosyncrasy always extreme and sometimes
alien. We too have persuaded ourselves to move as much as
possible by the unaided intelligence alone. In James, when we
read him with good will and for all he is worth, we see the richest
possible historical example of our own motion.

What impoverished it? What, in its own nature, limited its
authority? What but its exaggerated self, its achieved and guarded
exclusiveness, its taint of the absolute? James reproached Baudelaire for his *Flowers of Evil* by saying that it was as if he had
written Flowers of Good and represented nothing but bon-bons;
from which we extract, not the judgment of Baudelaire which was
offside, but an analogue for the judgment of James. If evil is not
evil unless veined with good, nor good good extricated from evil,
neither is intelligence intelligent unless it cooperates with those
other factors of personality—those other aspects of life—which
are not directly amenable to intelligence. To refuse to cooperate,
to insist on independence, may be indeed to perfect your instrument—here the intelligence—but it is a perfection secured only at
the expense of the authority—here over the whole of life—which
you meant to assert. A good half of the substance of that life, say,
is not only beyond your control since you are unwilling to attend
it, but is also beyond your knowledge since, willfully, you will
not see it. In arrogating intelligence you come to be, in fact,
unintelligent about stupidity. You will mistake reaction for response and confuse response with deep assent. The intelligence is,
when lifted above daily needs and daily use, no more than a
principle of control, a *habit* of awareness; it is indeed a kind of
routine for behavior or action; but it is neither a source of judgment nor a compendium of value, however it may be *used* in
making judgment and ascertaining value. It is the most intelligent who, when they are nothing else, are most prone to hysterias
at one extreme and to thinness at the other; and it is to these
extremes—hysteria and thinness—and precisely because of the
inevitable abdication of the intelligence at critical points, that

James runs. Pressed beyond its scope, intelligence alone cannot judge; it either gives in or gives out.

This consideration is pressed not in order to get rid of James or to belittle him, but rather in the effort to get at him, first to suggest an explanation of why so many people rid themselves of all James except the feeling of human belittlement they find in him, and, second, repairing *that* damage, to suggest a criterion for cutting away the clutter of the excessive or the inadequate (only at worst the hysterical or the thin) which obscures the actual great accomplishment that is there. It is in effect, whatever it may be in principle, a mere pruning for strength and fruit; which brings us smack on our second and definitive consideration—the consideration of just what the unaided intelligence does do when it is neither inadequate nor excessive, but rich and restrained. This is, and whether we like it or not, the simplest version of the great question of our time.

It has fallen out that we live in a new era; not by plan, by will, by need, but by discovery; we have discovered that we live, as western man has never been able to live before, in a single world. Vision, faith, conviction upon which the intelligence used to rely for direction, fortitude and discipline are now discovered to have no more sanction than the intelligence itself. I do not wish to be misunderstood. It is not the world that is new. The old world survives, and the old insights; those, no others. What is new is merely that the individual has not only, as always, to recover that world and those insights, but has also to regard them, once recovered, as without order or authority beyond that of his own mind. What is new is the absence of supernatural order.

There is a great sense here that the human mind stands at last on its own feet, and a desperate sense, following, that there is no footing not quicksand in the end and in the meantime precarious, shifting, and provisional. Hence, in the general, the rash of reason and the inflammation of emotion terminating either in fanaticism or caprice; and hence, too, in those able and willing to make extraordinary effort, the opportunity *and* the necessity for the constant deep exertion of the individual imagination upon the maximum field of the intelligence. That effort amounts in the artist (and in the statesman, the scientist, the philosopher, and the religious if there come again to be any) to this, that each man must make, in the strong, poetic sense of that word, the shape and substance of his own allegiance. This which society formerly did for him, giving his work significance, he must now do for himself, giving significance to society. This which was spiritual or imaginative certitude, whether supernaturally or mythically derived, is not now derived at all but made and when made is not certitude but experiment, subject everywhere to the test of experience and to the revision of renewed imagination. The effort of the imagination—the coadunating faculty, the faculty of so uniting the elements of experience that they work together—is no longer to survive as ideal, but rather to reach the actual.

It may be that this has always been so; looking backwards we seem to see that it was when Christianity or Shakespeare reached the actual that their real significance appeared, and not at all when they entered the ideal; but that was not how men thought as they went about their work. Churchmen and poets alike had the realm of the ideal as the availing source of conviction, even in heresy, and as the available authority of judgment, even when they refused to judge; and their works were submitted to it whether they liked it or not. Even today we cannot judge Dante without referring him to medieval Christianity; which is a primary part of his actuality. But, today, in judging such a man as T. S. Eliot who has made for himself Christianity as his central allegiance, we do not judge his work in terms of his religion; we judge his religion, if we touch it at all, in the degree that he has made it actual in his work. I take it that in some sense Mr. Eliot does so himself; at any rate to think so explains his remark that intellectual assent to Christian dogma is easy, but emotional assent is hard and slow. Emotion thrives in the field of the actual, where intellect inhabits the ideal. Thus we will deceive no one if we insist that Mr. Eliot has *made* Christianity his central allegiance in almost exactly the same sense that, in *Ulysses*, James Joyce *made* the plot of the *Odyssey* his animating frame, or that Thomas Mann has been lately *making* the story of Joseph a satisfying myth to order his sense of the conflict of human values.

I speak of relative successes; the point may be clearer if we think of a relative failure, in this sense only. There is W. B. Yeats who made a symbolic framework based on the phases of the moon and a system of arbitrarily (magically) systematized insights, not all his own by any means—hardly more than Christianity is Eliot's or Joseph is Mann's—but all alien to the experience of his readers, so that it is harder to see the degree that it envisages the actual. Thus Yeats's work succeeds as poetry in spite of the difficult allegiance which for him made it practicable. This we might distinguish as the making of a peripheral, rather than a central allegiance; and in fact Yeats supports that view himself in many of his late dubious qualifications of his system. (Critically, we might put the difficulty of Yeats's allegiance as this: that we have no means of knowing whether we are in a position gradually to exhaust the full significance of a poem or indeed whether it is fully there at all. Better still, perhaps, for our point would be an example of plain failure, such as *The Bridge* of Hart Crane, where the allegiance was deep as the "tribal morn" but never articulate enough to touch; Crane's success was not in spite of his allegiance but altogether beside it, in passages; what he set up as the godhead of imagination, being as it was only primitively human, could hardly have been more, even for him, than a roughly integrating force, like war or famine. The point is, that if we assume some allegiance is necessary to a writer if his work is to have magnitude (an assumption clearly born out in *most* great writers) then, to be effective, that allegiance must, for us, in our time, be made actual, or immanently actual, somehow *presiding* in, that work.

This may seem a far cry from Henry James; really, it is as near as night. James made his allegiance primarily to the general, apparently abiding conventions of society as he found it; but to those conventions taken seriously, to the full reach of their imaginative worth: just *as if* they were fruitful in action, rich in judgment. That is to say, he looked conscientiously, scrupulously, re-creatively at what men and women did, for the most part, by rote, and at what they failed to do through some fatal inability to conform to rote. In short, he refreshed the conventions of society by taking them as actual. Here he reversed, for the sake of imagination, the common procedure of the liberal moralists of his times. His skepticism, discrimination, refinement, were turned upon the conduct of individuals; his assent was full and generous and almost blind for the conventions of conduct. He took the best face values of society (not the worst, except for evidence of deterioration) as principles and seriously applied them, in much the same sense that people have in mind in making the assertion that no one knows whether Christianity will work because no one has ever tried it. James tried the conventions of society, feeling the whole detail by detail; and tried it, as it were, on his own, without, as *we* can see, the benefit and support of any general conviction in the society itself, quite as the case would be were some rash kindred imagination to try Christianity to its utmost.

How much he missed the general conviction may be seen roughly, I think, on the one hand in his increasing emphasis on form, in the narrow, imposed, coercive sense, and on the other hand in his finally almost fanatical development of detail beyond the price in terms of attention his readers were able to pay. That was his version of the self-achieved penalty to which the heretic— every mind on its own—must submit. With James the penalty like the heresy was extreme. He made far less of the values of society actual in his art than he thought because the very nature of his allegiance prevented him from feeling those values fully, and because he was wrong for his readers, whatever he may have been for himself, in believing that the force of form in what he did feel would make up for what he did not feel. The gap was wider though no deeper, than he thought. What he did feel was insufficiently connected with what he knew must be there, and he only weakened his authority—thinned his putative strength—by straining after what he could not touch. What remained, what persisted, had he known it, was enough; to the extent that the conventions of society to which he was addicted *did* work, his authority was absolute because both the conduct displayed and the judgments come to were represented as actual. No man ever made the merely conventional illuminate so much of the actual as Henry James did; and he did it, to repeat, by the imaginative experiment of fastening upon the conventional as the actual itself.

It is in the light of these considerations that we shall proceed to sample the spoils of Henry James, neither asking a different provision of victuals nor pretending any polite dispensation of grace, but patiently eating the dish as served; which is to say that for the most part we shall ignore the considerations that move us as we ignore the act of breathing, and for the same reasons, that otherwise we might lose them. "What are all those fish that lie gasping on the strand?"

[Handwritten draft, early 1940s]

A BIBLIOGRAPHICAL NOTE:

BLACKMUR'S ESSAYS
ON HENRY JAMES

"The Critical Prefaces of Henry James." *Hound & Horn*, 7 (1934), 444–77. Reprinted in *The Double Agent*. New York: Arrow Editions, 1935. Also in *The Lion and the Honeycomb*. New York: Harcourt, Brace & Company, 1955. Used as introduction to *The Art of the Novel: Critical Prefaces by Henry James*. New York: Scribner's, 1962.

"*The Sacred Fount.*" *Kenyon Review*, 4 (1942), 328–52.

"In the Country of the Blue." *Kenyon Review*, 5 (1943), 508–21. Reprinted in *A Primer of Ignorance*. Ed. Joseph Frank. New York: Harcourt, Brace and World, 1967.

"Henry James." *Literary History of the United States*. Ed. Robert E. Spiller et al. New York: Macmilan, 1948, 1953, 1963, 1974, 1039–64 in 1974 edition.

"The Loose and Baggy Monsters of Henry James: Notes on the Underlying Classic Form in the Novel." *Accent*, 11 (1951), 129–46. Reprinted in *The Lion and the Honeycomb*.

"*The Golden Bowl.*" Henry James. *The Golden Bowl*, Introduction, New York: The Grove Press, 1952, v–xxi.

243

Introductions to the Laurel Henry James series. New York: Dell,
1958–64.

> *The Wings of the Dove* (1958), 5–17 [Also used, in slightly
> modified form, as the introduction to *The Aspern Papers and
> The Spoils of Poynton* (1958), 5–18].
> *Washington Square* and *The Europeans* (1959), 5–12.
> *The American* (1960), 5–13.
> *The Portrait of a Lady* (1961), 5–12.
> *The Tragic Muse* (1961), 5–15.
> *The Golden Bowl* (1963), 5–13.
> *The Ambassadors* (1964), 5–12.

INDEX

Abélard, 93, 180
Accent, 243
Adams, Henry, 1–2, 4, 9, 46, 107; *The Education of*, 2; *Mont-Saint-Michel and Chartres*, 2
Adams, Marian, 45
Aesop, 48, 50
Arabian Nights, 34
Aristotle, 133, 148, 228; *Ethics*, 205; *Poetics*, 15
Atlantic Monthly, 94

Balzac, Honoré de, 30, 94, 102, 108, 117, 130, 164, 177, 181, 182, 215, 223, 233, 235
Barry, Philip, 148
Baudelaire, Charles, 237; *Flowers of Evil*, 237
Beach, Joseph Warren, 5; *The Method of Henry James*, 5
Beardsley, Aubrey, 3
Bennett, Arnold, 97
Blackmur, R. P., "The Critical Prefaces of Henry James, 6–7, 15–44, 243; "A Critic's Job of Work," 6; *The Double Agent*, 5, 243; *The Greater Torment*, 221, 221n; *Henry Adams*, 2, 12; "Henry James," 10, 91–124, 243; "In the Country of the Blue," 8–9, 13, 69–90, 243; "Introduction to *The Golden Bowl* (Grove Press)," 10, 147–60, 225n, 243; Introductions to the Laurel Henry James, 10–11, 14, 161–230, 244; *The Lion and the Honeycomb*, 243; "The Loose and Baggy Monsters of Henry James," 9, 125–46, 243; *A Primer of Ignorance*, 243; "The

Sacred Fount," 7–8, 45–68, 243; "The Spoils of Henry James," 13, 14, 231–42; *Studies in Henry James*, plans for, 12–13; "The Swan in Zurich," 2
Blake, William, 180
Brieux, Eugène, 148
Brooks, Cleanth, 5
Brooks, Van Wyck, 4–5; *The Pilgrimage of Henry James*, 4–5
Browning, Robert, 27; "The Ring and the Book," 17
Byzantium, 143

Cameron, Elizabeth, 46
Carlyle, Thomas, 93
Cervantes, Miguel de, 130; *Don Quixote*, 49
Chaucer, Geoffrey, 130
China, 143
Coleridge, Samuel Taylor, 27, 131, 149
Congreve, William, 112
Conrad, Joseph, 97, 161; *Chance*, 97; *Under Western Eyes*, 97
Coward, Noel, 148
Crane, Hart, 240; *The Bridge*, 240
Croce, Benedetto, 126

Dante Alighieri, 79, 127, 128, 134, 135, 142, 151–52, 166, 239; *The Divine Comedy*, 49, 138, 151–52
Dickens, Charles, 94, 102, 164, 181
Dickinson, Emily, 104, 191
Donne, John, 98
Dos Passos, John, 111
Dostoevsky, Fyodor, 95, 130, 136, 149, 158; *The Brothers Karamazov*, 136; *The Idiot*, 215

Dumas, Alexandre (fils), 148
Dumas, Alexandre (père), 9, 130;
    The Three Musketeers, 129

Edel, Leon, 93n; *Henry James: The
    Untried Years*, 93n
Egypt, 143
Eliot, George, 164, 181, 222
Eliot, T. S., 3, 4, 6, 128, 221–22,
    229, 233, 239–40; "Ash
    Wednesday," 221–22, 229
Emerson, Ralph Waldo, 93
Everyman, 48

Faulkner, William, 97
Fergusson, Francis, 224
Fielding, Henry, 130
Flaubert, Gustave, 95, 102, 108, 109,
    130, 181, 187, 233, 235; *Madame
    Bovary*, 109, 121
Follett, Wilson, 47, 62, 65
Ford, Ford Madox, 45, 97; *The
    Good Soldier*, 97; *Some Do Not*,
    97
Freud, Sigmund, 163, 168, 199, 225

Gainsborough, Thomas, 211
Gide, André, 76–78, 105, 145; *The
    Counterfeiters*, 76–77
Granville-Barker, Harley, 164
Greene, Graham, 97

Hardy, Thomas, 104, 161, 222
Hawthorne, Nathaniel, 4, 74, 94,
    102
Hay, John, 46
Heloïse, 180
Hemingway, Ernest, 73, 97, 111
Homer, 128; *Odyssey*, 239
Hound & Horn, 5, 243

Howells, William Dean, 16, 91, 97,
    104, 215
Huxley, Thomas, 222
Hynes, Samuel, 14

India, 143
Ingersoll, Robert Green, 222, 222n
Irving, Washington, 94
Isaiah, 67

James, Henry, Sr., 93–94, 96, 98–99,
    102, 110, 122; *Society the
    Redeemed Form of Man*, 99, 110
James, Henry, Jr.; "The Altar of
    the Dead," 26n, 27–28, 35, 48,
    55–56, 101, 108, 117, 119, 225;
    preface to, 26n, 27–28, 35; *The
    Ambassadors*, 7, 9, 11–12, 13, 14,
    26n, 30–32, 35–36, *37–43*, 49, 71,
    72, 96, 103, 107, *114–16*, 117, 119,
    121, 129, *131–42, 145–52*, 165,
    166, 171, *183, 213–20, 226*, 229,
    235, 244; preface to, 7, 26n, 30,
    31–32, 35–36, *37–43*, 121, 235;
    The American, 11, 26n, 28–29,
    30, *114, 164–65, 176–84*, 225, 229,
    244; preface to, 26n, 28–29, 30,
    176–77; *The American Scene*,
    3, 96, 97, 117; "The Art of
    Fiction," 17; *The Aspern Papers*,
    14, 26, 26n, 27, 34, *166–68*, 167n,
    168n, 244; preface to, 26, 26n,
    27–28, 34; "The Author of
    Beltraffio," 26n, 27, 33, 34–35;
    preface to, 26n, 27, 33, 34–34;
    The Awkward Age, 13, 26n,
    32, 36, 37, 59, *112–13*, 117;
    preface to, 26n, 32, 36, 37; "The
    Beast in the Jungle," 48, *54*, 101,
    119, 225, 234; "The Bench of
    Desolation," 72, 103, 119; *The
    Bostonians*, 13, *117–19*, 165;

Daisy Miller, 26, 26n, 33, 35, 36, 105, *164–65*, 179, *187–89*, 192; preface to, 26, 26n, 33, 35, 36; "The Death of the Lion," *84–85*; *The Europeans*, 164, 179, *185–87, 188–92*, 244; "The Figure in the Carpet," *81–82*, 106, 234; *The Finer Grain*, 71, 97, 123; "The Friends of the Friends," 48, *52–53*, 109; *The Golden Bowl*, 9, 10–11, 13, 26n, 30, 32–33, 36, 49, 71, *72*, 96–97, 101, 103, 104, *114–16*, 117, 119, 121, *131–42, 147–60*, 166, 171, 186, 192, *221–30*, 244; preface to, 26n, 30, 32–33, 36; "The Great Good Place," 86, 112; "An International Episode," 164; *The Ivory Tower*, 3, 7, 71, 97; "The Jolly Corner," 48, *56–58*, 99, 119; *Julia Bride*, 35; "Lady Barbarina," 26, 26n; preface to, 26, 26n; "The Lesson of the Master," 26, 26n, 27, 33, 34–35, 77–78, *87–88*, 106; preface to, 26 26n, 27, 33, 34–35, 77–78; *The Letters of Henry James*, 3, 5, 89–90, 99, 102, 107; "A London Life," 26; "The Madonna of the Future," 103; "Maud-Evelyn," 48, *53–54, 108–109*, 112; "The Middle Years," 34–35, 106; *The Middle Years*, 3; New York Edition, 6–7, 15–44, 97, 121, 123; prefaces to, 6–7, 15–44, 61, 121, 140, 205. See also prefaces to individual volumes; "The Next Time," *85–86*; *Notebooks*, 134, 181, 208, 218; *Notes on Novelists*, 17; "The Novel in 'The Ring and the Book,'" 17; *The Outcry*, 226; "Owen Wingrave," 48, *50–52*, 53, 55; *Partial Portraits*, 17; "A

Passionate Pilgrim," 103; *The Portrait of a Lady*, 2, 11, 13, 24 26n, 32, 36–37, 44, 59, *71*, 96, 101, 107, 109, *114–16*, 117, 119, 161, *164–66*, 181, *193–201*, 225, 229, 244; preface to, 26n, 32, 36–37, 44; *The Princess Casamassima*, 26n, 30–31, 33, 36, *117–19*, 165; preface to, 26n, 30–31, 33, 36; "The Private Life," *83–84*; "The Pupil," 225; *The Reverberator*, 26n, 34; preface to, 26n, 34; *Roderick Hudson*, 16, 26n, 29–30, 32, 33–34, *164–65*; preface to, 16, 26n, 29–30, 32, 33–34; *The Sacred Fount*, 7–8, *46–48*, 50, 55, *59–68*, 71, 103, 117, *119–20*, 121; *The Sense of the Post*, 3, 71, 97; "Sir Edmund Orme," 48, *52*; *The Spoils of Poynton*, 13, 14, 19, 26, 26n, 30, 31, 34, 59, 96, 107, 117, 166, 168n, *170–71*, 232, 235–36, 244; preface to, 26, 26n, 30, 31, 34, 235–36; *The Tragic Muse*, 9, 13, 26–27, 26n, 30, 32, 34, 35, 37, 107, *109–110*, 117, 128–29, 165, *202–12*, 244; preface to, 26–27, 26n, 30, 32, 34, 35, 128–29, 204–205, 207–208; *The Turn of the Screw*, 11, 13, 28, 48, 101, 103, 117, 119, 166, *168–70*, 234; preface to, 28, 48; *Washington Square*, 105, *109–110, 164*, 179, *185–87*, 188, *190–92*, 225, 244; *What Maisie Knew*, 13, 16, 26n, 28, 30–32, 37, 59, *112*, 117; preface to, 16, 26n, 28, 30, 31–32, 37; *The Wings of the Dove*, 2, 9, 11, 13, 14, 26n, 30, 31, 32, 34, 36, 37, 39, 49, 68, *71–72*, 96, 101, 104, *114–16*, 117, 119, 129, *131–42, 147–52, 161–63*, 165, 166, 168n, *171–75*, 182, 186, 192, 223, *226–27*, 229, 234, 244;

James, Henry (*continued*)
  preface to, 26n, 30, 31, 34, 36,
  37
James, William, 50, 93–94, 98–100,
  101, 102, 123, 162; *The Varieties
  of Religious Experience*, 99, 101
Jesus Christ, 211
Josephson, Matthew, 5; *Portrait of
  the Artist as American*, 5
Joyce, James, 19–20, 47, 75–78, 80,
  92, 105, 127, 145, 239; *A Portrait
  of the Artist as a Young Man*,
  75–76, 77, 92; *Ulysses*, 75–76, 77,
  239
Jung, Carl, 168

Kafka, Franz, 47, 82, 145
Kant, Immanuel, 46; *The Critique
  of Pure Reason*, 46
Kemble, Fanny, 208
Kenyon Review, 243

LaFarge, John, 94
Lawrence, D. H., 164
*Literary History of the United
  States*, 10, 12, 243
The Little Review (Henry James
  Number), 3–4
Litz, A. Walton, 14
Lubbock, Percy, 3, 5, 8, 89, 99, 107;
  The Letters of Henry James, 3,
  5, 89–90, 99, 102, 107

Malraux, André, 164
Mann, Thomas, 62, 76, 77, 105,
  142, 145, 146, 240; *Death in
  Venice*, 76, 77; *Doctor Faustus*,
  146; *Joseph and His Brothers*,
  240
Marlowe, Christopher, *Dr.
  Faustus*, 48

Matthiessen, F. O., 134, 134n; *The
  Notebooks of Henry James*,
  134, 134n, 181, 208, 218
Maughan, W. Somerset, 45, 148
Mayne, Ethel Coburn, 3
Melville, Herman, 104
Meredith, George, 104
Milton, John, 128, "Lycidas," 55;
  Paradise Lost, 128
Mistral, Frédéric, 163
Montaigne, Michel de, 150
Moore, George, 104
Murdock, Kenneth B; *The
  Notebooks of Henry James*,
  134, 181, 208, 218

Nabokov, Vladimir, *Lolita*, 187–88
The Nation, 94
New Critics (New Criticism), 5–7, 9
New Directions, 12
New York Times Book Review, 47
Niebuhr, Reinhold, 72
The North American Review, 41
Norton, Grace, 16

Ortega y Gasset, José, 163, 228
Ovid, 50

Parnassiens, 143
Pirandello, Luigi, 105
Plato, 76, 102; *Phaedo*, 76
Poe, Edgar Allan, 28; *The
  Narrative of Arthur Gordon
  Pym*, 28
Pontius Pilate, 211
Pound, Ezra, 3–4, 7; "The Notes to
  The Ivory Tower," 4, 7
Proust, Marcel, 19–20, 35–36, 47,
  62, 98, 105, 108, 145; *Remem-
  brance of Things Past*, 35–36

Putnam, Peter, 14
Pythagoras, 131, 208

Rachel (Élisa Félix), 208
Raleigh, Sir Walter, 230;
    "Walsinghame," 230
Ransom, John Crowe, 5
Richardson, Dorothy, 97
Rembrandt Harmenszoon van
    Rijn, 211–12
Rome, 143
Rubens, Peter Paul, 211

Sand, George, 181
Santayana, George, 102, 155, 222,
    225
Sargent, John Singer, 124
Scott, Walter, 102, 130, 177, 181
Scribe, Eugène, 148
Shakespeare, William, 135, 164,
    202, 223, 239; Antony and
    Cleopatra, 180; Hamlet, 179;
    Othello, 227
Shelley, Percy Bysshe, 27, 167;
    "Adonais," 55
Smollett, Tobias, 130
Statius, 138
Stendahl (Marie Henri Beyle), 223
Stevenson, Robert Louis, 104
Swedenborg, Emanuel, 222
Swift, Jonathan, 98, 224

Tate, Allen, 5
Tennyson, Alfred; "In
    Memoriam," 55
Thackeray, William Makepeace, 9,
    130; Vanity Fair, 121; The
    Newcomes, 129

Thomas Aquinas, 179
Titian, 211–12
Tocqueville, Alexis de, 74, 80;
    Democracy in America. 74
Tolstoy, Leo, 9, 103, 129–30, 133,
    202, 205; Anna Karenina, 133,
    205; War and Peace, 129, 133
Trollope, Anthony, 181
Turgenev, Ivan, 36, 95, 102, 164,
    181, 233, 235
Twain, Mark (Samuel Clemens),
    104

Valéry, Paul, 163
Van Doren, Carl, 165
Virgil, 128, 138

Wagner, Richard, 229; Tristan and
    Isolde, 229
Warren, Robert Penn, 5
Wells, H. G., 97
West, Rebecca, 46–47
Wharton, Edith, 97, 103
Wilde, Oscar, 27, 112
Wilson, Edmund, 47
Woolf, Virginia, 47, 97
Wordsworth, William, 128

Yeats, William Butler, 13, 128, 229,
    240; "Three Movements," 13
The Yellow Book, 3

Zola, Emile, 91, 95, 177

ACKNOWLEDGMENTS

Grateful acknowledgment is given to the publishers of books where the essays reprinted here first appeared. Introduction to the Arrow edition of *The Double Agent* by R. P. Blackmur (Copyright 1935 by R. P. Blackmur) reprinted by permission of Florence Codman. Introductions to the novels of Henry James in the Laurel Henry James series: *The Ambassadors* (Copyright © 1964 by R. P. Blackmur); *The American* (Copyright © 1960 by R. P. Blackmur); *The Aspern Papers/The Spoils of Poynton* (Copyright © 1959 by R. P. Blackmur); *The Golden Bowl* (Copyright © 1963 by R. P. Blackmur); *The Portrait of a Lady* (Copyright © 1961 by R. P. Blackmur); *The Tragic Muse* (Copyright © 1961 by R. P. Blackmur); *Washington Square/The Europeans* (Copyright © 1959 by R. P. Blackmur); *The Wings of the Dove* (Copyright © 1959 by R. P. Blackmur): All reprinted by permission of Dell Publishing Co., Inc. Introduction to *The Golden Bowl* by Henry James (Copyright 1952 by R. P. Blackmur) reprinted by permission of Grove Press, Inc. "In the Country of the Blue" (Copyright 1943 by The Estate of R. P. Blackmur; renewed 1971 by The First National Bank of Princeton) reprinted from *A Primer of Ignorance* by R. P. Blackmur by permission of Harcourt Brace Jovanovich, Inc. "The Loose and Baggy Monsters of Henry James" (Copyright 1951 by Richard P. Blackmur; renewed 1979 by Elizabeth Blackmur and Mrs. Helen Van Eck) reprinted from *The Lion and the Honeycomb* by R. P. Blackmur by permission of Harcourt Brace Jovanovich, Inc. "Henry James" from Robert El Spiller *et al., Literary History of the United States,* Fourth, revised edition (Copyright © 1946, 1947, 1948, 1953, 1963, 1974 by Macmillan Publishing Co., Inc.) reprinted by permission. "The Sacred Fount" first appeared in *The Kenyon Review;* "The Spoils of Henry James: A Special Case of the Normal" first appeared in *Grand Street.* Seven lines from "Ash Wednesday" in *Collected Poems* of T. S. Eliot (Copyright 1936 by Harcourt Brace Jovanovich, Inc.; copyright © 1963, 1964 by T. S. Eliot) reprinted by permission of the publisher.